Advanced Acclaim for

"Sheri McGregor has written an incredibly powerful, helpful book for those who have experienced parent-child estrangement. Through real-life stories and her own insight and expertise, she offers tips, tools, and resources to help parents navigate through difficult emotions. The book includes many self-help exercises that guide the reader toward better health, healing, forgiveness, and acceptance. *Beyond Done* helps parents change their thinking and their actions so they can move forward in their lives with self-compassion to find meaning, fulfillment, and yes, even joy. I highly recommend this book to anyone who has experienced, or has an interest in, parent-child estrangement."

—Janet Singer, author of *Overcoming OCD: A Journey to Recovery*

"Sheri McGregor has conducted hundreds of interviews and done extensive research on the subject of estrangement. From the data she collected and from her personal experience, she explores the many challenges of estrangement. This book is an important contribution to understanding and navigating this surprisingly common family tragedy. *Beyond Done* offers invaluable support and guidance for those seeking a new life of purpose, self-respect, love, and peace."

—Nancy Lee Klune, author of *Banished, a Grandmother Alone*

"A must-read for parents of estranged adult children. An essential book for the professionals who work with them. This new book by Sheri McGregor is a valuable addition to the literature available for parents and families who have experienced the pain and trauma of estrangement. The tone is one of a compassionate and dear friend, sharing hard truths with you and letting your pain wash away.

At some point the *why* is not as important as the *what*. The cruel behavior, the lies, the on again off again infrequent contact, the rewritten history, the untrue accusations, the merry-go-round of hope, and the baseless demands combined with a culture that tends to blame and shame parents, especially mothers, cause a deep grief and a hole in the heart. What *this* book does is realign the facts with the behaviors and offers solutions to parents who are hurting and traumatized. All parents make mistakes. Few parents make ones that are so egregious that estrangement is the best solution. All in all, Sheri offers a blueprint for bouncing forward from this trauma and strengthening one's resilience."

—Mara J. Briere, MA, CFLE, Grow a Strong Family, Inc.
(https://growastrongfamily.org/)

"In her new book, *Beyond Done With The Crying*, Sheri McGregor addresses the sorrows and triumphs of estrangement through the real-life stories of people doing their best to survive the trauma of estrangement. To help with the goal of acceptance, and to gain strength and understanding in recovering, the author introduces several exercises. These help readers recognize and examine their thoughts and actions and gain awareness on a journey of understanding and self-growth. Sheri encourages us to take charge of our own lives and our own health, which is key to our well-being.

Whether you are just now beginning this journey or you are moving steadily toward acceptance of estrangement and your own wellness, this book gives you various avenues to self-exploration and healing. I, for one, am eager to more fully explore these exercises, remembering that taking care of me will equal a happier future."

—Claire L. Cunning, author of *Poems from the Heart for Hope and Healing:*
For those who have experienced estrangement from a loved one

"Sheri McGregor's latest book, *Beyond Done With The Crying: More Answers and Advice for Parents of Estranged Adult Children*, builds on her original, *Done With The Crying*, in which she shared her personal story of how she became the parent of an estranged adult child and how she and her family coped with it.

This time around, McGregor takes a more expansive approach, sharing what she's learned after conducting hundreds of interviews with other parents of estranged adult children. Immediately acknowledging that 'estrangement is a messy business,' she begins by acknowledging that just as there are no perfect children, there are no perfect parents, and continues by sharing gritty realities readers won't find in other books on this subject, including cases of child sexual abuse. Throughout the ten chapters, which cover important topics like taking care of your mind, body and spirit, the impact on the greater family—including grandparents and other children, and situations where only one parent is rejected, McGregor includes reflection exercises, and a plethora of resources. Perhaps one of the biggest takeaways is the realization that if you dig deep enough into just about any family tree, you'll find instances of estranged adult children. McGregor's research reveals that adult estrangement is much more common than most people are aware. This, because it's been one of those 'dirty laundry' family issues no one wants to discuss publicly. Just as acceptance or recognition of LGBTQ sexual orientation, alcoholism or spousal abuse formerly were, before they were 'outed.' Highly recommended."

—Anne L. Holmes, APR, "Boomer in Chief,"
National Association of Baby Boomer Women

BEYOND
DONE WITH
THE CRYING

More Answers and Advice for
Parents of Estranged Adult Children

SHERI McGREGOR, M.A.

Sowing Creek Press

Shingle Springs, California

Sowing Creek Press
Shingle Springs, CA
E-mail: info@sowingcreekpress.com
www.sowingcreekpress.com

Beyond Done With The Crying: More Answers and Advice for
Parents of Estranged Adult Children/Sheri McGregor. —1st ed.
ISBN: 978-0-9973522-5-2 (paperback)
ISBN: 978-0-9973522-6-9 (ebook)

Library of Congress Control Number: 2021947412

Book cover design by Cathi Stevenson

For smart readers everywhere.
Enjoy your life.

Contents

Author's Note

As previously stated in print and elsewhere, revealing my name as a mother who has suffered the anguish of an adult child's estrangement has been a part of my healing. The problem of estrangement is widespread and largely beyond the parents' control. It is my belief that hiding perpetuates the misperceptions that are so prevalent toward parents whose adult children choose to sever ties, and that's one reason I have stepped out of the shadows to try and help.

While I have chosen this route, I readily empathize with those who won't, or who are not yet ready, to talk openly about the matter. I'm familiar with those feelings of wanting to protect myself, as well as my estranged child, from others' harsh judgment. To that end, I chose a pseudonym for my estranged adult child and continue to use it. Additionally, I have changed the names and identifying details for the individuals and families whose stories fill these pages—stories of heartache and tears, insight and wisdom, regrets and hard-won peace. Any similarity between fictionalized names, locations, and other details and those of real individuals and families is strictly coincidental.

While all the stories are based upon my telephone and in-person interviews, survey responses, exchanged e-mails, social media and other communications, in many cases, composites were formed for clarity in conveying common scenarios and opinions, as well as for readers' ease.

This book is not a substitute for medical, spiritual, legal, or psychological advice. Content is based on the author's personal experience, as well as studies and research, but is the author's opinion.

Readers should contact a licensed physician, psychiatrist, psychologist, or other licensed practitioner for diagnosis and care, and an attorney for legal advice.

Although care was taken to ensure the research and information in this book was correct at the time it went to press, the author and publisher do not assume and hereby disclaim any liability to any party for loss, damage, or disruption due to any errors or omissions—whether the result of negligence, accident, or any other cause.

# Introduction

In an undergraduate classroom, the bearded professor told a roomful of young students to write about something bad from their family. He gave examples of dysfunction: addiction, a nasty divorce, or abuse. In all her innocence, my 18-year-old daughter raised her hand and asked, "What if you've never had anything like that in your family?"

Little did she know that our family would soon suffer a rift that would leave us in shock and emotionally traumatized. Although we have all moved forward, we are forever changed. Oh, we're okay, really. We're stronger, wiser, and better equipped to appreciate the good things in life. But just as long-healed injuries may flare up on rainy days, we learned that psychological scars can flicker to life when we're overtired, stressed out, emotionally triggered, or not communicating well. That can affect a family.

My first book on estrangement, *Done With The Crying: Help and Healing for Mothers of Estranged Adult Children* (2016), included a chapter titled "Managing the Effects on the Family." As space permitted, attention was given to common concerns. These included managing matters that arise among couples whose children are estranged, how men and women relate, parenting our other children despite the shadow of estrangement, extended family factors, conundrums around social media, and taking a positive view of the changes to the family unit.

After hearing thousands of stories from families a lot like mine, as well as experiencing effects on the family firsthand, I've concluded that estrangement can leave a confusing legacy. Possible twists and turns ahead aren't always immediately apparent. Concerns that later reveal themselves may be traced to roots that involve the estranged one or connect to history that began long ago. There is much more to say about the post-estrangement family. That's why and how this book came about.

What's Included

To date, more than 50,000 people have answered my original survey about parent-and-adult-child estrangement. Hundreds of hurting parents and other family members reach out to me every week. Their sorrows and triumphs give voice to the vast complexities of estrangement. In the pages ahead, you'll find very practical ways to address the footprints left on your life.

This book takes a thorough approach to parent-and-adult-child estrangement. I have included people who are semi-estranged, fully disconnected, and even parents who reconciled or made the tough choice not to continue the relationship. The wide array of circumstances, ranging from common scenarios to lesser-known aspects of dealing with estrangement, can provide insights for all of us.

Helpful observations are included from parents, grandparents, grandchildren, and the siblings of adults who chose to estrange. Commentary, tips, and advice derived from my education, work, and research to support parents' emotional and physical well-being round out the book. Topics are comprehensive and relevant to parents' needs. Any subjects in common with my first book are covered from new perspectives to provide additional information.

Some of the ways family members are intertwined include genes, history, business, and beliefs. In this book, you'll find the million dollar question—*why?*—is covered subtly, through real-life stories that get at root issues, family patterns, and parents' individual experiences. The practical answers, advice, and solutions *from the trenches* make this book unique.

One fact I discovered along the way is that rifts as deep and cutting as these can teach parents much about themselves. My emotional recovery included recognizing my place in the world as I grew up, became independent, and began raising a family. Like many parents who have shared their stories, my whole life relates to how I could find a way to move forward, heal, and grow. In this book, I have more fully stepped into my role as supporter and friend to caring parents. Sometimes, that requires pointing out the nonsensical and debunking common advice. At times, my positions make me the lone dissenter, but then standing up for ourselves as decent, loving parents in a world that doubts us is a lesson for us all (and covered in the book).

When things get muddled, it helps to remind ourselves that we've been through a trauma. Occasionally, we must pause and tend to ourselves and our treasured relationships. This makes us stronger in stepping forward again.

How to Use the Book

Before reading this book, I encourage you to start with my first volume on this topic. *Done With The Crying* shares my story and is designed to move parents beyond the murky landscape of the paralyzing questions, self-blame, and doubt into the solid territory of acceptance over what is beyond their control. *Done With The Crying* offers a gentler approach to facing reality and venturing forward for your own well-being. This resonates with hurting parents who can begin to take charge of their own lives yet still hold out hope for the return of a much-loved son or daughter.

Here, with more than a decade of estrangement under my belt, I've taken an expansive approach. In the pages ahead, I share gritty realities you won't find elsewhere. Such as what reconciliation really looks like, how the siblings are affected, and ways to overcome or manage those issues. Parents are encouraged to see themselves as whole persons, with real needs and feelings, rather than the "good parents" so often described by those who judge and direct.

A big step toward healing is laying bare things we may have been afraid to admit. This includes thoughts and feelings about our own children, which are natural given the circumstances, but difficult for loving parents to accept.

There are no perfect parents. We all make mistakes, and those are reflected in the real stories of people doing their best in the imperfect science of family life. One chapter is dedicated to parents who characterize themselves as having somewhat "bigger" regrets, like not recognizing an ex-spouse's pedophilia, parents' substance abuse, and unrealistic expectations for a child. These stories can benefit *any* parent. They offer much to learn about how we forgive, cope, and heal.

Estrangement is a messy business. It's sad, devastating, traumatic, and cruel. To move beyond its painful grasp, parents must face the very real ways it has, and sometimes continues, to impact themselves and their loved ones.

Chapter topics and reflection exercises build on one another and are best completed as you encounter them. However, your resistance toward any one activity should not stop you from reading on. A subsequent story or exercise may lead you back to what you skipped. Ultimately, how the book works best will be unique to each reader. I respect you as you are. Give yourself the same loving acceptance. This journey may have begun because of another person's behavior, but the path forward is all about you.

CHAPTER ONE

Getting Real

"When I discover who I am, I'll be free."
—Ralph Ellison, *Invisible Man*

In a moment of conflict, Madelyn told her 19-year-old daughter, Amy, "If you're going to leave us anyway, just do it now." Then, to reaffirm her own strength and prepare for another estrangement, she said, "I survived your sister going. I can get through it again." When Amy turned to her with a look of horror, Madelyn immediately regretted the statements.

"Oh, that's great, Mom," said Amy. "Just lump me in with Nicole."

Madelyn knew her younger daughter had been hurt by her older sister's estrangement. She wanted to hug Amy and make it all right, but she was scared. Amy might reject her. "If the shoe fits." She hated the cold words even as she spoke them but was compelled to protect herself. She shut the door behind her and went to her own room to cry.

"It was a turning point," says Madelyn. "I realized how much my older daughter's estrangement had changed me."

Although Madelyn knew she could survive another estrangement, she didn't want one. She didn't really believe her younger daughter did either, but the conflict between them was building. Madelyn found herself wondering if she had the gumption to keep trying. She loved Amy, but the situation was vaguely familiar. Madelyn was exhausted just remembering the awful pain from four years earlier when her older daughter, Nicole, had cut all ties with the family. She had expended so much energy for what was, ultimately, a losing battle. Madelyn wondered, *If Amy will just eventually estrange like Nicole did, then why should I even try?*

I can relate to Madelyn. It's not easy to parent other children when the glossy dream of motherhood, unconditional love, and "family forever" has been shattered. Other facets of our lives also become tarnished and complicated.

We'll pick up Madelyn's story in Chapter 4: Shaping the Family. For now, let's focus on her realization. An adult child's estrangement can cause profound changes to parents and other family members. If we're to overcome disillusionment, negativity, bitterness, fear, and dread, we must get real with ourselves about the effects. Awareness opens pathways to renewal and growth, which are necessary if we're to thrive.

The Trauma of Betrayal

Estrangement is traumatic. As a loving parent, the very foundation of who you are is wrapped up in your children. When that identity is ripped away, everything shifts. Suddenly you're adrift, wondering who you can count on and where you fit. Distress and distrust can permeate the present. Fear and dread can infect the future. That's why when other relationships get difficult, parents like Madelyn may wonder: *What's the point?* If doing your very best, giving time, energy, and love won't make a bit of difference, what's the motivation to try?

Whether the feeling is a steady current that tugs you along or pops up in a time of stress, as it did for Madelyn, a *what's-the-point* attitude is damaging. Losing faith in other human beings causes issues in all sorts of relationships: family, work, marriage, friendships, spiritual, and even country. Distrust is insidious.

When we're emotionally traumatized, perhaps especially by an unexpected source, it's easy to fall into negative habits or rely on safe routines. Learning to trust ourselves and others takes effort and commitment. Some of us have worked so hard to please a child and reconcile that we've lost touch with ourselves. That makes for shaky ground on which to base our future.

Let's turn to Paul, whose wife divorced him after twenty-seven years. He suffered horribly when his two adult daughters sided with their mother and refused to see him. "My world collapsed overnight," says Paul, who "sucked it up" and did what he does best. "I worked."

For six years, Paul kept busy in his career. He telephoned his daughters on birthdays and on holidays. He sent money, apologized in long, heartfelt letters for whatever hurt he may have caused, and told them he would always love and be there for them when they were ready to talk. Nothing changed. Then a health scare put Paul in the hospital. His daughters were notified but didn't come. Embarrassed and angry, Paul decided he'd had enough. It was too painful to hear their vicious words or be ignored. At that point, ceasing to contact them was an easy decision. He tucked away a sliver of hope and left possible reconciliation in their hands.

Building a life beyond the safe refuge of his work proved difficult. Paul's social life had narrowed to occasional dinners with his happily married brother and his family. Paul always felt like the odd one out. Knowing he needed change, Paul got a dog to take on long hikes, enrolled in an art class, and joined a dating site. Two years later, he was married, but within a few months, the couple faced a hurdle. His wife wanted to go places and make friends they could join for hobbies. Paul couldn't warm up to her ideas. He'd built a wall around himself and was comfortable in its confines. He'd allowed his new wife in, but when she wanted to expand their world, he grew anxious.

Paul's wife insisted they see a marriage counselor, and the problem quickly became evident. Emotional trauma from the abrupt end to Paul's first marriage and his daughters' continued rejection had taken a toll. Paul had not been fully aware of how deeply his circumstances had affected him. When pushed out of his safe routines, he had panicked. Becoming aware helped Paul chip away at the protective coping techniques that no longer served him.

Let's meet Donna, a divorced mother of two estranged adult children who describes herself as "numb." Donna had worn herself out working full time to support her family. When her husband's business failed, his verbal tirades grew more contentious. He blamed her for everything that ever went wrong. "The abuse had always been there," says Donna. "But it used to be wrapped in sugar."

Donna divorced him when her children were in grade school. He paid sporadic child support but rarely visited. Donna did well for herself and put her son and daughter through college. "Those were hard years," she says, explaining that her children were A-students, and to the outside world looked stellar. At home, though, they were unkind. "They could be sweet when they wanted something," she says. "Then they lashed out the way their father always did." When they graduated, took jobs, and moved out, they began seeing more of him. Donna's son hasn't spoken to her in nearly four years. Her daughter calls occasionally but can be mean.

These days, Donna does IT work remotely. She spends most of her time cloistered in a home office, serving clients around the world. Donna sometimes longs for more companionship but, for now, avoids the risk. On her exercise walks, she shares snippets of conversation with neighbors, but avoids getting close. Keeping her distance is a coping strategy. She even switches grocery stores to sidestep clerks who become too friendly. She explains, "This way, I don't get hurt."

Estrangement between Parents and Adult Children: How Common?

A handful of studies reveals that parent-and-adult-child estrangement is not a rare occurrence. Differences such as sample size, participant demographics, how estrangement is defined from study to study, and even the intended purpose of research aren't always clear when reported by popular media. I've included specifics from a few of the studies below.

- *A study consisting of 354 graduate and undergraduate students from several Northeastern colleges found that 29 participants were estranged from a father, and five participants from a mother.*[1]

Limitations include a small sample size and narrow demographics. Among this mostly single and mostly female student participant population, more than 80% were under age 27. Additionally, for purposes of the study, "estrangement" was defined narrowly, with a complete and deliberate cutoff of all communication.

- *A U.S. study conducted over an 18-month period beginning in 2001 found that 11% of mothers in a 566-family sampling from the greater Boston, Massachusetts area were estranged from at least one adult child.*[2]

The narrow geographic location may not be representative of a wider area. It's also helpful to look at the criteria for defining estrangement. Mothers included only those between the ages of 65 and 75 who had at least two living adult children. The study excluded mothers living in care facilities rather than in the community. Estrangement was defined as meeting at least one of the following criteria as reported by the mother interviewed: (a) no contact with the child in person or via telephone in the past year, or (b) no contact of any sort with the child within the last month and judging the relationship quality at 4 or below on a scale of 1 to 7, with 1 as very distant and 7 as very close.

- *A U.S. study conducted in 1990 with 971 adult-child participants over a 48-state region, found that 7% of adult children had infrequent or no contact with mothers. Using the same criteria for contact with fathers, the frequency jumped to 27% of adult children.*[3]

That this study was conducted three decades ago (as of this book's first printing) is an obvious limitation. Regardless, it's frequently cited, even in newer material. The researchers note that the much higher figure for detached relationships with fathers than with mothers could be rooted in traditional nurturing roles, as well as influenced by divorce-custody decisions that more frequently favor mothers. Over the last several decades, though, fatherly roles include increased involvement in children's day-to-day lives. Shared custody among divorced parents is more common. A more current study might reveal different results.

It may also be important to note that of the studies mentioned here, only the first one was intended to measure the frequency rate of estranged adult children. The second study examined the role differing values may play in relationships, while the third studied familial solidarity as it relates to aspects such as geography and divorce.

Dirty Little Secret

Even if your estrangement was of a cut-and-dried variety without verbal assaults or mind games, being thrust into a group that's often looked down upon is traumatizing and dashes confidence. It's tough to go from good parent to one who's rejected.

I remember vividly the first few awkward times I told anyone beyond my closest circle that one of my five adult children, a son, was estranged. Arms folded. Smiles dropped. People looked, or even stepped, away. I imagined they thought I was a monster, and for a while, I retreated to a place of silence and fear.

Parents feel tremendous pain and grief but will often suffer alone rather than open themselves to blame or judgment. But as estrangement continues, parents must find ways to move forward. Honest communication about their circumstances can be a healing breakthrough and, for many, enlightening others about the problem of estrangement and how common it is holds meaning.

Since I first started speaking out in late 2013, the light of knowledge about estrangement has brightened. In a broad sense, the subject is no longer taboo. Estrangement is frequently reported among celebrities. The media capitalizes on estrangement-related sadness during holidays, and advice columnists routinely field questions on the subject. News sources from disparate countries report about parents suing for filial support from adult children who have abandoned them. Legal professionals offer commentary on disinheriting ungrateful offspring. "Estranged" has become a known term.

Many people recognize that estrangement happens even in the nicest families. That's good, because when people feel judged and perceive discrimination, as many parents of estranged adults do, their physical and mental health can suffer.[4] Society is still biased against parents, though, and blaming them is often slipped into the discourse. The overbearing mother, know-it-all dad, or domineering in-law are overused examples and clichéd fodder for the easy solutions some experts like to convey.

Estrangements caused by extreme, abusive parents are valid and understood. The media provides a big stage for adult children who come from abusive backgrounds, and rightly so. Child abuse is a serious problem and deserves attention. Yet the abuse of parents by adult children also exists. It's just not talked about much. That's partly because it often goes undetected. Parents themselves frequently hide the verbal, financial, emotional, and even physical abuse committed against them by their adult children. They may not get real with themselves in admitting what's happening to them or in honestly labeling the behavior. They may fear retribution, feel responsible somehow, or not want to get their son or daughter into trouble.

One terminally ill mother said her son's physical abuse started decades ago, when he was in his twenties. In a fit of rage, he smashed her hand beneath the top-load washing machine lid. For days, she hid the injury from everyone, including her son. "I tucked my bruised, swollen hand into my sweater pocket so he wouldn't see the extent of the injury," she says. Other incidents included pushing and shoving, as well as verbal abuse. Years later, her son stopped coming around. For more than two decades, she didn't tell a soul about the abuse. She confided in me because, as she puts it, "Before I die, I want other parents to know they aren't alone."

While the public conversation about parent-and-adult-child estrangement and even elder abuse is beginning to change, the loudest voices may still be the most hurtful. Rejected parents complain that experts still blame them, characterize adult children as more psychologically sophisticated, explain away or even excuse bad behavior they say derives from societal change, or tell parents they must have emotional wounding of their own that infected their ability to parent. The never-give-up and eggshell-walking advice that set parents up for endless stress still exists, as does the theme that "good" parents must take responsibility for reconciling.

When these voices come from the helping field, it can be especially hurtful. The side effect is that some parents who might benefit from therapy find the "help" off-putting. I still hear from parents of estranged adult children who have tried everything to make things right, yet when they seek help to get past the pain and move forward for themselves, it's tough to find a clinician who gets it. These parents complain that they're guided toward reconciliation despite their history of trying. Often, they're told, "Let's consider your child's feelings . . ."

Reflecting on the part we may have played in a situation is always wise, and in some cases, can lead to reconciliation. If reconciliation is not the goal, though, parents usually have good reasons for that. They deserve a compassionate ear. Yet the reality of the situation—that the "child" is often in their thirties, forties, or fifties, and the parent is getting elderly and is finally done with the episodic, no-contact tantrums that have gone on for a lifetime—may not be heard or is dismissed.

Despite the complaints, empathetic, sensitive therapists who are familiar with this issue and can help do exist. To find one, you may need to do some interviewing and trial runs. (See the box in chapter two titled "Tips for Finding Support.") One mother shared that her therapist has been a huge help. When she approached this therapist with her concerns about past bad advice, the therapist told her that the mental health field hadn't yet caught up to the estrangement epidemic. Hopefully, her explanation indicates more knowledge will be gained, ultimately leading to more help. However, to achieve that must begin with not only listening to those who are affected but really hearing them.

It's sad when mental health professionals tell me they are embarrassed to admit their own sons or daughters have rejected them. They worry they'll be viewed as frauds, helping other families when they themselves have "failed," despite all their knowledge and expertise. The truth is all the "good" parenting in the world, all the techniques and strategies suggested by child development experts and followed to a T, may not make a difference when it comes to raising children to adulthood, when they make decisions for themselves. Parents influence only a fraction of their children's lives. Additionally, if these therapists were better able to process their own emotions and cope, their experience and understanding of estrangement could position them to be of particular help. A recent study confirms that those who seek help find their counselor's knowledge and understanding of the subject valuable in shaping a positive counseling experience.[5]

With beliefs and opinions skewed toward shaming parents, it's no wonder so many avoid talking about their circumstances. Avoidance is a sure symptom of emotional distress, perhaps to the level of trauma. Life is fleeting. Why not live it fully engaged? Remaining in a state of hurt won't change what has happened to you. Hiding behind emotional guard walls won't bring back an estranged son, or prove you're deserving of love by a daughter who has deserted you.

Donna purposely avoids social entanglements. Paul had fears he didn't fully discern. Madelyn's distress showed up in a moment of intense frustration with her younger daughter. Do you recognize yourself in any of these scenarios? Are any of the feelings or concerns in this chapter familiar to you? Estrangements, with or without abuse, whether prolonged or in cycles of repeated reconciliation and rejection, can have profound effects. With awareness, support, and a commitment to yourself and your happiness, you can overcome challenges. Stepping toward renewal and strength helps you and the ones you love. Any work is worth the effort.

Talking Tips

Talking to others about estrangement doesn't have to be difficult.

- **Create a few short scripts**. Prepared answers boost confidence and help you keep your emotions in check.

- **Plan answers that fit various events or situations**. Small-talk situations don't call for details.

- **Let your relationships guide your words**. Aunt Sally may require a brief update with facts. A nosy meddler can be put off. A friend who cares wants to know you're okay.

- **Consider your goals**. One mother knew she wouldn't see a cousin for a while due to the COVID pandemic. When asked about her daughter in an e-mail, she replied by saying there had been a falling out and, for the moment, the situation wasn't improving. Her goal was to inform the cousin so the news wouldn't later be a shock.

- **Consider your boundaries**. You're not obligated to share information when asked. You could say that it's a painful subject or even that you'd rather not discuss the matter out of respect for your child's privacy. One mother begins by appealing to the questioner's heart: *Surely you understand that this is difficult for me to talk about . . .*

- **Prepare statements with a purpose**. Your words can serve as conversation stoppers, add levity, inform, or assure.

- **Practice and rehearse**. The words will come easily when needed.

 # Shine a Light

The following questions are intended to offer insight. Whether you've been estranged for years or are new to the heartache, awareness can help you to take action for your own well-being. Each group of questions may trigger thoughts or memories about the estrangement, or even about other circumstances. As you go along, use the lines to write down your feelings, including any surprises. Referring to these later may be helpful to you.

How do the questions in each section specifically apply to you? Circle the number that most accurately describes your response using the following scale:

1 = never   2 = occasionally   3 = often   4 = very often   5 = always

1 2 3 4 5   Are you on edge?

1 2 3 4 5   Do you find yourself suddenly angry?

1 2 3 4 5   Are you sometimes overcome with sadness for no apparent reason?

1 2 3 4 5   Do you suffer from guilt or shame?

_____

_____

_____

_____

1 2 3 4 5   Are you troubled by the past, unsettling memories, or images?

1 2 3 4 5   Is your sleep disturbed by insomnia, nightmares, or early awakening?

1 2 3 4 5   Is your focus or concentration impaired?

1 2 3 4 5   Are you struggling with an addiction of any sort?

_____

_____

_____

_____

1 2 3 4 5 Are you compelled to stick to specific routines?

1 2 3 4 5 Do you suffer from panic attacks?

1 2 3 4 5 Are you obsessive or hypervigilant?

1 2 3 4 5 Are you compulsive?

_____

_____

_____

_____

1 2 3 4 5 Do you have difficulty saying no?

1 2 3 4 5 Do you put other people's feelings or choices before your own?

1 2 3 4 5 Do you worry about or try to solve other people's troubles at the expense of your own loss of time, energy, and opportunities?

1 2 3 4 5 Do you make decisions and participate in activities that you later wish you hadn't?

_____

_____

_____

_____

1 2 3 4 5   Would people consider you calm, but you feel anything but?

1 2 3 4 5   Do you feel detached from life or other people?

1 2 3 4 5   Do you feel like an imposter?

1 2 3 4 5   Are you just going through the motions?

_____

_____

_____

_____

1 2 3 4 5   Are you fearful of letting people get to know you?

1 2 3 4 5   Do you shy away from relationships in general or beyond a point?

1 2 3 4 5   Have you lost interest in activities that used to bring you pleasure?

1 2 3 4 5   Do you avoid getting involved (with people, in groups, etc.)?

_____

_____

_____

_____

Consider your answers. You can tally up an overall "score" if that's helpful. However, the purpose of this exercise is to find connections. Where have you circled the higher numbers? Sometimes patterns emerge. Maybe you recognize that your anger or mood-shifts indicate where the pain of estrangement still stumbles you. Perhaps you are more aware of intrusive thinking, negative self-talk, or just how much sleep you continue to lose. Or maybe you notice that you're too involved with other people's problems, possibly even to your own detriment. Pause now and look back at your notes. Jot down a few more thoughts about what you may have discovered. Awareness is the first step to change.

_____

_____

_____

_____

_____

_____

When you're done, take a few deep breaths and stretch. Open your mouth wide and purposely yawn. Recognize any tension you feel and let it go. For some, this exercise will be a big step. Being honest about how we're affected can be stressful. Shining a spotlight on dark places can be scary. Give yourself credit for following through.

Scarred for Life?

Emotional traumas can leave scars. That's why it's important to gain awareness. Hopefully, the "Shine a Light" exercise provided some useful insight.

To better understand emotional scars, let's begin by looking at physical ones. Scars are the body's way to heal and rebuild damaged tissue. But some scars go beyond the original injury, impair movement, affect nerve sensitivity, and create new problems. Emotional scars can be the same. Someone with aggressive physical scarring may sit differently or avoid clothing that rubs against a tender spot, much like Donna avoids close social contact to protect herself from anxiety or hurt.

Even when a person heals well, an old physical injury might bother them when they're tired or stressed. Emotional wounds, though healed, can also flare up at times. Most parents who've suffered an adult child's rejection will be emotionally triggered at some point. Maybe hearing about a publicized celebrity estrangement prompts grief or anger about your own. A serious illness (your own, a family member's, or your estranged adult child's) might bring a dilemma about whether to call—and a tidal wave of crushing memories rolls in. Or, like Paul, you reach out and are humiliated by your child's lack of empathy or concern.

Happy events can also be trying. What if Aunt Edith wants everyone at a niece's wedding? Maybe you didn't tell her (or she forgot) that you don't have your son's contact information or that your daughter shouted obscenities the last time you spoke. Aunt Edith may wonder: *Why can't you just get along?* We'll talk more about extended family later, but the possibilities for triggered pain are many. The scars may not be visible, but that doesn't mean they don't exist. That's why it's important to get real about your experience.

Throughout this book, you'll find useful tips, tools, and resources. Stories of parents who overcame challenges provide positive examples and inspiration. However, when persistent issues interfere with functioning in work, relationships, or your well-being, seeking professional support is important to consider. Problems such as chronic sleep disturbances, addictions, mood swings, and irritability are no fun (for you or those around you). Estrangement can be grueling. There's no shame in admitting that you've been hurt and are seeking support to heal.

You should know that some parents experience Post Traumatic Stress Disorder (PTSD) after estrangement. If you have a history of trauma, you're more vulnerable because traumatic experiences can have a cumulative effect.[6] One mother of an estranged son said her therapist explained emotional hurting like balls in a box, bouncing against a tender, injured spot. The more balls of hurt get put in the box, the more a wound is bumped. I like the analogy because injuries don't heal well, or can even become worse, with repeated agitation.

It's also true that previous trauma you've overcome can resurface with later stress.[7] One mother, Joanna, grew up witnessing her father's abuse of her mother. When her parents divorced, and her father left them, she was troubled by nightmares. Joanna remembers waking up in terror and lying there until dawn, listening for her drunken, abusive father's return to the house. Eventually, the intrusive nightmares faded. Joanna grew up, married, and had a daughter. When Joanna's daughter was in her twenties, she developed a drinking problem and eventually became estranged.

In her midfifties, Joanna was plagued with a series of health problems requiring hospital stays and surgeries. Then her husband passed away. At that time, her estranged daughter reconnected for a short-lived, tumultuous reconciliation. It was then that Joanna began suffering again. Like a little-girl version of herself wrapped in a much older body, she awakened in the night from horrific dreams. Although her father was long gone and her daughter, who had been verbally abusive, had cut contact again, Joanna would lie in bed in terror, listening.

Joanna sought help. Her clinician referred her to a trauma specialist. She was diagnosed with PTSD and effectively treated with Eye Movement Desensitization and Reprocessing Therapy (EMDR) to address the trauma that had been reactivated by her circumstances.

Joanna recently moved to a community where she feels physically secure. She has made new friends, plans to travel, participates in a meditation group for senior citizens, and writes in a daily gratitude journal. She misses her husband and recognizes that his stable, loving presence was a buffer against all her life's stressors. "My husband is irreplaceable," she says. "But I'm taking care of myself. I'm really living. That's what he would want for me."

Eye Movement Desensitization and Reprocessing Therapy, or EMDR

EMDR is a form of psychotherapy used to alleviate the stress of traumatic memories. In brief sessions, clients focus simultaneously on the disturbing memories and an external stimulus, such as their clinician's hand movements, which they are instructed to follow with their eyes. The practice is believed to connect to the biological processes of REM sleep and allows for the reprocessing of trauma and the forming of new associations. EMDR is used on its own or in conjunction with other types of therapy.

Freeze and Fawn

Most people have heard of the first two *F*s of trauma in the stress response known as "fight or flight." This physiological response to a threat includes increased heart rate, blood pressure, and breathing rate, in preparation to either stay and deal with the situation or run to escape it. The response is thought to date back to ancient times, when encountering a dinosaur or a saber-toothed tiger required quick action to save one's life. The fight-or-flight response is helpful in acute danger, and the body is meant to quickly return to its pre-arousal state.

Today, though, the fight-or-flight response is most often discussed in relation to PTSD or sustained stress. In simple terms, the fight-or-flight response gets stuck in the "on" position and doesn't fade away as swiftly as it should. Things like traffic, work, or social pressures can contribute to a more constant state of stress arousal. So can the circumstances that frequently surround estrangement.

Not all parents think of estrangement as trauma but given the disorienting circumstances and shock that often accompany a cutting-off, estrangement qualifies. Some are all too familiar with verbal abuse, fear, or precarious situations caused by adult children that more blatantly fit into a trauma slot. These types of experiences, and the rift itself, further complicate parents' accumulated trauma. For the moment, let's leave the fight-or-flight response and get to the second two Fs of trauma: freeze and fawn. These responses make sense in life and death situations but become dysfunctional in everyday life.

Freeze Response

You might have seen a mouse play dead when caught by a cat. It's a primitive survival tactic. The mouse freezes, the cat loses interest, and the mouse can make a break for it. In human trauma scenarios, to freeze might be illustrated when a crime victim dissociates from what is happening or waits for a chance to escape.

A dysfunctional freeze response in everyday life means tuning out. Examples include habitual TV binge watching, excessive video gaming, using substances that promote mental escape and allow avoidance. Overworking or oversleeping can also be freeze responses.[8] These behaviors dull emotional pain and allow for the denial of an uncomfortable or unhealthy reality.

Fawn Response

You might think of Bambi when you hear the term "fawn response," but this is not about a baby deer. People with a fawn response surrender their wants and needs for another's. Fawning is used to keep the peace and is learned in high conflict or abuse situations. Bending to appease a volatile person keeps the pleaser safe but can also be triggered in less hostile situations. Fawning can become habitual. When this happens, personal boundaries can become blurred, leaving the fawner vulnerable to people who purposely exploit them.

Let's meet Roy, a divorced father of one daughter. For the last two decades, Roy has been caught in a trap of fawning—first with his ex-wife and later with their daughter. After the divorce, he only saw his daughter a few times a year. To avoid her temper tantrums when she was a teenager, he frequently gave in to her whims. If he didn't, she would refuse to visit him. In adulthood, she improved. He paid her tuition to a good school, and she entered a career path that suited her. She also moved within two hours of him, so saw him more frequently. But Roy says she is a lot like her mother and became increasingly self-centered.

When his daughter got married and had a baby, Roy found himself opening his wallet much more often, even to his own financial detriment. For a time, his generosity stalled his daughter's frequent use of the silent treatment and bought him time with his grandchild. Roy is disabled now and living on a fixed income. Without the means to indulge her expensive tastes, he says, "I've all but lost my only family."

Have you been snared in a pattern of striving to please volatile adult children so they will stay in touch or stay calm? Fawning is a way of pacifying others, thus maintaining the appearance of a happy family. If it sounds like walking on eggshells, that's because it is.

People pleasing may be a trauma response to something in your history, including a difficult adult child. Or fawning was learned in other situations and triggered by parenting a difficult child/teen/ adult child.

Becoming Self-Aware

Trauma responses can be triggered without full awareness. Recognizing your own behavior as codependent, people pleasing, or a way to tune out or enable denial, can help you change. Let's look at an example.

One mother called her tendency to repeatedly reach out to the adult children who ignored her "chasing." She felt the need to text again, even when they didn't respond to her previous text. If you are compelled into action that defies logic, take notice. Observing our own compulsions is a form of mindfulness. Once you notice, you can dig deeper for answers and begin to break old habits that might have once been useful but became dysfunctional hangers-on that limit you and fuel unhealthy dynamics.

To use this mother as an example, she could ask herself: *Why do I feel the need to send another text?*

One possibility is denial. She may not want to face the reality that:

- she is being ignored
- she is perceived by her adult children as a pest
- her adult children could be so inconsiderate to their own mother
- her grown children are not nice

If she can text again and prompt a reply, she doesn't have to face these painful truths. A non-hostile reply text, even if it's one word or an emoji, can be viewed as connection, thus keeping her safe from the reality of a non-existent or dismissive relationship.

Another possibility is her codependency and/or overly indulgent empathy. Maybe she sends the additional text because she fears being misunderstood. She frets that her adult children might think she doesn't care, is angry that they didn't reply, or some other fear-based worry that puts the adult child's feelings disproportionately ahead of her own.

It's fine to take on other's perspectives and to care how they feel. Those are normal responses when we love people. But when taken to extremes that are not appreciated and fuel our compulsions, fears, and distress, these behaviors become enslaving and dysfunctional. They do nothing for one's sense of dignity either.

I often hear from parents about their tenuous bits of connection with an estranged child. Often, they feel desperate to hold on and are walking on eggshells to try. I feel for these parents. Frequently, they're in the same position they were in when the estrangement began, when they apologized for gross exaggerations or complete historical rewrites, and sacrificed their own logic, wellness, and other relationships to chase after the one who so hurt them.

One more possibility to mention here is the sensitivity that can plague parents who have been rejected by a child. An unanswered text might be given more weight than it should. Even in healthy relationships, if an adult child is busy and under stress, they may not immediately answer. In today's world, with all our immediate connectivity, perceived slights may be more prevalent than we think.

For Your Growth

Whether you're fawning, freezing, chasing, or otherwise reacting, recognizing the unhealthy behavior provides a chance to grow. Ask yourself questions such as:

- *Has this happened elsewhere or in other relationships?*
- *Have I ever tuned out in some way?*
- *Have I tried to appease or please?*

Then ask yourself: *When and with whom?*

Mining our histories for the seeds of our own quirks, inadequacies, and overall character won't fix an estrangement. Awareness propels us toward positive change *in ourselves*. There is always room for improvement. Even so, beware of falling into the trap of always fixing oneself. Peace and joy along the journey should be on the agenda.

If we're fortunate enough to gain a caring, mutually respectful, and loving relationship with adult children who once rejected us, they will also need to have grown. Whether or not our adult children return to us, taking good care of ourselves and learning more about our history and how it shaped us, fuels a happier, more fulfilling future—with others and on our own.

Codependency

In the past, the term, "codependent" referred to unhealthy devotion, help, and enabling in a relationship involving substance abuse. The codependent person in such a relationship is preoccupied with someone whose substance abuse renders them inebriated and/or unable to function for themselves. Nowadays, the term is used more liberally, even within relationships separate from substance abuse.

A codependent person is overly preoccupied with another person's needs and wants, even to the point of self-neglect. Other telltale signs include poor boundaries, feeling responsible for another's mistakes, difficulty saying no, feeling compelled to take care of other people, a need for control over others' behavior, and wanting everyone to like you. Codependent people sometimes have difficulty asserting their own needs and may put themselves last on their own lists.

Codependency is probably the byproduct of dysfunctional relationships. The roots for codependency grow in households that feature substance abuse, dismissive caregivers, or the denial of issues when there are clearly problems. Simply by way of their nature, some people may be more at risk for codependency than others.

If you are a people pleaser, preoccupied with others' lives or problems, feel responsible for others' mistakes, or often put yourself last, codependency is worth exploring. For more information, consider an online codependency quiz. They're not foolproof, aren't meant to provide any sort of diagnosis, and may be attached to the marketing of a coaching or therapy program—but the quizzes may be helpful. Also consider books on the subject. I've listed a classic, as well as a newer book by the same author. An online bookstore search will help you choose books that best fit your experiences.

Suggested Titles

Codependent No More: How to Stop Controlling Others and Start Caring for Yourself by Melody Beattie

The New Codependency: Help and Guidance for Today's Generation by Melody Beattie

Bend and Bounce Back

You can learn much from traumatic experiences. So it's crucial to hold your history close as you step forward but not so tight that you get lost in it. The ability to learn from adversity, grow stronger, and bounce back epitomizes resilience, and that's what much of this book will help you to achieve. Gain really can come from pain, but resilience is unique to the individual and affected by a variety of factors.[9]

Below, we'll consider five aspects of resilience gleaned from research and tailored here to parents of estranged adult children. As you read, reflect upon how each aspect applies to you and your situation. Then, we'll look at an example of resilience.

1. *Choice: Make the decision to save yourself.* When parents receive the news that they're no longer wanted, shock is a natural response and can be paralyzing. You may think the cutting-off will be temporary because it's too painful to imagine it lasting. Ideals about unconditional love may hold you hostage—you're unable to get through to your child and reconcile but also unable to let go. We'll deal with those and more feelings in the pages ahead. For now, realize that to move forward, you'll need to make a choice to fight for yourself and your future. You'll need to want to save yourself.

2. *Honesty: See the situation for what it is.* It's tough to admit the truth. The son or daughter in whom you invested so much time, love, and energy has turned on you. Weren't you a good parent? Didn't you instill good values, exemplify decency and kindness, and teach right from wrong? The truth is that life is full of outcomes that don't fit expectations and payoffs that are worked for but not achieved. Even if you have felt all alone, you are not the only one who never imagined this could happen to a good parent. Although painful, you must look honestly at what is happening. Accept the facts: your child(ren) rejected you, unfairly blamed you, and/or even abused you. Your child may have left without explanation. Or you are one in a vast family who fits the modern vernacular that is so carelessly applied: One of the so-called "toxic" moms or dads who did their best but were abandoned anyway.

3. *Focus: Look to a new life.* Getting beyond the shock and pain requires a shift in perspective. Stop focusing on what you have lost and longing for what no longer exists or isn't currently possible. Instead, focus on making a life for yourself. If you were shipwrecked on a deserted island, you would have a choice: mope around wishing things were different or find what you need to survive. You might not know how long you'd be there or what the future held, but despite the uncertainty, you'd make a life for yourself, at least for now. Think Tom Hanks in the movie *Cast Away* and his volleyball friend, Wilson. Focus on what you'll do now and next.

4. *Creativity: Be on your own path.* Resilience is unique to the individual.[10] Parents' forward paths may be similar but will have their own twists and turns. Some people have ready resources such as self-confidence, social support, and vibrant physical health. Others must seek the help of a therapist or require

medical treatment. Whatever your limitations, you can be resilient.

One mother with multiple sclerosis learned about goal setting in my book, *Done With The Crying*, and reached objectives that supported her health, thus helping her journey forward after estrangement. Another mother has a physical disability that severely limits her mobility. She considers her strong imagination a resource and uses it to fight against despair or envy. By using your limitations and strengths in creative ways, and by seeking support, you can move forward, resilient in your own way.

5. *Flexibility: Be willing to change.* What works at one point may not work forever. Early on, closely held hope for relationship restoration may keep you going. Later, hoping for what never materializes can be debilitating. There are seasons of estrangement and turning points when your attitude can change. Resilience requires flexibility in your expectations and thinking. The cliché of the tree that bends in the wind, rather than breaks, fits.

Resilience in Action

Forward momentum isn't always a straight line. Sometimes we waver or bounce backward a little before making leaps ahead. "The Boat," one story from my blog at RejectedParents.NET, has become a reader favorite. Because it illustrates resilience, I'm sharing a version of it here. As you read, imagine the described scenes. Immerse yourself. Will you remain in the wake of your son or daughter's rejection? Or will you save yourself?

The Boat

Imagine the adult child who has rejected you is on a boat. You're looking up from the water below. See your son or daughter dropping all sorts of poison off the back of the boat. Imagine the angry, stinking words your son or daughter flung at you. See those poisonous words hitting the water with a splash. Acrid smoke rises from them. It stings your eyes and fills your lungs so you can barely breathe. You feel as if you'll choke.

You cough and gag, but your child isn't done yet. A net appears in the murky depths and stretches across the open water. You can't swim to the boat without getting caught and entangled. With the barrier between you, your child is still not done. He throws out hooks and spills out chum that attracts vicious sharks.

"Wait!" you call out. Dazed and confused, you holler and plead. "Help! Can't we talk?" But your child takes the helm. The boat speeds away. There is no denying this. Your child has hurt you and left you behind.

See the wake of the boat. Feel the choppy waves. Smell the acrid fumes rising from your child's spiteful words. Notice the sharks.

Now, what? Do you:

- Stay in the spot, paralyzed, struggling to keep your head above water? The sharks lunge and bite at the net to try and get to you.
- Wait there, expending precious energy treading water but resolute that you can fix this no matter what? Meanwhile, the horrible toxic clouds fill your lungs . . .
- Swim toward the net, planning to cut through and follow the disappearing boat despite your grown child's rejection? You'll put yourself in shark-infested waters.

Those are all options, but as you float there, your legs and arms tiring in the choppy waves, you consider another. You could turn and swim to shore. You could save yourself.

In the distance, the shore looks lonely, and you're uncertain. It's a brand-new world over there on dry land. Not what you expected to be facing at this point in your life. You don't know what a future on or beyond that beach holds without your child. Should you swim to shore?

You look back at the boat, which is getting smaller on the horizon. The sharks bite at the net, their dolls' eyes staring. The toxic cloud of angry words your child has dumped is settling into the waves, spreading, an ugly, contaminating slick. Despite the danger, you feel compelled to swim after the boat. Isn't following your child, despite the horrors, what a truly good parent would do? Isn't a parent's love unconditional? Shouldn't your devotion be tireless?

You waver there, swallowing some water as the waves swell and the poison cloud drifts near. You want to swim to safety, but is it safe on those unknown shores? And . . . what will people think if you give up on your child?

The water is cold. Your legs are numb. Your arms are tired. The cloud of poison burns your lungs with every breath. You can see your estranged adult child getting smaller and smaller as the boat is nearly out of sight. How can someone so distant loom so very large?

The boat turns. It's coming back! It roars close, and your child tosses out a life ring. Relieved and grateful, you laugh for joy as you reach for it. This nightmare is finally over!

But then your child snatches back the rope. Once again, the boat speeds away. You're in its wake, growing weary as the water closes in. What do you do? *Make a choice to save yourself.* Get out of the water. Turn and swim to the shore.

You may find sunny beaches, creative sandcastles, and refreshing waterfalls. Don't look back. *Focus on what's ahead.*

Expect a storm or two. Gather resources to weather them. You may see other parents climbing cliffs to a new beginning, but you're not able to. Ask for help. Find some vines to hoist yourself up the cliff. Or, bush-whack a trail all your own. Get creative and make your own way forward.

It won't be all work. You reach the top of the cliff and wait there where you can still see the boat in the distance. You find sweet fruits, coconut trees, perhaps even pineapples, and a few good friends. From the clifftop, you send out messages. You write them on paper, stuff them in bottles, and toss them into the sea. You radio the boat, sending messages of love and hope that are never answered.

Then, one day, you realize the clifftop resources are dwindling. It's time to move on. You bend and flex. Glad for your life, you walk away, ready to treasure every day.

Can you recognize yourself in the story? Maybe your son or daughter didn't hurl accusations. Regardless, you've been left in the wake of rejection. I know that feeling of treading water but fearing the shore. In the pages ahead, you'll find the examples of parents and families who have faced estrangement, learned to manage them-selves, their families, and their future. Their experiences, as well as the information and exercises ahead, will help you bend and bounce back too—maybe even stronger and more resilient than before.

Lifetime Map

Examining your own history provides insight into how circumstances, events, and your emotional experiences may have worked to shape your outlook and how you cope. This powerful exercise can help to restore the self and clear a path to a future you design.

Before starting: Decide to commit. The Lifetime Map is best completed in a series of short sessions spanning several days to weeks. The basic idea is to create a timeline for your life, provide emotional context, and tell the story of who you are, where you've been, and where you're going.

What you'll need: While you could use a computer, I recommend a large notepad and a favorite pen. The act of writing by hand is known to deepen thinking, enhance creativity, and relieve stress. Why not glean those benefits in the process?

Set the stage: Choose a time when you're relaxed. Remembering the story of you can be fun. Recall your very essence and even reclaim it. Don't judge your memories, and don't discount them.

Whenever I ponder my early childhood, one memory always come to mind. Me waiting by the window for the rain to stop. When it did, I ran outside where a beautiful pink lily had bloomed during the storm. Now, more than fifty years later, that moment still holds magic. It also holds a clue about my affinity for the natural world. Being the youngest child, the last to go to school, and often "too little" to tag along with my siblings, nature became a friend.

Do you have specific memories that relate to your interests as an adult? You'll be finding connections as you reflect. Don't rush. Savor the wonders of your history no matter how small. Consider how they figure in to who you were and who you've become.

Words of caution: When a memory feels fuzzy, you may be

tempted to ask for help. While that could be a good idea, it's important that this be *your* history. Individuals remember things differently. Even siblings in the same family can have unique viewpoints on the same events. For your Lifetime Map, the point is to interpret your own experiences.

Digging into your history can stir up feelings you may not be prepared for. If at any time you feel overwhelmed, take a break. A few moments in a natural setting may soothe you. If you're stuck ruminating over an incident or memory, turn negative thoughts into positive ones. *Why did that happen?* becomes *It's in the past. Good things happen to me.* This may sound trite, but if negative thoughts can multiply, positive ones can be just as fruitful.

With hurtful memories, reflect on anything you handled well or can be proud about. Focusing on what you did right, even in a bad situation, reduces stress. You might also take a walk or otherwise move your body. The release of physical tension frees the mind.

If you can't find relief, consider seeking the help of a mental health clinician. Share what comes up and how you feel about it. This exercise is meant to help, not hurt.

Phase One: Get Started

Begin with your birthplace and date, then jot notes about your family at the time. Break your life into sections such as birth to age five, the elementary school years, and so on. If a certain period requires more attention, provide the space. Allow at least a page or two for every era, but don't worry if you end up leaving blank space. You may remember more later. Proceed through the years answering prompts such as these:

- Where did I live? (e.g. city, neighborhood, house, circumstances)
- What did I accomplish? (e.g. learned to ride a bike, got my first job, etc.)
- Who do I remember and what did we do together?

- Did anything special happen?
- Did I start a new hobby?
- What situations feel uncertain or incomplete?

Consider major events whether good or bad, remember your pets, vacations, school days, deaths, holidays, family relationships or strife, a divorce, your own friends or those of the family. Note anything that comes to mind as significant and give it a spot on the Lifetime Map. Don't judge, just jot. Add thoughts and feelings but don't stress about recording every detail. Aim for a basic outline. You can fill in more later. Often, as you progress through the years, new memories will surface. Page back and add your thoughts.

Once your basic Lifetime Map is complete, let it rest. Allow yourself to add in events as they come to you. You may find that you had completely forgotten about an upsetting event that happened in the third grade. A lost pet, a bullying incident, or when your new bike was stolen and you got blamed for leaving it somewhere.

Feel-good events may resurface. Be sure to savor those memories, too. A prize in an elementary school art show, a first kiss, winning a sports trophy, or your correct guess of how many jelly beans were in the jar. Write them down.

Phase Two: Feel Your Way Through

Here, you'll expand on your basic timeline. Thumb through your notes. Embellish your thoughts and add in feelings. You won't remember your birth, but maybe you were told about it. In my family, there was a short film clip to commemorate my arrival. My mother's handwriting was on the little box that held the reel: "Sheri coming home from the hospital." I remember feeling loved when my family occasionally watched that clip. That memory leads to other home-movie memories, all within family context.

We used to play a black and white rodeo film backward—and laugh at the rider falling *onto* the horse instead of off. Films of our

Yellowstone trips in two consecutive summers show my mother's bleached blonde bob and Bermuda shorts era. The happy films ended abruptly. My father's job changed, resulting in tougher years for my family.

Follow the rabbit holes of your memories. Jot down your feelings as you go. Put them in context.

PHASE THREE: Find Your Story

Take your life in sections and look for themes. Note revelations that come to mind. What circumstances or events helped shape you into who you have become? What roles did you play? Once you have pondered your story with these thoughts in mind, you're ready to leverage your history for your future. Capsulize your life using emotional language. Tell your history and who you are.

Beth's childhood with a long-haul-trucker father and a mother left to parent her and two younger siblings, shaped Beth into a quiet, helpful sort. Never one to complain, she pitched in at school and in the community. Becoming a teacher seemed the perfect fit.

Beth married a man she saw as "larger than life." He took advantage of her loyal nature. At 26, she found herself alone with two children to raise. Embarrassed she'd fallen for him, Beth steeled herself to the pain and put her children first. She provided a decent life, saw them through college, and was understanding when they decided to look for their father. She didn't badmouth him or complain when they saw him regularly and visited her less.

Meanwhile, she retired from teaching and helped her mother through a protracted illness. Soon after her mother's death, Beth's adult children confronted her. Their father had blamed her for the divorce and told them she kept him away from them while growing up. When she refuted his revisionist

*history, they abandoned her. Beth was devastated. Despite all
her service to other people, she had somehow become isolated.*

By doing her Lifetime Map, Beth gained insight into how her personality contributed to her circumstances. She takes pride in her integrity and goodness but learned she needs to practice better self-care, to
speak up more often, and even to put herself first. She's become mindful of that need on a daily basis and is making plans to do more for herself in bigger ways, such as tours to beautiful locations, in the future.

Alternatives

If the idea of writing about your life doesn't resonate, you can still
benefit from your Lifetime Map. Below are a few alternatives for
this exercise. Use as is or borrow elements for a method you create.
You're in charge.

Voice message: Once you've completed a basic history, perhaps
as simple as a bulleted list with dates, embellish by voice. Use your
phone or computer to record your spoken story. When you play
the recording back, you may be surprised how your story resonates
or matches up to other of your life's puzzle pieces.

Hobby time: One father, Gabe, chose to recall his history with
biking as a fun context. He catalogued his bicycles throughout his
child- and adulthood, remembering friends, the different routes
he used to ride, and why. He remembered ramming his first tri-
cycle repeatedly into the back fence and connected that memory
to the rage he felt when his father left the family. At age 12, he got
a newspaper route, and his bicycle represented freedom. In adulthood, when his marriage hit a rough patch, his long, solitary rides
allowed him time to think. When his son became estranged, bicycling provided escape. Now in his sixties, he and his wife plan to
splurge on motor-assisted bikes and cycle together.

What hobbies have you enjoyed? If you've spent time traveling, memorable locations might give your Lifetime Map structure.

Maybe you've always loved artwork, photography, or handcrafts, and you can create your Lifetime Map around those pursuits.

Book it: Enjoy scrapbooking? Consider using old photographs to make your pastime your Lifetime Map in keepsake form. Add stickers, poems, and notes-to-self. Make it for you alone or perhaps to share.

Collage: Use your own photos or those cut from magazines as visual representations. Glue them to poster board and add snippets of text about your life. A soft rose with dewdrops on the silky petals might represent a time you saw as a new beginning. Ditto a sunrise. A stormy sea can punctuate text you write about a difficult time. Bring the end around to an image to represent a future you design. Choose a calm lake for peace or a strong tree for your endurance. If you prefer to work on the computer, you could do a digital collage (and there are online courses for this).

It's Your Life

Whichever way you complete your Lifetime Map, end on a positive note. Come up with at least one forward action that's within your reach. Be specific. Deciding to take better care of yourself sounds good but is too generic. It's better to come up with details such as getting your hair styled regularly or adding colorful vegetables to every meal. Joining groups to make friends sounds fine but deciding on a group type and planning conversation starters is a better plan.

This is your life. When it comes to living, there is no "one size fits all." You can choose and implement a plan for your best way forward. What chapters would you like to add? The ending isn't written yet. It's your choice.

Notes

CHAPTER TWO

Take Care of Your Mind, Body, and Spirit

"I have chosen to be happy because it is good for my health."
—VOLTAIRE

Divorced mother, Linda, began to suffer physically when her two daughters were teenagers. Her body ached all over. "Some days even my bra straps would hurt me," she says. Yet test after test came back negative. Her doctor finally diagnosed her with fibromyalgia, but Linda wasn't so sure. She believed her pain was caused by stress. Her ex-husband, who had moved to another state and didn't see the girls much, had decided he wanted a more active role in their lives. "He began to undermine my parenting," Linda says.

As her daughters grew and the visits with their father became more frequent, a new symptom appeared. "Little pink areas on my arms," says Linda. "Like the bruising you see on old people. And they would take a long time to heal."

There was no physical trauma to cause the spots, but as the lesions became more frequent, Linda recognized a connection. The dark pink and purplish areas appeared whenever she argued with her oldest daughter, Diedre. Unfortunately, their quarrels were worsening. Diedre was spending a lot of time visiting her father and stepmother. She would come home angry at her mom.

At that time, Linda's younger daughter, Tina, was refusing to visit her father. So, she wasn't affected directly but did witness the fights between her sister and mother. "She would hide in the basement and cover her ears," says Linda. "But she overheard."

By the time Diedre was sixteen, Linda was rarely going out. She wore long sleeves and long pants to cover the discolored areas on her arms, legs, and back. In pain, embarrassed about her appearance, and desperate for peace, she agreed that Diedre should go live with her father. Linda was sad but admits that having Diedre out of the house was a relief to her and to Tina.

With her health improving, Linda could once again enjoy the lifestyle that her previous career in television afforded her. She and Tina traveled to cities around the world to visit the filming locations of their favorite movie and TV shows. Linda wished things were different with Diedre, but she wanted nothing to do with her. She still had Tina, and for a while, they got on with their lives.

When Tina started college, she made a trip to visit her father and sister. "She came back saying her dad and stepmother had tried to brainwash her like they had Diedre," says Linda, who was grateful Tina was on to them. She knew Tina would continue to become more independent in adulthood but couldn't have predicted the changes in her to come.

The summer Tina was twenty, she returned from college with an attitude of blatant disrespect. She had parties in the home and left the mess, took Linda's car without permission, and laughed when she busted the side mirror as she backed out of the garage. Linda says, "When I asked her to help out with chores, she'd say that's what *I* was for and then go off with her friends."

That summer, Linda's health took a nose dive. She wondered if she might be dying of some mysterious condition. Doctors hadn't helped.

Then one of them listened as she described the stress in her life, connected it to her symptoms, and diagnosed her with psychogenic purpura. The condition is one of intense bleeding under the skin, triggered by emotional distress. Though somewhat rare, and often associated with anxiety, depression, or other mental illness, it is also real.

Seeking to calm her environment for her health, Linda told Tina that she could no longer stay with her on summer breaks. Tina laughed, but for the first time ever, Linda was determined to stand up for and care for herself. "She told me I couldn't afford to lose her because she's all I've got," Linda says. "But I told her I'd rather be alone than with someone abusing me."

The Stress Connection

Most people rarely face life-and-death situations, but as was discussed in Chapter One, our bodies sometimes respond as if we do. Traffic that makes us late, an unexpected bill, or some other modern-day mishap can put us in a physical and mental state of alarm. Day-to-day aggravations can add up, and when there's no clear end to stressful events, our physiological response doesn't get the chance to calm itself. The anguished uncertainty of estrangement can be like that.

Parents who are cut off by adult children worry and fret. *Where did I go wrong? How will this affect the rest of our family? What will this do to my estranged child's future?* Such ruminating causes anxiety, anger, and even depression. Sporadic contact that gives hope or dashes it, a feeling of being powerless to repair the relationship and embarrassed that your own kid disowned you, or not understanding why the estrangement occurred, becomes a recipe for sustained stress.

Experts agree that stress is linked to cardiovascular disease, diabetes, arthritis, cancer, and other ailments. Estrangement, whether episodic, enduring, or shockingly fresh, is hard on health. Learning ways to mitigate the effects and putting those techniques into practice could be lifesaving. This chapter will help.

Mind Over Matter

"We become what we think." *Buddha*

"Pessimism never won any battle." *Dwight D. Eisenhower*

"Whether you think you can, or you think you can't—you're right." *Henry Ford*

Mind Your Mind

How we think about stress can make a difference in how we cope.[1] Our thoughts work with our emotions and can lead us forward or hold us back. If we're focused on our sadness, we can feel powerless to help ourselves. If we're grateful for whatever is good in our lives, we're more likely to make an effort and to utilize our existing resources, such as social supports, that help.[2]

People routinely attribute ill health to the stress of estrangement. I regularly hear parents say, "This is killing me." I made a similar statement when my son called after a year of separation, and then didn't follow through with the continued contact he promised. At that point, my health dipped to an all-time low. My doctor warned me I was a prime candidate for a heart attack. Needing to take charge rather than wait around feeling helpless, I called my son to discuss our situation. The conversation proved fruitless. My decision to take care of myself, something I could control, and to let go of what I couldn't—his actions—may have saved my life. I got serious about recovering from the devastation. I had been a good mother to him. I had a life to live. Dan would not steal my joy, my peace, or my future.

Linda came to that point twice. First, when she let Diedre go to live with her father, and later, when Tina became so disrespectful. She set up boundaries to care for her health. With a wry wit that reveals optimism, Linda says, "Diagnosis? I'm allergic to my kids." Linda is committed to lifestyle changes that make her symptoms manageable. Meditation, walking, and exposure to nature help. So does her attitude. "The road to a happy destiny is paved by focusing on gratitude and joy," she says. "Those thoughts and feelings can triumph over grief and loss."

Evaluate your view of the estrangement. Turn negative thinking around. For example, consider what you don't miss. Is their absence freeing in some way? Wondering what sort of mood your son or daughter will be in can take its toll. Perhaps you've been distressed over requests for money, or weary of forceful opinions over your political or religious views. Or your life may have been a constant tightrope because you knew that one innocent statement could turn a happy day into a nightmare where you were always wrong and always to blame.

Does the estrangement promote your growth in some way? In my tech-savvy son's absence, I learned how to use content management software, install it on an Internet domain, and then add functional plugins. The result was the support forum for rejected parents that became a healing lifeline for so many, including myself. It was an opportunity to expand and grow. The outcome has been more confidence and enthusiasm for future projects that require learning. And I'm not the only one. Many parents tell me they have moved beyond the daze and shock of early estrangement, seizing control of their thinking and then their lives. They have branched out into all sorts of directions. Healthy growth fosters positive feelings, but it starts with how you think.

Reshaping our thinking about stressful situations decreases negative emotions and increases positive ones. On the other hand, altering behavior to hide our emotions (suppression) decreases positive feelings and can heighten negative ones. That's important because so many parents "walk on eggshells," sometimes for years, to keep the peace. They say that if they talk about their own troubles, they're ridiculed, put off, or even blamed by unempathetic offspring who say the parents brought the problems upon themselves. Some parents are afraid to state a differing opinion for fear the son or daughter will keep the grandchildren away. These parents hide their frustration, anger, and dismay, yet feel the stress in their bodies. They know first-hand that suppressing emotions can harm health.[3]

Consider how your own thinking may be mentally and physically impacting you. Ancient and modern philosophers are right: We are what we think.

 # Your Turnaround

In the example below, read the negative statement on the left. On the right is an example of turning the thought around.

NEGATIVE	POSITIVE TURNAROUND
My grandchildren will never know me.	*One day, maybe they'll come looking. For now, I'll do everything I can to make myself strong. When they ring my doorbell, I'll be dressed and ready!*

When you read each statement above and consider its implications, note what images come to mind. The sad statement, "My grandchildren will never know me," lacks hope and fuels a sense of powerlessness. I imagine slumped shoulders and a lack of will. Its turnaround, however, motivates an energetic response. Thinking like the turnaround, you're more likely to get up and going, to exercise, eat right, and learn new things. If the grandchildren do show up, you'll be ready, relevant, and have things to talk about. Which statement best supports well-being? There is no downside to living with a positive frame of mind. You're not disloyal for choosing happiness.

Below are a few more examples. Review the negative statements and their turnarounds. Then come up with your own. For

BEYOND DONE WITH THE CRYING

negative examples missing their positive counterpart, write one in. It's good practice.

At the bottom, use the blank space on the left to write in any negative beliefs that have personally plagued you. Turn them around on the right.

NEGATIVE	POSITIVE TURNAROUND
I'll never get over this.	*I'm moving beyond the hurt. I've been through tough situations before. Even baby steps move me forward.*
A good mother would never give up on her own child.	*I'm not giving up. I'm giving in. My son's decision is beyond my control. For now, giving in allows me to better care for myself and be present for the ones who love me.*
I must be a failure if I raised someone who could hurt us like this.	*I raised my daughter to be kind and caring, but she has changed. Despite her decisions, I will remain a person of integrity. Her failure does not define me.*
I can't be happy until my family is restored.	*I owe it to myself and those who love me to make the most of my life now. I can hope for the future while finding joy in the present.*
Everything I did was for him/her. My life is over now.	

NEGATIVE	POSITIVE TURNAROUND
This is taking years off my life.	
If my own child can reject me, then no relationship is safe. I'll never be able to trust anyone ever again.	
I can't face another holiday without him.	
I'd like companionship but no wo/man could understand this situation.	

Negative	Positive Turnaround

Changing your mind is an ongoing process. Here are a few more options to help.

- Transfer any of the turnarounds that inspire you onto notecards or a bookmark. Place them in prominent places where you'll see them often. Or keep them handy to pull out for a reminder.

- Try this exercise at the mirror. Really feel the part as you say the negative statements aloud. Notice how you look and feel. Then take a cleansing breath and smile before saying the positive ones. Infuse your voice with conviction. See and feel the difference!

- Set versions of the positive turnarounds to familiar tunes. Sing them when you're under stress in traffic or on your way to an important event. I'm always singing in the shower or on a busy day. Try it—you'll feel the fun!

Finally, visualize your "turnaround" in a bigger way. Close your eyes and imagine yourself pivoting from a dark cloud that represents emotional distress (worry, dread, frustration, anger . . .) and lifting your face to warm spring sunlight. See yourself plucking a bright, scented flower or a ripe, sweet fruit from an abundant garden. Smile as you walk forward on a sunlit path. Memorize that image of yourself stepping forward, happy and fulfilled, your senses alive with the scents, sounds, and scenery. Now, call up that vision if you ever feel down. *Be your turnaround.*

"Social" Security

Decades of research show that social relationships fortify well-being. Positive social connections reduce high-risk behaviors, raise self-esteem, increase feelings of belonging, and promote effective coping skills. A trusted friend can help you see a situation from a better angle. A lighthearted companion or an uplifting group elevates mood. It's also true that a happy spouse is a strong predictor of better health for their mate.[4]

Let's meet Serena and Dale, whose thirty-four-year-old daughter, Vannie, refused all contact two years ago. Sad and embarrassed, the sexagenarian couple stopped socializing. Then Serena was diagnosed with breast cancer. She felt isolated in her neighborhood—and in her marriage. "When I talked about Vannie, Dale would get mad," she says. "He has quite a temper. So, I'd stick to safer topics." Unfortunately, Serena can attest that bottled emotions have a way of popping up later to wreak havoc. "I'd lie awake at night," she says. "My mind wouldn't shut off."

As part of her cancer treatment, Serena joined a support group for patients to share their feelings. "It helped," says Serena, who didn't speak of Vannie directly but says, "People relate to family stress." After the second meeting, Serena came home and took down every picture of Vannie. "Seeing her face all around me made me sad," she says. "But I also realized I was mad."

The support group nurtured Serena to more freely express her emotions. In the short term, getting angry works as a motivator, perhaps especially when it replaces debilitating sadness. But persistent anger threatens relationships and tends to unravel social supports.

Her husband's temper had stifled Serena's and may also have slowed their forward momentum after the estrangement. Frequent outbursts can cloud judgment and inhibit positive coping skills.[5] Serena recognizes this in Dale. She wanted to sell the home where they raised Vannie and move to their home in Florida for "a fresh start." Whenever she mentioned it, Dale would just get mad. "It was like he was stalled," she says. "But I knew we couldn't keep waiting around for her. When do we get to put ourselves first?"

If Serena asked that question in my peer support group, the answer would be a resounding, "Now!" The group is filled with people who realize they wasted too much time waiting and wish they'd have taken care of themselves better all along. That doesn't mean parents must give up on the possibility of a restored relationship either. They can hope for the best, continue to reach out if they feel that's right, but also tend to their needs and future. The best, most stress-buffering support groups include valid information and the wisdom of personal experience from empathetic people who are willing to share.[6] Look for those elements in any group. Also consult the box "Tips for Finding Support" in this chapter.

Another benefit of the cancer support group was that Serena realized how much she needs friends. She and Dale rehearsed how to answer possible questions about Vannie and have begun rekindling existing friendships. It's working for them. Not everyone is so fortunate. Some parents discover that they must look elsewhere for a supportive network. In *Done With The Crying*, there are some faith-based and other stories to help. Here, let's talk about a single mother who says her social network in a small town all but dissolved with her son's estrangement.

Myrna's son was a star high school basketball player in the quaint community she'd moved to years ago as an unwed mother. They were both well-loved. Or so Myrna thought . . . Then her son met a divorced woman six years his senior while working in a nearby city.

The trouble started the first time the woman came to Myrna's house. Her son introduced Myrna to his girlfriend, who stepped inside, pinched her nose, and complained of a smell. Myrna says, "I have always kept a clean house." Even so, Myrna hunted for any possible source, took out the half-full kitchen trash, and lit a scented candle to cover the odor she didn't detect. "My son was so happy," says Myrna. "I wanted to get along."

After hearing so many thousands of stories of adult children who estrange after meeting a love interest, what happened to Myrna next has become familiar to me. The typical scenario goes down something like this:

- Adult child calls after a casual meeting to ask why the parent was unkind to the romantic friend, disrespectful of the friend's family, or asserts some other unsettling accusation.

- Although baffled, the parent apologizes to keep the peace.

- The parent continues to try to get along and may even go over-board to welcome the friend. The adult child's happiness over-shadows the parent's own.

- Things go better for a time. The parent ignores red flags such as conversations that just don't feel quite right, words that return to the parent's ears slightly altered, frequent last-minute plan changes, or the feeling of always being the one who must bend.

- A wedding is planned (often at the parent's expense), and things get more heated.

Variations include a honey-sweet future in-law whose attitude makes a U-turn with the wedding ring. Or there's a last-minute blow-up that includes a wedding disinvite.

Myrna's son eloped just after he was hired for a coaching position at his old high school. Myrna wasn't invited to the ceremony. He moved his wife and her two children to Myrna's hometown.

"Over the course of a year, my daughter-in-law all but erased me," says Myrna. "She gossiped about me, cried to everyone, and convinced people I'd known for years, including my son, that I was a horrible person to her." Myrna adds, "Those Lifetime TV channel movies where the nanny steals someone's family must be based on people like my daughter-in-law. She assassinated my identity."

Myrna remembers feeling all alone. "I was sick, too. For the first time in my life, I got asthma and allergies. Some days I could hardly breathe. I ballooned up to two hundred pounds, was prediabetic, depressed, and bitter. I stopped caring about things, too." She laughs. "I woke up one day and realized my daughter-in-law must have been psychic that first day we met. That morning, I realized my house really had begun to stink."

Irritated, Myrna cleaned up, joined an online weight loss group, and used a treadmill. As she lost weight and felt better, she began to contemplate her future. *What do I want for myself? What can I do? What expectations will I need to let go of?*

Myrna ended up selling her home, taking her small pension from decades working at a discount bakery, and moved to another town. "Moving was stressful," she says. "It's not for everyone, and I spent at least six months just getting used to a new place. It also took time to make friends, but I worked at it." That included looking at past relationships and thinking about what she wanted from new ones. Her new location provided a fresh start where she could choose hobbies and friends based on her own needs instead of always the needs of others. Myrna took classes, adopted a little rescue dog for walks with a community group, and slowly got close to a few people. "It was scary," admits Myrna. "But it was right for me."

Myrna's only regret is being too nice—first to her son and then to the woman he chose. "I should have stuck up for myself from the very beginning. Instead, I tried to keep the peace with my son." She still misses him but says, "He changed. And I'm okay. I have a life today, and you know what? Even without him, it's pretty darned good."

Making New Friends

Friends are part of any social network but making them isn't always easy. You may have spent so much time devoted to family that you don't know how to start. If you find yourself needing new connections, it pays to first reflect on how you define a friend.

Ask yourself:

- *What does friendship mean to me?* A writer friend of mine once said she has her tennis friends, her art friends, her book club friends . . . Her social network is based on mutual interests around which their activities revolve. Her description contrasts with another pal who considers group-related friends "associates," and counts few people as actual friends. What's your distinction, if any?

- *How much time and energy do I want to devote?* Some hope for constant companions. Other people are happier with friends they see at planned intervals or even infrequently.

- *What are my boundaries?* Do you want friends who call at all hours or drop in for unexpected visits? Or do you consider evenings your own and weekdays off limits? How about borrowing your things?

Knowing what you want out of friendships will guide you in building your social network. Some social situations seem closer by nature. A small church might expect and foster more open-door friendships than a mega-church. Both might provide more close-knit opportunities to socialize than a classic car club. A book discussion group is a much different social space than a bicycling meet-up. Which environment is right for you?

If your self-esteem has taken a hit or you're feeling anxious, try situations with low-interaction expectations. A class where your hands are busy provides the security of a prop. You're not expected to say much if you're listening to a presentation. Over time and with effort, interest groups can lead to close relationships. If you feel anxious, it's okay to skip a pre-meeting mingle. You can rush out right after the session, too. In time, though, you'll need to set goals for more interaction if you want to make friends. Plan a few short scripts you can vary from and introduce yourself. In an interest group, you already have something to talk about.

Making friends can take time and requires patience. A recent study found that it takes around fifty hours for someone to go from an acquaintance to a casual friend, and another ninety or more to grow even closer.[7] Show an interest. Ask what's been happening since the last time you were together, and then actively listen. The next time you meet, you can build on the conversation.

Be an observer, too. Most of us know someone who makes friends easily. What can you learn from how they interact? While it may not feel natural to comment on someone's clothes or hairstyle, most of us can come up with a conversation starter. Try the weather or something about how quickly the year is passing—everyone can relate.

Finally, don't be afraid to move on. I once worked hard to cultivate a friendship that went nowhere. Upon reflection, I can see that I mistook her social outreach as personal. She was only networking. Our goals didn't mesh. The same may be true of groups and organizations. Some groups aren't conducive to forming relationships. Don't take it personally. I once joined a professional organization thinking I'd make friends. Unfortunately, I could never seem to crack the code and left the meetings feeling socially inept. What to do with that realization was my choice: take it personally or chalk it up to a mismatch. I chose the latter.

Ghosted

Rejected parents can be nervous about telling new people they're estranged from a child. I once was, too. Now, I refuse to hide this part of my life and am occasionally judged for it. Usually, I plow past bias, realizing that people are uninformed about the growing numbers of adult children who cut off loving families. Most times, people eventually come to see me for who I am rather than an arbitrary initial idea based on their own biases. That includes the need to believe that, as good parents, estrangement couldn't happen to them.

Hostility can come from adults who have estranged from their folks, too. I've been the recipient of nasty looks or snide remarks. They're best ignored or responded to with kindness. The adult child whose eyes grow cold may hate their own mother, *but she isn't me.*

These encounters don't bother me for long. That may be why they always catch me off guard. Like recently when I joined a community group and volunteered to help. The founder, a woman with grade school aged children, ignored me. Then she asked again, publicly, if anyone wanted to fill the specific roles for which I'd offered to help.

I did a doubletake. Was she *ghosting* me? My gut affirmed the thought, but I questioned myself anyway. Rejected parents can get a little sensitive to any whiff of rejection. Then I remembered our first conversation. She'd asked for a service company referral on a local social media site. I posted a name, and then she sent me a private message, saying she had looked me up. She knew about my work and said her brother was estranged from her mom.

Surprised by the private message and its topic, I replied that, of course, I didn't know the circumstances, but that estrangement was sad. She shot back a reply: "Yeah, well, she's estranged from a lot of people right now."

It wasn't until she ghosted me in the community group that I realized the "a lot of people" might include her. She might also be estranged from her mother.

In that group, I took a step back, stayed a member because its focus is important to me, and decided to work behind the scenes where I could. My quick networking with a close contact helped accomplish one of her initial goals. Because of the circumstances, she may eventually find out the role I played, but it's not something I'll reach out to convey to her.

In all honesty, I can't know for certain that she ghosted me because of my estrangement and hers, but similar scenarios have happened to other parents. One mother joined a small women's group and was told outright she wasn't a good fit. Others have suffered the cold shoulder.

If you're ghosted, consider first your possible sensitivity and, with a calm head, weigh that possibility against the facts. Then, plan your response. Is standing up for yourself worth the aggravation? Would insisting on recognition hurt or help? Sometimes it's easier to walk away.

Although sidelined, I decided the group's goals were more important than my personal feelings. The experience taught me about my values. I don't know what sort of mother this younger woman has, but I do know this gal has made a positive difference in the community. I choose to see that good.

Friends Forever?

"Life's too short." As people get older, a diminishing time horizon adds a hefty dose of reality to this phrase. In younger years, bigger social networks helped us share responsibilities like carting kids around while balancing educational and career pursuits, but not all of those "friends" are close. Later in life, meaningful relationships are more important. It's common to drop some social ties and seek out others that satisfy an increased quest for meaning.[8]

Rejected parents often worry they're becoming bitter. They have nothing to add when friends sometimes drone on (insensitively) about seemingly perfect adult children and "grands." It can hurt when friends misunderstand or forget the deep pain a son or daughter has inflicted. And as rejected parents move beyond family as their main source of enrichment, others' domestic joys or struggles may bore them.

Taking a pause or limiting some associations is a normal life process. The circumstances are unique, but people's needs and interests change, which shifts what's important to them. When children grow up, parents no longer connect through the kids. People retire and lose touch with coworkers. Some friends die. Others move in new directions emotionally and relocate geographically. Forever friends for our whole lives are few, but it's never too late to start and nurture friendships that offer personal meaning and joy.

Tips for Finding Support

Almost daily, I hear from a parent who had thought they were the only one. When something so devastating occurs, just knowing you're not alone is a relief.

Online Support

There are free and fee-based support forums hosted by websites and on Facebook. Some groups are solely for parents, others for adult children, and some for a mixed bag of estrangements. To find a group, use search phrases such as "support forum for parents of estranged adults" or the word "estranged" or "estrangement."

Before joining, read a few postings to determine the tone. Are members considerate? Do arguments detract from the purpose? Is the exchange of information what you need or want?

Study the FAQ or any informational topic threads. Is the group moderated? Do members use their own identity or usernames? Is members' contact information private? Who runs the group? Is there a specific focus such as reconciling, information, or healing? Is it a match for you?

Depending on your needs, consider forums for parents of adult children specific to mental health disorders, which may include discussions about estrangement. Or try groups about parental alienation, grandparent alienation, or those that advocate for grandparents' rights.

In-Person Meetings

Search for in-person groups at meetup.com or on the web using terms such as "parents of estranged adults" connected to your city ("parents of estranged adults"+"Los Angeles"). Some groups have formed based on the concepts in

Done With The Crying, so consider putting a search in combined with that title and/or my name, too. Some churches have hosted those meetings, as have life coaches and therapists. These are sometimes free and sometimes fee-based and run over a period of several weeks.

Closed-Door Support

Seeking a therapist who can help you with this specialized issue requires fore-thought, research, and effort. Your patience in the search will ensure you find the right match for your individualized needs and save you time and grief later.

Start with online directories that list therapists for your area (easily found by searching "therapist"+"city name"). Then consider your needs. Depending on your history and circumstances, look for someone who knows about estrangement, ambiguous loss, grief, life transitions, family relationships, or trauma. You can glean a lot from the tone of a therapist's listing. Ditto their experience and training. Today's therapists may also make videos about what they know and how they serve, which may be helpful in deciding who to call.

Ask yourself questions such as these:

- Does gender matter to me?

- How about religious affiliation?

- What do I intend to get from therapy?

Shop around. Scheduling introductory meetings with two or three therapists is ideal. Go in with clear expectations and communicate them. Then, listen closely to the clinician's response. There's no need to commit to a therapist or program right away. Feel free to go home and consider the meeting, the clinician's perspective, demeanor, and any stated goals or ideas. In restating your issues and expectations with different professionals, you gain insight into your own experience as well as varying viewpoints and support styles.

Finally, ask questions. It's fine to go in with a list of things you want to know. Things like hours, cost, insurance, specific questions about how they might support you, how much they know about estrangement, or how informed they are about another issue that complicates the estrangement or how you are affected by it. The therapeutic relationship requires open dialogue that leads to understanding, flexibility, and trust. Caring clinicians desire rapport and seek to build it with their clients. Your questions are part of that.

Is a Life Coach Right For You?

Life coaches help clients progress by first listening to their desires and understanding their obstacles, and then by helping to devise goals and implement ways to achieve them. They're supportive and realistic but maintain high expectations for clients to follow through on.

If you're wondering if life coaching is right for you after estrangement, ask yourself if you're ready to move forward. Making progress toward specific goals is what life coaching is all about. Your feelings won't be ignored, but unless you're willing to accept them and step forward anyway, life coaching won't help. The most successful clients are goal-oriented people, doers with high levels of self-awareness. Many have worked with a therapist in the past and found it useful yet have reached a transition point and recognize that goal setting, accountability, and action are the only way through.

If you're contemplating hiring a life coach, consult the information under the heading "Closed-Door Support" in the box called "Tips for Finding Support." Much of the advice for finding the right therapist will apply here as well.

Most life coaches work by phone and offer a free introductory session to explore the client-coach match and whether the coaching is right for you. My advice is to beware of salesy pitches that ask for long, expensive commitments. Coaching is about action. A handful of sessions may be all you need.

You Belong to You

There's an old television jingle that goes, "Take good care of yourself, you belong to you." It's a variation of an old song called "Button Up" in which the lyrics are directed to a loved one because "you belong to *me*." Either way works. Taking good care of yourself is good for you and good for those who love you. Here, we'll look at information to support your well-being.

Physiologically, the aging body doesn't cope with and recover as easily from stressful exchanges as it once did.[9] That's one reason it is, in my opinion, unethical for those in the helping fields to put a strong emphasis on reconciling and the onus of cultivating what is an unhealthy relationship, on aging parents. Abusive behavior from adult children to their parents must be seen for what it is. Denying its existence or seriousness, ignoring the deleterious effects, and continuing with the old saws, "never give up" and "keep trying," or even "some contact is better than none," can place vulnerable parents in harm's way.

You're in charge of yourself, your life, and your happiness.

Even so, many of you know estrangement as the unwanted gift that keeps giving. News from afar can be unsettling. Hearing about a new grandchild you didn't know was on the way and may never know can bring sorrow tumbling back. News of a worrisome lifestyle or troubling circumstances can keep you up at night.

Make yourself a priority. Bolster your well-being to buffer the negative effects. Here are a few tips:

- *Be consistent.* As with physical exercise, healthful eating, social support, positive perspectives, or anything else that's good for you, consistency is key. Results may not be immediate, but over time, you'll feel better about yourself, be less stressed, and bounce back with more vigor.

- *Get green.* Nature is good for you. Purposefully notice the way the wind ruffles through leaves, the repetition of lilting birdsong, and the rainbow prisms formed in dewdrops lit by morning rays. Follow the wisdom of trees that release their leaves in preparation for winter, so the burden of snow will slip past their limbs. Bring nature inside, too. A potted plant that has minimal needs can improve productivity and lift mood. House-plants also cut interior air pollution and fight against molds.

- *Think "doable" rather than "extreme."* The outdated "no pain, no gain" motto isn't wise. Axioms of health emerge, persist for a time, and are often later debunked. As an example, even the 10,000 steps a day rule, preached with the rise of fitness apps and trackers, is no longer the default. The idea may have roots in the marketing strategy of a Japanese company that used the number in its pedometer's name. Apparently, the Japanese language characters for the written number look like a man walking! In a 2019 study of more than 16,000 older women, just 4,400 steps per day was associated with significantly lower mortality rates over the next four years. Benefits did increase up to 7,500 steps, then leveled out. Even 2,000 steps a day has benefits.[10]

- *Learn to adapt.* You are more than any illness or its limitations. Find solutions and compromises so you can participate in life. Revising your identity to fit your abilities is required for successful aging.[11] Work with your fears and limitations. A writer friend with a severe acrylate allergy wears gloves to handle printed pages. If you're unsteady when walking, use a cane—and show it off! Online, you can find inexpensive canes in happy patterns and bright colors. If you worry for your safety, you could take a self-defense class or arm yourself with mace. Or rely on the strength in numbers with a travel or day-trip group (there are many for seniors). Take action in some way. Try a bicycle with pedal assist. Alter your schedule to avoid the jostling of crowds. Take advantage of stores' senior hours and days or get curbside delivery. Get special accessories so you can see to thread a needle—or try a new hobby altogether.

- *Add purpose.* The quest for meaning becomes increasingly more important to people as they age, and people find meaning in the moment.[12] Take part in things that you enjoy and are fulfilling to you. Add purpose to your healthy habits, too. Particularly as people age and sedentary modes tend to increase, incorporating a sense of purpose to exercise provides motivation and increases success.[13] Attend a healthy cooking class with a friend—even if it's an online event—and enjoy companionship while doing something good for you. Give your daily walk a destination: to wave to or visit a neighbor, participate in a fitness class, attend a religious service, feed the ducks in the park, or pick up dinner.

- *Cultivate your creativity.* Try your hand at poetry, take up painting, or join a theatrical group. You'll meet new people. Plus, you'll reap the benefits of improved psychological well-being. Expressive pursuits can help process trauma too.

- *Get breathing lessons.* Those with yoga experience will know about belly breathing. Qigong and tai chi also introduce purposeful respiration to enhance wellness. There are many useful breathing techniques. Try inhaling deeply to the count of four, and then exhaling to a count of six or eight while lightly constricting your throat (it makes a whooshing sound). This activates your parasympathetic nervous system for a sense of calm. Look up Diaphragmatic Breathing Relaxation, find a wellness practitioner who incorporates use of the breath, or follow a smartphone app or YouTube video. It's beneficial to escape the chest breathing that's appropriate for acute stress when a fight-or-flight response is needed. Too bad shallow breathing becomes a habit and may even continually trigger the body's stress response. Tons of research validates what ancient Chinese medicine has known forever—mindful breathing is physically and emotionally transformative. If you have a specific health syndrome, look for research on how breathing can help. You may be surprised what you find.

- *Nurture your sense of humor.* The Internet provides alternative views for every experience, even illness. When a back issue recently got me down (pun intended), I searched for "bad back jokes" and found cartoons.com where you can search by keyword. One comic hit home: A doctor told his patient who sat on an exam table, "I can cure your back problem, but there's a risk that you'll be left with nothing to talk about." Laughing at myself lessened my pain. It's no joke—laughter is good for your health.

Your body presents you to the world. Your figurative heart, your mind, and the things you say and do are who you are. You're worth your own good care and keeping. That's why this chapter is placed near the front of the book. Your physical and emotional wellness connect. Take good care of yourself. You belong to you.

Start now. What are your takeaways from this chapter? What tips or ideas make sense to you? What will you do for your health and wellness? Set goals for yourself, break them down into doable pieces, and get started.

 Notes

CHAPTER THREE

Face-Off

"The emotion that can break your heart is sometimes
the very one that heals it."
—Nicholas Sparks

This chapter explores the grittier emotions parents face in the wake of estrangement. The families included represent a cross-section of estrangement scenarios and how parents cope. Depending on your circumstances, you may be shocked, surprised, or even comforted by them. You're not alone and, though painful, admitting and accepting your feelings can be a pathway to heal.

Let's first meet Gigi, a mother who raised her daughter alone. Fearful of breaking down, she avoided coworkers and shut her office door. Instead of the confident woman who managed a team of workers with an approachable style, Gigi became quiet and isolated herself.

Are you on the verge of tears like Gigi? Perhaps it's your anger that scares you. Or you're envious of others' wonderful relationships with their adult children and grandchildren—but then are ashamed of that feeling. Guilt, frustration, hate, worry, doubt, bitterness . . . emotions can be scary, unpleasant, or something you've been taught to hide. Even the fun ones can get you into trouble if expressed at the wrong time.

After two years of no contact with her daughter, Gigi still gets weepy on birthdays and holidays—and that makes her mad. When Gigi's daughter married, she cast her mother aside. "She has a new family now, and they don't make room for me," Gigi explains. "But my job requires leadership. I can't sit at my desk in tears or go around in a snit about how unfair my life is. Not if I want to stay employed."

Maybe you can relate to Gigi's need to keep her emotions in check. An adult child's rejection brings emotional baggage. Hiding feelings doesn't make them go away. At the book's outset, you met Madelyn, a mother who worried that her younger daughter would walk away like her older one did. Madelyn's fear and complacency exploded and hurt her younger daughter during a tense moment between them. Your emotions may ambush you at inopportune times, too.

Reflecting upon your emotions in the safe space of this book can provide valuable insight to smooth out this bumpy ride. So, settle in for a face-off with your feelings. If you're squirming at the thought of examining your emotions, take a breath and set aside any judgment or resistance you may feel. Commit to reading through the scenarios, look for similarities in your own experiences, and try the presented strategies.

An Enemy in The Mirror?

When your son or daughter's behavior desecrates the rosy image you have always held of them, you might wish you'd had a head-ache on that long-ago romantic night (as one mother says). Or you may scrutinize your return on a mountainous investment of time, energy, and heartache, ponder likely future gains, and withdraw your unconditional love (as one father puts it).

No loving parent wants to hate their own daughter or wish their son had never been born, but if you've ever had those feelings, you can be certain that you're not alone. Especially if estrangement continues and is wrought with meanness, you may question whether you even want a relationship or whether you could ever trust your child again. Even so, these kinds of feelings can be so foreign and repulsive that they turn you against yourself.

Divorced mother Paulette knows that sort of confusion and hurt. Her son, now thirty-three, was unruly and unkind from his early teen years. He berated her for her "lousy" parenting skills, called her crazy, ugly, and fat, and blamed her for his every problem. Paulette dreaded his verbal assaults. She no longer liked him but was conflicted between the logic of wanting him out of her life and a deep sense of shame. "He's my son," she says. "That's not how a mother should feel."

Then Paulette met other parents whose adult children treated them badly. A few said outright that if they had it to do over, they wouldn't have children. Their honesty made Paulette's feelings seem more normal. If anyone else had treated her so viciously, she wouldn't have tormented herself for how she felt.

In reflecting upon her life, Paulette recalled that her son had problems in school and then with employers. She hung in there with him, even when he was arrested at age twenty-seven and she bailed him out of jail. She was his mother. She believed in him.

He lived with her until age twenty-nine, and Paulette recalls how it felt for her, each time she arrived home after her two work travel days per week. On her way home from the airport, a familiar tension always gripped her. What sort of mood would her son be in? "I used to think if I could just say the right things, show just the right interest level, and not guilt him with too many questions, everything would be fine," she says.

Sometimes, Paulette succeeded in appeasing him, and they would have a pleasant dinner or even a few weeks of peace. That is until her son no longer needed her. When he moved out to his girlfriend's house, Paulette says he stopped calling. "But for a long time, I still called him." Her son was never pleased to hear from her. Deep down, Paulette believed some defect in herself was to blame.

He had been adept at convincing her she was no good. It was how he manipulated her into taking his abuse.

Paulette was so accustomed to suppressing her emotions that she could barely hear her inner voice. To drag out her feelings and deal with them was unknown territory. With the help of a therapist and an online support group, she came to see that she had been a good mother. Her son had repaid her love with abuse. Her coldness toward him was nothing to feel guilty about. Rather, it was her inner voice helping her to survive.

To some of you, Paulette's case may sound extreme. Even if your child did not berate and abuse you, strong emotions may come in waves or hit you unexpectedly. Emotions such as anger, guilt, envy, hate, and regret can be harsh companions, but sitting with the truth can be liberating.

For almost all parents, there is an element of disbelief when a child cuts them off. As parent-and-adult-child estrangement has become more known, psychologists, sociologists, and historians are speculating on the issue. Some proffer the idea that parents expect they will be "repaid" by their children for raising them. It's a harsh word. In my experience, parents hoped to remain friends and get to know their grandchildren. The last thing most parents want is to become a burden on anyone, let alone their children. I believe that when adult children cut off loving parents, it's completely normal for moms and dads to look back on all their time, energy, love, and heartache—all the fond memories they expected to add to—and feel disappointed, angry, and hurt.

Looking back on our lives is a natural part of growing older. People hope to enjoy the fruits of their labor. Believing that the children we have loved so much might like us, or even love us, is part of that. When they don't, we can still face the mirror. We don't have to reconcile their uncaring, unkind, or dismissive behavior with our own reflection.

Your emotions about children who have hurt you are normal. They may also be fleeting. Wishing at some point that a child who has grown up to hurt you so deeply had never been born does not make you a monster. You can work at accepting your losses and adjust your expectations for the future. By recognizing and accepting your feelings, you validate yourself and your experiences. Completing the next exercise can help.

Call It What It Is

Just as the Inuit and Yupik (Eskimo) languages have a variety of words to describe types of snow, the emotional landscape of estrangement isn't all "sad." The ability to name feelings with specificity is a vital skill for emotional wellness and diminished distress. Labeling feelings draws energy away from your emotional brain and gets your prefrontal cortex buzzing.[1,2] That means if your daughter says she's found a substitute mom, your emotions don't have to hijack your mood. Using rich, specific language to identify and express your feelings triggers complex thinking for a calmer, more even-keeled response.

More about Specific Words

In the body, fear, terror, and anxiety affect you the same way, with increased heart rate and the urge to run or to defend yourself. But the words themselves fit for different situations. Anxiety may come on prior to an important test or meeting, while terror connotes a scarier scene. To do this exercise, consider broad emotional categories, and then add related words. Anger as a category could include words such as rage, indignance, and irritation. Each of these can similarly affect physiology but these words don't mean the same thing.

Get into the habit of naming your feelings in the nuanced ways that best fit. In the table, I've suggested five broad categories. Write in as many related words as you can think of, and then use a thesaurus to find some more. The website www.thesaurus.com makes this easy. A few words are included in the table to get you started. There's also an optional category you can name if that makes sense to you. Or make all your own categories—it's up to you.

Don't get caught in an emotional storm. Using rich language helps. In doing this exercise, you train yourself to respond to upsets with a calmer head. Instead of cursing in traffic, tell yourself, "I'm feeling frustrated because I'm worried that I'll be late." If holiday music makes you cross, stop glaring at shoppers and consider what's really ailing you: "I used to love all the shopping and fun. Now that my son is gone, holidays are lonely and embarrassing."

Bonus: Once you're in the habit of labeling your feelings, let them lead you to a fix. If you find yourself dreading the holidays, focus on solutions. Plan something new and fun to do. If you're often stuck in traffic, arrange your schedule to leave earlier, try a new route, or find a podcast or audiobook to make use of the time. Don't forget to label your feelings about those things, too. "This book is so funny," or "Daydreaming about traveling to Santa Fe for Christmas and imagining the luminaries lit up all over town makes me feel serene, joyful, and at peace."

Option: As you seek out new words for your emotional word families, note which ones resonate with your situation. Use the lines at the end to reflect and write about how you feel.

HAPPINESS

Elation

Satisfied

Contentment

SADNESS

Anguish

Mourning

Heartbreaking

FEAR

Dread

Jitters

Anxiety

ANGER

Rage

Exasperated

Irritation

DISGUST

Repulsion

Self-loathing

Shame

OPTIONAL CATEGORY YOU CHOOSE

Emotions at Work

There are many situations where emotional displays are unwelcome. Will an upcoming event or important meeting require nerves of steel? The ideas in this section are aimed at the workplace (even if that's a video call from your home office) but also fit many other situations where emotions must be checked at the door. Adapt the ideas to your own life circumstances.

Gigi's open-door policy was one of her strengths as a leader, but when her daughter shut her out of her life, Gigi was consumed with worry. "Not only would I cry at my desk," she says, "but I was never sure when my emotions might tumble out to wreck my mascara, my day, and my reputation." If she wasn't sad, she might be angry. When people talked about family, her tension would rise. "They'd complain about some silly inconvenience," she says. "I'd be standing there, blood starting to boil, thinking they weren't half the mother I am, but they're still loved." Sometimes, Gigi found herself responding with an edge of sarcasm she knew wasn't good for her work team, adding, "And it wasn't good for me either."

Brad, the father of an estranged son, had similar feelings. "I'm not usually so cynical," he says. "But I had a hard time not saying out loud what I was really thinking when somebody down at work waxed on." If a coworker showed adorable baby pictures, Brad might offer an acceptable comment: "He'll be a heartbreaker." It was his added, "It's your heart he'll break one day," that made him realize: "Nobody likes a grump. Even I didn't like me."

It can be difficult to remain congenial when the stability of all you believed in is reduced to shards. It's tough to put in work time when all you really want to do is curl up at home and cry. Even so, with advanced planning, you can be productive on the job without jeopardizing your reputation or your career. In fact, with a shift in thinking, work can become a haven to escape the pain. Your livelihood is important, so use the tips below to devise solutions and then apply them.

Physical Preparation

It's tough to feel confident and in control when you're exhausted and unwell. Be kind to yourself with rest, nutrition, and movement. Your body houses your precious being—and that includes the part of you that works.

Gigi drank calming tea before bed, sprayed lavender oil on her pillowcase, and then rose a little earlier so she wouldn't feel as rushed each morning. She knew that when she was tired and rushed, she was more prone to emotional displays.

What can you do to sleep better, eat healthfully, and exercise? If you need to, turn back to Chapter Two for ideas. On the lines below, jot down a few techniques you can implement—then put them into practice.

_____

_____

_____

_____

_____

Mental Preparation

Brad found that listening to music on his work commute helped. "Usually Neil Young or AC/DC," he says. "I admit to tearing up behind my sunglasses on the Neil Young days, but my head was in a better space by the time I punched in."

Brad's music choices are from times he recalls as "simpler." Favorite songs stir anticipation as melodies ebb and swell to crescendos. That the expectation always pays off is a comfort. Something you can count on, maybe at a time when little else is steady.

Gigi settled into a religious radio habit on her morning drive. Upon arrival, and as needed throughout the day, prayer provided focus.

How can *you* prepare mentally to put your emotions aside for the workday? Some parents give themselves a mental pep talk that they are kind, confident, and have a good attitude. They tell themselves that the next few hours are for work, and that they can cry or rant later, on their own time. Recognizing a set number of hours makes feelings more manageable and provides a countdown to releasing emotions again. Setting a goal of being cheerful and then succeeding, even for an hour at a time to begin with, bolsters confidence and provides a template to then repeat.

Some parents tell me they prepare for the day by reading positive quotations, a short passage they find meaningful, or even their own profound words in a written response created for one of the exercises or prompts in *Done With The Crying*. Others listen to the audiobook (or choose another that helps) during their commute. Before getting out of her car for work, Gigi reminds herself to *Bookmark it!*[3] The technique is one that helps a person leave an issue at rest for the moment.

What can you do to get mentally prepared to keep your emotions in check? Take a moment to jot down a few ideas, and then follow through with trying them.

_____

_____

_____

_____

_____

Workplace Sanctuary

Some parents keep a meditation app on their phone and turn to it during breaks. Others set up their desktop computer with a scrolling screensaver that features beautiful nature photos, an inspiring quotation, or a reminder (*inhale, exhale, breathe...*).

Gigi's open-door policy meant she couldn't close other workers out. In the early haze of her daughter's rejection when her emotions were the most unpredictable, she had to find another spot in the building where she could duck in and pull herself together. A public restroom stall was her go-to. Where might you hole up for crying eyes beyond prying eyes?

Is there a short trek in or outside the building you can use as a sort of racetrack, assuring yourself you'll be steadied again at the finish line (back at your desk or station)? A brief change of environment works wonders. Just to get away, one father routinely volunteered for deli, food truck, or coffee kiosk runs.

One mother related that she took breathers outdoors where glimpses of the sky, the chattering of birds, and the sound of rustling wind in the trees had a calming influence. "The guard at the door saw a lot of me," she says. "His polite smile and friendly greeting became a sort of therapy. I knew it was his job, and that made it better, because there was no pressure to chat." She laughs. "After a while, I'd look at him say, 'Get me out of there,' or whisper, 'Escape.' It became a sort of joke, so he'd tell me, 'Enjoy the moment,' or when I returned, 'Back to the asylum, huh?' That tiny connection of understanding helped."

The thread of humor in this woman's experience with the doorman brings up an important point about people in your work environment. For a time, it may be necessary to change up who you hang out with. Coworkers with whom you used to have much in common may no longer be a comfortable match. The coworker who used to bore you with his groaner jokes might provide a unique perspective or even comic relief that you need just now.

Refer to the discussions about friends in Chapter Two and apply as needed for the workplace. It's okay to be "busy" for previously social lunch hours. You may belong to others on the clock, but breaks are required by law. With appropriate excuses if needed, use your break time to take care of *you*. Write out a few ideas about possible changes to make your work environment supportive.

_____

_____

_____

_____

_____

_____

No matter your job or environment, you can make a difference for someone else, too. The tiniest kindnesses affect others in ways we may never fully know. For anyone, the world can seem like a cruel place from time to time. Make the effort to sincerely greet those whose paths you cross. Your polite smile, like that of the guard at Gigi's building, may be just what another person needs—and the connection will be good for you.

When it comes to the problem of estrangement, ceaseless worry and overanalyzing often make zero difference. Setting aside your emotions and staying focused to best serve in your job role keeps your hands busy and your mind occupied. Clock in at work and enjoy a shift-long vacation from estrangement-related chaos.

Who's in Your Corner?

Think of a benevolent historical figure, a loving individual from your childhood, or anyone you admire for their wisdom and kindness. Do you have a role model or mentor? (Examples: A caring grandparent, a friend who has endured hardship and come out smiling, Jesus Christ, Gandhi, Mother Theresa, Dr. Drew . . .) Choose one person or several.

Now, imagine turning to that person whenever you feel down about yourself or your situation. What advice might you get? What would that person do or say to help? Role play. Give good care and advice.

What You Didn't Know Can Hurt

The roots of estrangement can run deep. Sometimes, parents are left to contemplate history they wish they'd have known about earlier. Then they wonder how they didn't know and suffer guilt or regret. Here, we'll look at one specific example, where the parents found out many years later that their daughter had been abused.

Bonnie and Mike raised three bright, happy kids. Their only daughter, Brynn, is now estranged. Her history includes a two-year high school romance with a boy who was as likeable and involved in school activities as Brynn. When they broke up, Brynn seemed fine. She continued in chorus, track and field, and graduated with honors. After graduating, she went to work for a promotions company. She dated some but not seriously.

"She was a strong girl and mature for her age," says Mike. "We were surprised when, at twenty-five, she brought home a loser in his late thirties who drank too much and didn't treat her well. She'd met him on a dating site."

Bonnie says, "We thought Brynn would figure him out, but a month later, Brynn moved in with him an hour's drive away."

Mike says, "We stayed in touch and did our best to see the good in him. What else could we do?"

Over the next several years, they saw less and less of Brynn. She stayed in touch via sporadic texts and phone calls. She attended only a few family gatherings—usually alone.

"She was skinny," says Bonnie. "She lost her job, too, but was looking for another. We tried not to worry, and we had a lot to contend with anyway. Our daughter-in-law was diagnosed with cancer. I took on most of our granddaughter's care. Our younger son was planning a wedding, my mother needed assistance, and Mike's work with the city involved his business in a lawsuit."

Two days before their younger son's wedding, Brynn showed up back at home with a suitcase. Her parents were shocked and relieved, but the night before her brother's wedding, the situation took a dark turn. Brynn said they were right about the man she'd been living with but that he'd seemed to read her from the moment they met. Bonnie adds, "Then she explained why she thought she had been so susceptible to him."

The parents were horrified to hear that Brynn's high school boyfriend had manipulated her emotionally and then controlled her physically. "In unspeakable ways," says Mike. "You don't wanna know."

The next day, they attended their son's wedding like zombies. Brynn dressed inappropriately and overdrank. "It was embarrassing for her brother," says Bonnie. "And we were so exhausted and upset we could barely keep a smile and get through the day. I still can't look at our younger son's wedding photos without tearing up."

"We managed," says Mike. "And the next day looked for the silver lining. We had our daughter back."

As the weeks passed, more came out about the gravitas of all that happened. Bonnie was traumatized by her daughter's sometimes detailed revelations of sexual abuse as a teen, and later at the hands of the man she'd been living with. The older boyfriend had also threatened to kill Brynn.

Bonnie managed to keep the abhorrent images out of her head when she was busy, but when out in the car alone, her thoughts wandered. She suffered bouts of rage so powerful that she would pull over and scream and cry. "I beat my fists on the steering wheel," says Bonnie, "but I was powerless to change a thing."

She also suffered guilt over not having spotted any signs of abuse. Brynn even yelled at her, asking why she hadn't protected her. Bonnie felt horrible. How could she have missed it? And why hadn't her daughter told her? It was two sides of a tortuous coin.

As time went on, Bonnie looked back and forgave herself. Brynn was always such a happy teen. She and the boy had been involved in school activities and part of a bigger social group. Bonnie came to realize just how good her daughter was at hiding. Nothing had been awry during Brynn's high school years. Her daughter got good grades, had lots of friends, and was a favorite of her teachers. Apparently, *no one* suspected what happened.

After a few months at home, during which Brynn saw a therapist a few times and then insisted she was over it all, she landed a good job where she was quickly promoted. Brynn seemed fine until she began staying out all night. Bonnie and Mike were aghast when Brynn confessed that she'd been seeing the older man again. She even denied that he had done the awful things she had earlier told them he had. On her thirtieth birthday, Brynn moved back into his house.

"It's been nearly six years now," says Bonnie. "Brynn used to text me a little heart emoji or something short. She never answered her phone though. We went to the house a few years ago and knocked. Nobody answered, but we were visited by the police a few days later. Brynn said we were harassing her. "The officers were sympathetic but as powerless as us," says Bonnie.

Mike has suffered tremendous anger. "I wanted to find that schoolboy and kill him at first," says Mike. "Then the lowlife she's living with, but Bonnie set me straight."

Mike and Bonnie believe substance abuse plays a role in Brynn's current choices. Their sons echo the concern. The family has pulled together and, although they miss Brynn and worry for her, they have gotten on with their lives.

These days, the couple's daughter-in-law is cancer free and their younger son and his wife have a baby on the way. Mike and Bonnie have come to terms with the past they didn't know about and can't change. It's the future they worry about now.

They hope Brynn will wise up, but they know that many victims return to their abusers repeatedly. The parents have accepted that they have no influence over Brynn. They're also troubled by the statistics they've read about the problems of child sexual abuse victims even in adulthood. (See "By the Numbers" in this chapter.)

"Our life plan was for Mike to work two more years and then us move closer to the city," says Bonnie. "We're worried that Brynn will need help though. And then what? The three of us in a little condo? We decided to keep the house for three more years and then reevaluate."

Like many parents, as time passes, Bonnie and Mike have developed reservations about any reconciliation. Do they even know their daughter anymore? With no contact, that feeling becomes entrenched. Brynn's substance abuse complicates matters, as does her later denial that the man she is living with had abused her. Trust has a way of eroding.

Bonnie and Mike believe Brynn's past abuse is at the root of her issues. Unfortunately, when children are abused, the parents may be the last to know—if they ever find out. A family friend, an uncle, a brother, a schoolmate, an online friend . . . perpetrators run the gamut and often commit their crimes under the guise of innocuous roles and behind faces of innocence.

Given the frequency of childhood sexual abuse, and that so many victims wait at least five years to tell or even *never* tell, it's reasonable to assume that hidden sexual abuse exists in at least some adult children's estrangements. A variety of fears, issues of shame, and worry make telling difficult, even for an adult. Victims of childhood abuse have higher incidences of psychological disorders than the general population, too. For some, estrangement may seem like a better choice than exposing a dark truth.

If you suspect this could be true of your child's history, consider whether a danger to other children exists. Children can't always speak up for themselves. They need adults to intervene.

When You Suspect Child Sexual Abuse: Resources

- Darkness to Light. Support and information about child abuse, reporting, and prevention. https://www.d2l.org/

- LACASA Center. Education and support: child abuse, domestic violence, and sexual assault. https://lacasacenter.org/

- National Child Traumatic Stress Network (NCTSN). Information and advocacy organization. https://www.nctsn.org/

Even when parents didn't know about the abuse, affected children may harbor resentment. Brynn bluntly asked why Bonnie hadn't protected her. At first, Bonnie felt blamed but managed to set aside her feelings and continued to listen as Brynn bared her painful history. In shock and heartbroken for Brynn, Bonnie assured her that telling was the right thing to do. Abuse victims often lament the loss of their childhood years. Bonnie came to realize that, at the time of the abuse, Brynn couldn't express her anger. She was confused by her feelings for the boy who mentally and emotionally coerced her.

As a pragmatic sort, Bonnie took her heartache and dismay to the safe space of a journal. She filled some of those pages with emotional rants. She used others to ask and answer questions that helped her analyze the time period when the abuse took place. By reflecting on the memories, she saw that Brynn really had been good at hiding. Bonnie forgave herself for not somehow knowing what was happening.

Keeping the Secret

When an adult son or daughter reveals that they were sexually abused many years earlier in childhood, parents often wonder: *Why didn't my child tell me?* A few of the reasons are outlined below.[4, 5]

- **Self-blame**. Children may blame themselves for not stopping the behavior, fighting, or screaming (or fighting or screaming more). A teen may believe s/he contributed by drinking alcohol, by flirting, or by participating to a point, and not knowing how to stop contact that became assault.

- **Shame**. In some cases, it feels safer for the child to believe s/he is at fault than to see a caregiver on whom the child is dependent as bad. In other cases, emotional coercion and control contribute to shame.

- **Fear**. Some kids worry because of threats of harm to the child or the family. Others worry about family disruption, marital breakup, ridicule, or punishment.

- **Protecting other people**. Often victims want to protect their loved ones. Even very young victims recognize that learning of the abuse will be emotionally painful.

- **The perpetrator's status**. Victims of well-respected figures of stature within the community or the family are typically less likely to tell (or be believed). Cases in point include the Penn State sports scandal and the child victims of Catholic priests.

- **Traumatization**. Children who are hurt in this way may be in shock. The thought of revealing what happened and of recounting the events may be too much to bear.

By the Numbers

Child Sex Abuse

- About one in ten children in the U.S. will be sexually abused before their eighteenth birthday. That's approximately one in every seven girls and one in every twenty-five boys.[6]

- In a 2009 phone survey of more than 800 adults who had been sexually abused as children, 21% had never revealed what happened to them. Of these, twice as many men (34%) than women (16%) had never told.[7]

Future Effects

- A 2009 study among 9,170 female and 7,823 male participants concluded that men and women who were sexually abused as children are more likely to be physically, psychologically, or sexually victimized by intimate partners as adults.[8]

- Women who were sexually abused as children are twice as likely as others to suffer from depression than those who were not.[9]

- Females who experienced childhood sexual abuse are at a substantially higher risk of developing a wide range of psychiatric disorders than those who did not.[10]

- More than twice as many adults with a history of childhood sexual abuse report a suicide attempt.[11]

- According to statistics reported by the organization Darkness to Light (www.D2L.org), adult criminal behavior, and problems including eating disorders, obesity, and substance abuse, are more prevalent in child sexual abuse victims than in the general public.

It may be important to note here the long history of blaming mothers when a child has been abused. Even the psychological literature sometimes subtly blames mothers for failing to protect their children. Mothers are expected to apologize for something they were unaware was happening or couldn't prevent.[12]

The reality is that mothers are often secondary victims who are traumatized by learning about the abuse. Still, society, and even psychology, has some catching up to do. It's possible that "mother blame" is at the root of at least some estrangements where childhood sexual abuse has occurred, whether it's revealed or not. At the very least, feelings of blame toward a mother (or parents) may add to a survivor's confusion and factor into estrangement.

Mothers and fathers often blame themselves, too, thinking they should have known or recognized what was happening or that someone they trusted was unsafe. Guilt is a valuable emotion that can guide us to feel for other people or make amends when we're wrong. However, guilt serves no purpose when it's irrational and aimed toward something you didn't know about or couldn't have reasonably foreseen.

Processing emotions around something you didn't know about and cannot change requires self-compassion and a realistic view of your own culpability. For Bonnie to get past this, it was necessary for her to reinforce that the regret she felt over what happened to Brynn was not due to her own culpability or responsibility. She had been kept in the dark about it.

Fathers, too, may have secondary trauma. The above is not intended to exclude fathers for the very deep hurt, anger, or sense of guilt they may feel upon later learning their child had been abused. Mike expresses that when he asks, "Wasn't it my job to protect my family?" Mike's immediate anger may be a cover. When Mike found out what happened to his daughter, he felt helpless. His anger made him feel a little more powerful.

Professional counseling is helpful in situations such as this. Those with past trauma of their own may be especially vulnerable due to triggered memories or attempts to avoid them. In the aftermath of estrangement, it's important that you take care of yourself. Refer back to "Tips for Finding Support" in Chapter Two.

Helping the Parents of Child Sex Abuse Victims

- TAALK: https://www.taalk.org
  U.S. nonprofit with information and support groups.

- MOSAC: https://www.mosac.net/
  Help for mothers of sexually abused children.

- MOSAC UK: https://www.mosac.org.uk/
  Serves all parents and caregivers.

- Stop It Now!: https://www.stopitnow.org
  Founded by a survivor. Resource guides and support.

Anger: Simmer Down, Boil Over, or Stew

The subject of this section is anger. We'll begin by continuing for a few paragraphs with how Bonnie and Mike productively dealt with theirs. Then we'll move on to show anger, and its management, from different angles.

Mike's anger, first at the boy who hurt Brynn, and later at the older boyfriend she said had manipulated and abused her, was white-hot and boiling. Although not as vocal about it, Bonnie had a similar response. They both knew denying their anger wasn't productive, but also that letting it stew or erupt wasn't good for them.

A hands-on sort, Mike expelled negative energy through physical work. He would pick up a shovel or rake and work. He dug out a path in the front yard and lined it with pea gravel, created hypertufa pots for a crop of lemon grass, and redesigned the side yard. He added a bubbling fountain and a bird feeder, transforming what began in anger into a sanctuary of nature.

Physical activity reduces stress hormones in the body and increases feel-good ones. That's one reason exercise is a stress-buster. Mike went a step further by channeling his energy into creating beauty and function that was true to himself. Directing the energy of his anger into something good increased his self-esteem and helped to validate him as husband and father at a time when he felt like he'd failed.

Bonnie banged her fists on the steering wheel. The behavior hurt her fists and her psyche. She didn't like feeling out of control, and rather than express the anger and it dissipate as she thought might be the case, it impaired her focus when she pulled back out on the road. She began to dread driving anywhere alone for fear the feelings would overtake her.

Bonnie realized her anger was normal but also that it didn't help. In the job from which she had recently retired, she had often been required to organize and direct projects. She had always turned to paper and pen to get this done. By using her journal at a time when her personal life had taken a turn into chaos, she was able to identify her emotions. She devised positive affirmations and used them to bolster her self-esteem, which led to organized behavior and a calmer demeanor that felt like her old self.

Old-school advice to express anger by acting out, primal screaming, throwing pillows, or hitting something has been relegated to the psychology trash bin. These sorts of behaviors are not helpful and make anger a habit. The *practice* of anger, like any habit, becomes more entrenched and difficult to stop. If you're beating your fists on anything, yelling at the dog or your spouse, or otherwise expressing rage in ways that are not helpful, first admit it, and then steer yourself in a better direction.

Bonnie and Mike relied on their inherent natures and strengths to effectively deal with the very real and understandable anger they felt. After reading about how they moved beyond anger, how might you best manage the anger you're feeling? On what history and experiences can you lean? What personal strengths will help you recover an even keel? Pause for a few moments and ponder these questions. Use the lines to jot down a few thoughts.

_____

_____

_____

_____

_____

Earlier, you met Brad who realized nobody likes a grump. He used music to reach a better headspace for his workday. Kudos to him for dealing with his feelings in a way that supported his livelihood. Unfortunately, as estrangement continues or deepens, it can be like an endurance race. Anger you once controlled or processed on one level can have deeper roots that surface later to trip you up. To illustrate, let's look more closely at Brad's situation and how his anger simmered.

After Brad's wife divorced him, he focused on being a good father to his fifteen-year-old son, Denny. But he knew his ex-wife had given Denny an earful of lies. She'd had an affair, yet blamed Brad for their divorce. Brad refused to badmouth her the way she did him. He did his best to stay in touch, paid child support, and then Denny's college tuition.

When Denny graduated and relocated for a job, Brad reached out but was mostly ignored. He attended his son's wedding but, seated at a side table with his ex-wife and the man she'd left him for, Brad felt like an outsider. A year and a half later, his ex was conspicuously absent from their new grandson's christening, and when Brad asked about her, Denny admitted he hadn't invited her. He thanked his dad for coming, clapped him on the shoulder, and left Brad standing alone. Denny joined his wife, baby, and a crowd of in-laws for photos on the church steps.

After that, Brad focused on training for a promotion that kept him busier than ever. He still reached out, but Denny didn't respond. When Denny changed his cell phone number, Brad was angry but says, "He's my son. I figured he was confused. I know I was."

On Denny's thirty-fourth birthday, Brad called his son's work. "The receptionist first said he was in but then said he wasn't," Brad relates. "She put me through to voicemail, and I sang 'Happy Birthday' and asked him to call." After three weeks with no response, Brad felt so empty, he contemplated suicide. "I didn't want to die," he says. "But I needed a change. I was sixty-four, overweight, and tired." Brad penned his resignation.

Within a year, Brad had sold his condo and relocated to a rustic lakefront community. He fished, established a wave-and-smile relationship with neighbors, and enjoyed his freedom. Still, sitting on his deck as sunset turned the lake pink, memories drifted in to torment him. Things his son said as a child. How Denny's dark eyes blinked when he was deep in thought. How proud he was to see Denny graduate college with honors. As the sky faded into night, Brad wondered: *What could I have done differently? How could I have kept Denny close? Why did God give me a son if I'll only die all alone?*

Brad saw a therapist a few times but says, "He talked a lot, but he didn't say much that helped. I didn't need to hear about how many parents come to him and cry. I needed solutions." Brad took matters into his own hands.

As late summer lent fiery color to the tree leaves, Brad joined a gym and walked the shore paths. He breathed the fresh air and was thankful for his blessings. He appreciated the comical coots and the pelicans' gracefulness on wing and on water, despite their clunky ways on land. By the next summer, he'd lost thirty-seven pounds and was seeing the widow who ran the tackle shop. Maybe he didn't have his son in his life, but his life wasn't over. The tranquility of the lake soothed him, and for the first time in years, Brad was content.

Then someone bought the lot next to his cottage and began to build. Saws buzzed, hammers pounded, and Brad's anger boiled. "I'd accidentally drop my keys and be infuriated," he says. "I'd snap at my girlfriend. I'd drive through the post office loop and cuss people slow to put their letters in the slot." He was "cheesed off" all the time. "One morning, my bait was mushy and kept falling from the hook. In a rage, I snagged myself and couldn't get free."

At the urgent care clinic, a nurse got him talking. When he told her about the construction that had ruined his little heaven on Earth, she patted his shoulder and said, "Life isn't fair."

Those three words brought a surge of anger so strong that Brad wanted to slap her. The intensity of his rage shook him. On the way home, he stopped for a double cheeseburger. As he pulled into his gravel driveway, he flipped the bird to the construction site full of workers next door. Then he went inside and slammed the door.

Brad's girlfriend urged him to try a life coach she knew. He didn't want to, but she was irritated at his outbursts—and worried about him. He reluctantly agreed. With the coach's support, he came to realize that his lack of control over outcomes and a deep sense of injustice fueled his anger. When Brad had married, he insisted they establish a solid foundation before having a child. He'd done everything right, yet the marriage crumbled. After the divorce, he maintained his integrity, loved his son, and never badmouthed his ex. Even so, his son disowned him. After retiring, he recognized the danger of becoming mired in regrets and began to take care of himself. As a result, he felt successful and in charge of his life once again. Then the construction, with its noise and chaos, pierced his fragile new start. Working with a life coach helped him to acknowledge a truth he hadn't faced before: That try as he might, something or someone could come along to spoil his peace. He would have to learn to manage his response to that reality.

Anger can be white hot and immediately connected to its source, as it was for Bonnie and Mike. Or it can be more sweeping. Anger can be processed in a way that suits the situation for a time, like Brad's earlier management for the workplace, yet be rooted more deeply and later triggered to a boiling point.

Anger, too, can simmer or be purposely repressed. You'll recall Serena and Dale from Chapter Two. For years, Serena kept her feelings under wraps. That way, she didn't trigger her husband's volatile temper. Yet inside, her feelings stewed. When she joined the cancer support group and finally admitted to being angry at her estranged daughter, she progressed toward positive change, and also helped Dale get unstuck.

Brad's more generalized anger rose like a bright red flag. By better understanding that his irritation over the new construction had triggered deeper anger over the reality that life isn't always fair and holds uncertainty, he was better equipped to change his response. He started by remembering those early days when he labeled himself a grump. "This wasn't much different," he says. "Only I had more free time and no long commute or job at stake." He chuckles. "I didn't realize it at first, but I had something more important at stake. My life."

By labeling himself as grumpy, Brad had shifted his feelings from the realm of the emotional brain to the more complex thinking that takes place in the prefrontal cortex. Then he could devise plans for managing his emotions. That had worked for him at the time. Although his recent anger was different, the solution could be the same.

With the help of his life coach, Brad came up with behaviors to manage his temper. If the construction noise irked him, he could turn up his music and sing along. He could choose to take a walk by the shore, visit his girlfriend at the tackle shop, do a chore, or otherwise distract himself. Brad discovered a world of audiobooks he could plug into and found that historical accounts of trials and triumph helped. "A lot of great men and women have miserable lives," he says. "They still do good things."

Brad also shifted his thinking to more helpful perspectives: *The construction won't last forever.* Better self-talk also worked for unexpected situations like the mushy bait. Life wasn't always perfect but had good surprises, too. He could remind himself of things that made him happy. His girlfriend, the funny coots, the strength he felt since losing weight and getting fit.

"My anger could snag me like a fish on a hook," Brad says. "So I made a game out of staying free like the legendary big bass in the lake." This idea helped Brad to see that he had a choice to slip away from the "hooks" life tossed his way rather than feel sorry for himself and rage over any misfortune.

Brad likes thinking of himself like that big bass legend so much that he uses it whenever he gets down about Denny, too. He knows his son was hurt by the family breakup and his mother's very vocal blaming of him. Denny chose to avoid them both rather than work to understand or fight for either relationship. Maybe one day his son will come around. Maybe Brad will even reach out to Denny again. For now, though, he plans to avoid the bait of hope and remain free like that legendary fish. On the rare occasion he gets caught up in sad thinking or anger, he says, "I imagine what I'd do if I caught that big boy. I'd throw him back." Brad can let himself off the hook, too.

The Bitter Truth

On the tails of estrangement, it's common for bitterness to pay a visit. The trouble starts when an embittered outlook settles in to stay. With awareness and support, you can learn how to show any bitterness the door.

Most of you have known people you could describe as "negative." Neighbors you avoid because they always bring you down.

The friend whose constant complaining you can take only in small doses. Or the relative whose call you send to voicemail because it's always a repeating refrain of pain. Rather than reporting on progress in moving forward, or asking for support or feedback, an embittered person clings to past hurt and seeks validation about its injustice—over and over and over.

Distrust can be another aspect of bitterness. A modicum of cynicism as people age can be classified as wisdom or critical thinking. People learn from experience. It's wise to recognize that not *everyone* is honest and well-intentioned, but a pervasive distrust of the world and everyone in it is probably bitterness at work.

In Chapter One, we met Gabe, the father of an estranged son. He and his wife live next door to a young family and see their younger selves in the young neighbors' adoration and pride for their children. Gabe is a little envious of their naïveté. When Gabe's son was young, not even teen angst was a worry, let alone estrangement. Of the couple next door, Gabe says, "They're living the dream. Something most parents do when they have little ones."

My husband, Brian, has said this very thing. *They're living the dream* reflects the way many of us can look back at times when life seemed simpler. These were the eras of our own innocence.

Gabe calls this insight "cynical," but I consider it realistic. He and his wife wouldn't try to warn their neighbors about what could lie ahead. They enjoy the little family and wish their neighbors the best. They're like me and Brian, who know that to sparingly impart advice from experience can be helpful, but raising a stop sign for every potential problem on the horizon isn't.

In the first chapter, we met Donna, who has described herself as "numb." Donna protects herself from potential hurt by keeping her social distance. Living first with an emotionally abusive man and then the children who grew to display similar cruelty and eventually estrange contributes to her lack of trust. Seeing the political division, unrest, and violence in the streets over the last several years, especially during the COVID-19 lockdowns when she was glued to the news, didn't help. In a way, Donna lost her faith in humanity.

Bitterness can impair physical health, foster depression, promote a sense of helplessness in one's life, weaken drive, and cause social isolation. Being bitter can become a perpetuating cycle, too. Friends and loved ones grow weary of hearing about how unjust the world is. They may withdraw, furthering a sense that no one is loyal or cares. Doling out negativity keeps you focused on misery and can make you unlikeable. It's no way to live.

Even if you're not a negative person, I hope you will take a few moments to do the following exercise. "The Bitter Test" will help you identify if and where even a little bitterness may have crept into your outlook. It's another way to gain awareness. You can use what you learn to challenge or shift your perspectives, as well as create new and helpful habits.

The Bitter Test

A cynical, embittered view can sneak up on a person. Are you bitter? Read the following questions and rate your responses. Use a scale of one to five, with one meaning "strongly disagree" and five meaning "strongly agree." Don't spend a lot of time deliberating. There are no right or wrong answers, only your truth.

1=strongly disagree   2=disagree   3=undecided   4=agree   5=strongly agree

_____ I'm eager to try new things.

_____ My hard work rarely pays off.

_____ When others are joking around, I rarely join in.

_____ People consider me sarcastic.

_____ I lament about other people's choices.

_____ Bad things usually happen to me.

_____ I'm spontaneous.

_____ Things seldom turn out like I wish.

_____ There's no point in going out of my way to help.

_____ I'm optimistic.

_____ New ideas put me off.

_____ I envy people's joy.

_____ No good deed goes unpunished.

_____ People are only friendly when they want something.

_____ I talk and/or think about the past often.

_____ Just because someone seems nice doesn't mean they are.

_____ Most people would lie for material gain.

_____ No one cares much about me.

_____ People are quick to discard the tried-and-true for the next big thing.

_____ You can only count on yourself.

_____ I often start sentences with, "Yes, but . . ."

_____ It's a dog-eat-dog world.

_____ People are only in it for themselves.

_____ It's best not to trust anyone.

_____ I'm irritated when other people talk about their joy.

_____ People always think they have the answer to my problems.

Now, look back and identify the statements you agree with the most. Paying closest attention to those you've marked with the highest and lowest numbers, patterns may emerge. Are you cynical about the world at large? Do you believe you can or can't influence what happens to you? Have you lost faith in people? Do you feel as if life is unfair?

Now, let's work on it. Use the next set of lines to jot down a few thoughts about the exercise, your feelings about individual statements, and what you've learned. As you write, remember to use specific words. Be as descriptive as possible. Also, don't judge yourself. This is for your eyes only. Estrangement is a disheartening experience—one that can permeate your very identity and leave you questioning who you are, what you stand for, and whether your beliefs make sense. Awareness allows for positive change. Don't censor yourself.

Reflect upon what you've written. Did you have these same attitudes before the estrangement? No matter how long ago the estrangement started, think about how your mood and outlook may have changed. Have other incidents or traumas added to your distress and shaped a more negative perspective? Was there ever a time when you were different, perhaps more carefree? Have the changes in you affected those around you? Think about the subjects you often talk about. Where is your focus? Are you curious about things, or are you set in your ways?

Write your thoughts in the next set of lines. Don't criticize yourself. For most of my life, people have called me a Pollyanna and happy-go-lucky. Estrangement changed that. For a while, Negative Nellie was more my speed. If I can admit it, so can you. Taking notice can make the need for change clearer. You may want to come back to what you've written a little later and use your thoughts for good.

_____

_____

_____

_____

From Bitter to Better

You have reasons for bitterness. So did Ebenezer Scrooge. But when he was directed toward the present and future, Scrooge was able to change. You can, too. In "The Bitter Test" exercise, you were asked to see yourself as you are. Now, we'll turn to the horizon and see what's ahead.

A few years ago, my home's septic system began to fail—and stink. The original 1950s-era concrete tank had been built to last and was sound, but tree roots had cracked the old clay pipes. A contractor bypassed those, dug a series of trenches for modern pipes, and created a new leach field with a specialized gravel pit. The project tore up existing hardscape, including foundational sidewalks and rock paths.

Not long afterward, I told my friends, "The system is all updated. Now, it'll outlive me."

"It's your legacy," one friend quipped.

We all laughed, but later, I got to thinking about her silly jibe. What *would* my legacy be? What will yours be? Ponder the question. There's more to your legacy than what you leave and to whom. There's your reputation, how you'll be remembered, and any lasting impact you make. Let's look at "legacy" where it really takes place: in the present.

Scrooge had the gift of a ghost to show him his future, but it was his behavior in the present that required change. It's the same for you and me. At the time of our septic issue, my husband and I were contemplating a move. The septic issue was a slow leak. We could have left a stinky legacy for the next owner, but that decision would have affected us in the present. Our property was large. So, we could have avoided the issue. Still, on a beautiful, blustery day (probably when we had guests), the smell might carry. If we dealt with the problem in the present, we could enjoy and take pride in the results now.

It's possible "The Bitter Test" brought surprises or shed light on an inner cynic. Even if you don't recognize an ounce of bitterness in yourself, read on about what it takes to change. We all have room for improvement, especially when it helps us and the ones we love.

Four basic steps for change:

1. **Awareness.** Always the first step, this requires *honesty*. You need to see the situation and yourself as you really are.

2. **A decision to change.** It's necessary to make the *choice* and be willing.

3. **A shift in *focus*.** Concentrating on what is and where you want to be rather than keeping the hurt alive.

4. **A new direction.** To take charge in a new way requires *getting creative* in what you think and do, and *flexibility* in what you try.

These steps are another way to look at resilience. The elements required for resilience from Chapter One are italicized in the steps listed above. Keep in mind that change for the better isn't an all-or-nothing prospect. Even tiny steps in a better direction is progress. Brad didn't change overnight. He used music to help him and later hired a life coach to help with his anger. Donna has recognized that she avoids people and understands why. It's a good first step. Give these parents credit—and then be as kind and generous with yourself.

Let's meet Eliza and Monte. For seven years, their daughter, Joelle, was episodically estranged. The first estrangement started soon after she married, at age twenty-one, and told her folks to "bug off." For the next six years, she made amends and cut them off again twice. She smeared her folks on social media and accused them of abuse. Yet Joelle was their only child. They had given her an idyllic childhood.

Eliza grew anxious, gained weight, and developed hypertension. Monte persuaded Eliza to take a vacation and they came home to a reset. Monte went back to work. Eliza joined a gym. She also took classes and contemplated returning to her teaching career.

At age twenty-eight, Joelle showed up on their doorstep and apologized, saying she'd left her husband and had been in treatment for addiction. Sober for four months, she needed a place to stay. Eliza and Monte let her take her old room. Joelle was moody but there were glimpses of normalcy. The parents were guarded but hopeful. Within a few months though, Joelle got a job, began staying out late at night, and had little to say to her parents. "She would shut her door," says Eliza. "If we tried to interact, she'd be mean or storm out of the house and not come home all night."

Eliza's health suffered again. Monte told their daughter she needed to move out soon. Joelle left in a hurry, telling Eliza, "Are you happy now? You got what you wanted."

A week later, the couple returned home one evening to find Eliza's car missing. They reported it stolen, and the next day, law enforcement said they had found the car with their daughter, who was bruised up and had a broken nose. Joelle claimed her mother had attacked her. She told police that she'd only taken the car to get away from her.

Monte was livid. He told Eliza, "She's gone too far. There is no coming back from this."

In shock, Eliza finally accepted that the relationship was toxic. Taking a hard look at the past seven years, and realizing they needed change, she and Monte made plans. Within a year, they had sold their home and moved to a smaller one with no spare bedroom.

In their new community, Eliza was afraid new friends would ask about family, so she spent a lot of time alone. When she talked to Monte, the subject always turned to their daughter. "He wouldn't go there," says Eliza. "He was sick of hearing about me being sad."

Craving interaction, Eliza joined a social media group for return-to-work educators. Her postings quickly garnered complaints. Upset, Eliza read back through her postings and realized her tone was argumentative and even ridiculing. She had become bitter. When she told her husband what happened, he shrugged, confirming the uncomfortable truth. He also told her he missed his partner in life.

Eliza was embarrassed and angry. "Joelle is our daughter. How could Monte just go on and not seem hurt?"

Monte assured Eliza that he was sad about Joelle, but he refused to keep dumping energy into something neither of them could fix. "Plus," Eliza adds, "he said he needed to stay strong so he could work and make sure we were safe in retirement. He loved our daughter, but he also loved me and us."

The couple vowed to spend more happy time together. Eliza joined an online group for estranged parents where she could talk about Joelle. "My husband also agreed to listen a little." Eliza laughs. "That meant about five minutes a month!" The date nights they committed to were at first awkward and included long pauses. "Thank goodness my husband has a sense of humor," Eliza says. "He broke down the icy wall between us with his goofy self, and I let him. I forgot how fun he could be. I forgot how fun *life* could be."

In time, Eliza joined a charity organization, made friends, and began substitute teaching part time. She wishes things were different with Joelle but is making progress and seizing what brings her joy. She still gets down at times but reminds herself of the good in her life. "No one gets to change me into a bitter old woman," she says. "Not even my daughter."

Eliza befriended an older widow whose son had been estranged for many years. That woman became an example for Eliza. She had done positive things with her life, had given to charities, and had made good friends. Recently, the woman died, and her forty-five-year-old son showed up at the funeral. He shook his head in judgment as good things were said about his mom. Many in the crowd knew of his mother's sorrow over his rejection of her. They assumed he had swooped in to claim an inheritance. Her son's badmouthing and blame could never sully his mother's legacy. Her life of kindness and generosity spoke for itself. Eliza aims to create a similar legacy.

Eliza is like many parents who don't recognize the alternative versions of themselves their estranged sons or daughters describe. I know that feeling, too. Most parents ponder the denouncements, attempt to understand and empathize, and try to reconcile the accusations with actual history.

Especially in the beginning, when the shadow of estrangement is so very dark, it can be difficult to see ourselves for who we really are and were. Hopeful things will change, most parents work to reconnect. Often, they don't tell anyone about the estrangement for fear they will be judged, or perhaps worse, their children will be viewed in a negative light. There's an exercise in *Done With The Crying* to help parents see history as it really was, give themselves credit for the good they did, and move beyond estrangement's gloomy eclipse. In that way, looking back can help, but it's in the present that we embrace our lives and create a legacy that cannot be sullied.

Remember my septic system? Repairs required tearing up foundational hardscape, digging out the root of the issues, and adding new connections. Similarly, estrangement disrupts parents' foundations and requires digging deep to clear out old attitudes. Or, as one mother said, realizing that the "tropes" of mother- and fatherhood are idealistic rather than realistic. To step out of the line of undeserved fire and save themselves, parents may very well need to *give in* to a child's decision. Then comes the rebuilding, one foundational piece at a time.

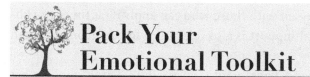

Pack Your Emotional Toolkit

People learn to "self-soothe," to calm themselves, beginning in infancy—or even in the womb. As children develop, tactics like thumb-sucking and stroking a blanket are typically abandoned, but people take on new habits to ease their nerves. Nail-biting and foot-tapping are examples, as are drinking alcohol or smoking cigarettes. Obviously, some of these pacifying activities have little to no benefit or can hurt us. Everyone needs an "emotional toolkit." Pack yours with care.

Just as any supply kit must be periodically examined, expired items culled, and new supplies restocked, an emotional toolkit requires maintenance. First, reflect on your go-to habits. When stressed, do you get angry and yell at your spouse? Treat loved ones or pets dismissively? Do you reach for a cup of calming tea? Does rock music help? Are you a walker? A smoker? An eater? A self-talker? Good or bad, consider what you turn to when emotionally distressed. Be honest so you can identify any need for adjustment and pack better supplies or tools to care for yourself. Give this some thought and become aware of your emotional rescue habits, good or bad.

On a recent walk, nature distracted me. Beautiful deer peeked from between oaks, turkeys meandered across the road, and squirrels chattered as they leapt from branch to branch. Happy and on alert for the next sighting, I stepped onto a rough spot and tumbled, face-first, to the ground. After pausing to see stars, check that nothing was broken, and regain my wits, I limped home feeling sorry for myself—and then I reached for my emotional toolkit.

"Crack some jokes," I told my husband. "Make me laugh, or I'll cry." Glad to oblige, he compared my fat-lipped profile to Donald Duck and told me I had kissed the ground. Humor is a go-to tool, and I surround myself with those who can apply it (at times too liberally!). The social support is also relevant. Find someone to laugh with. It helps.

Can you expand your emotional toolkit? Think about what works best for you, consider why, and how you might adapt so it becomes a habit or is within reach when you need it most. Anyone's life has upsets. Stressors can hit those who have suffered estrangement trauma with even more impact. I added a few emotional toolkit ideas below. Mark those you like. Then use the lines to make your own list—and pack in advance so you'll be ready.

- Calming herbal tea (keep varieties or a favorite on hand)
- Upbeat or inspirational music (handy CDs, or a music app already loaded)
- Old movies (on video, or know what channel features them)
- Talking (a supportive person to text, call, or e-mail; a local "warmline," versus "hotline," to call)
- Positive self-talk (have upbeat words on sticky notes ready; be your own cheerleader)
- A sweet pet to cuddle, train, or treat
- Nature (visit a refuge, watch birds at a feeder)

- Exercise (get things ready: weights, a treadmill, videos, yoga mat, gym membership)
- Meditate (have a quiet space prepared)
- A hobby (keep supplies on hand)
- Comfort foods (on occasion)
- Helping (volunteer, pick up neighborhood trash, pray for other people)
- Journaling (keep a special notebook or computer file)

Borrow from or adapt any of these ideas. Write down your own ideas. Begin to pack your emotional toolkit.

_____

_____

_____

_____

_____

_____

_____

_____

_____

_____

Notes

CHAPTER FOUR

Shaping the Family

"The really wonderful thing that happened to me when I was in space was this feeling of belonging to the entire universe."
—MAE JEMISON

In his 1980s "On the Family" lecture series (available on YouTube) the late John Bradshaw, whom some credit as the father of the self-help movement, stands alongside a heavy, six-foot, metal mobile. Each gleaming silver piece represents a family member. Nudge one and the others wriggle, and then settle into place. Bradshaw and proponents of "family systems theory" say that's how healthy families work. I prefer to think of that mobile like a wind chime. The stress of a little gust brings pretty music. When the breeze stops, the pieces calm, all at rest.

Estrangement is more than the stirring of a little breeze. Imagine the damage a gale-force wind can do. When a piece of the family mobile goes missing, the whole thing tilts out of whack. Members don't just wriggle back into place. Recovering balance can take bigger shifts to compensate for the loss. The thing to guard against is *over*compensating, and doing things like burdening family members by clinging too closely, being so hell-bent on staying strong that you become insensitive, or harboring self-doubt that clouds judgment and interferes with steering the family ship.

Adjustments are necessary, but the scenarios can be complex. A third-party adversary may have already been messing with family balance. The under-the-radar alienation tactics of an ex-spouse or absentee parent may have launched a sneak attack. Another relative may have secretly schemed, stirring up family friction. Substance abuse, mental illness, or chronic ill will may have created so much chaos that estrangement brings relief. The strong winds that corrupt a child's thinking and whisk away the person you once knew always hold an element of mystery, and the chasm that's left reverberates with the question: *Why? Why? Why?*

You may have come to conclusions, looked back enough to settle on an answer, even if it's a placeholder, and gotten on with the work of standing steady. You may be coping, having found a gentle rhythm as the chimes do their tune. But with enduring estrangements, there is always more to learn—about yourself, your family, and how you can move forward for the best.

Years ago, while attending a night class that required a long walk from the parking lot and up three flights of stairs, I broke my big toe. To avoid the pain of that bone striking the pavement, I put weight on the outside of my foot. That was normal behavior, a way to compensate for the injury, but not something I could keep up. I tried to anyway. At the time, admitting I needed help seemed like admitting failure. Instead of a little normal compensating, I *over*compensated. My odd gait threw everything out of whack, so my neck and hip began to hurt. That's how it is in the aftermath of estrangement. You might find yourself veering off track. You might realize when a storm starts in another branch of the family, that you've been drifting. One good thing to remember: You can always correct your course.

The issues of estrangement can bubble to the surface when you least expect them. Even when things are going well with other children, you may worry. A daughter going off to college triggers fear of abandonment because her brother rejected you during his first year at university. The sister you thought was supportive makes an uninformed statement or insensitive comment, and you realize she never really understood, or you fear she has been judging you all along. Setbacks can shake your confidence. A surfacing memory shifts more answers into place, yet heralds in new questions. Life can echo and trigger distress, but also teach you. You can grow more resilient still.

In the chapter ahead, I'll share a bit more of my own family's estrangement saga. We'll dig deeper into a variety of family-related issues, you'll witness patterns that repeat close to home, learn how estrangement affects the siblings, and more—all with the help of caring parents who've experienced this unique grief.

Picking Up the Pieces with Your Other Children

I frequently hear from parents who've been advised not to burden their other children. So, they don't talk about the estranged one. The trouble is the unmentionable hangs in the air like a bad smell. While pretending nothing's wrong, the parent unwittingly conveys that the topic is taboo—or communicates something unintended but hurtful.

Virgie learned how important communication is when her teenage son thought she didn't love him as much as she did his estranged brother. On the advice of a therapist, Virgie was so scared she'd "poison" their relationship (her therapist's word), that on her sad days she avoided her son. In the beginning, she had a lot of sad days, and her son began to believe he wasn't important to her. He confided to a high school girlfriend who was mature enough to tell Virgie. Mortified, Virgie quickly explained to her son the reasoning behind her behavior, and then corrected her course.

Children shouldn't feel the need to shoulder your sadness, but hiding your feelings goes too far. When Virgie finally shared her feelings, her younger son felt free to agree that he was also sad—and angry. Admitting to the hurt was a relief for them both.

After that, they could share that the holidays weren't the same, that they missed the rejecter's sense of humor, or that they squirmed when new acquaintances asked about family. Their openness helped Virgie's husband, too. In being strong for them, he had brushed aside his own pain. Over time, though, as his wife and son talked, he was freer to admit to his feelings as well.

Many fathers can relate to wanting to maintain strength for the family. In denying their own emotional pain, they may come off as insensitive to other family members. Victor, a middle-aged father of two young sons and an older daughter, kept unwavering faith. When daughter, Martina, rejected the family at age twenty-three, he believed she was a prodigal and would return with a change of heart.

"He'd tell me it was a phase and to pray that God would bring her back," says Victor's wife, Ruby. At times, Victor's reminders to "have faith" infuriated her. "He annoyingly whistled all through the day," she recalls. "I needed to talk about Martina. She abandoned her little brothers, and she hurt me."

After a year and a half of no contact, Martina phoned her father and apologized. He bought her a plane ticket home from Los Angeles where she had been living. Ruby wanted explanations but went along with Victor's admonition not to press Martina.

The reunion started out well. Martina was good to her little brothers and enrolled in community college. Over time, though, she changed. Martina started and quit three jobs during her eight months back at home. She met new friends and dumped old ones. Ruby wanted their daughter to see a therapist, but Martina accused her mom of thinking she was crazy and would slam her door. Victor would gently lead Ruby away, saying, "Patience."

The boys were confused but recovered from household upsets the way their parents did: with smiles, hugs, and what Ruby calls "blessed routines." Meals, homework, football practice, and games. The family was functioning as best it could.

When Martina left again, she blamed her folks for her "horrible life" and sped off in the used car Victor had bought her. Ruby needed to talk, but Victor clammed up. "He stopped whistling," says Ruby. Three months later, he suffered a heart attack.

"He's better now," says Ruby, nearly five years after the scare. "And he's opened up. I'm the one who told his doctor about our daughter." To the couple's surprise, the physician shared that he hears about estrangements often. "He said to Victor, 'It hurts, but you have got to let it go. She's an adult.' Then he told Victor he had a good wife and to lean on me. Victor was trying to be so strong, but his heart felt the pain."

In a way, Victor had been overcompensating. His good intentions inadvertently invalidated Ruby's feelings and shut her out. When she wanted Martina to get help, he took it as a sort of slight, as if he couldn't handle their family's needs. He carried the weight of their daughter's disruptive influence.

Although my family story is different, I can relate to a show of strength. It was during a turning point after my son's estrangement that I was attending that class when I broke my toe. I was determined to move forward, modeling perseverance and strength, and wasn't about to let my injury slow me down. My body soon said otherwise. I needed help and to do things differently. So, I corrected my course, finishing the class by asking my daughter to drive and being dropped off near the elevator.

Even the strongest people need help at times. I learned that lesson, and so did Victor. He followed his doctor's advice to lean on his wife and transitioned away from a high-stress job. Ruby restarted the work she had quit when their twin sons were born.

Martina still makes the rare call home, which disrupts their peace whether she's showing her sweet self that sparks hope or she's cursing them. "We're a work in progress," says Ruby. "But we're moving forward. The last time she called, we didn't answer." Ruby read the nasty texts that soon arrived and suggested Victor delete the ones sent to his phone. "A person can only take so much," Ruby explains. "Victor doesn't need the stress."

They have offered Martina counseling or even to go as a family unit. Martina has refused. They have decided not to pursue her. Meanwhile, her brothers are growing up. The couple hopes to remain close to their sons in adulthood. "We love all of our children," says Ruby. "But kids grow up. Our lives matter, too."

Let's turn to Patricia and her husband Matthew, who are like many parents whose issues with one child cause worry over the others. Molly, Matthew's daughter from a previous marriage, came to live with them full time when she was sixteen because her mother could no longer handle her. Matthew and Patricia's children, a son and daughter, were six and seven. Matthew looked forward to making up time he'd lost with Molly when his ex-wife had moved with her to another state four years earlier.

"Molly had a sharp tongue and was always using it on me," says Patricia. "We did our best to be kind and patient." Patricia understood Matthew's ambivalence about correcting his daughter. "Molly already felt like her mom threw her away," she says. "Matt worried she'd feel the same about us."

By the time Molly graduated high school, she ran with a rough crowd and used drugs. Molly is now twenty-three and, for the last four years, the only time she has called was when she needed help. They have bailed her out of jail, fixed her car, and lent her money numerous times. A few months ago, they paid her rent directly to her landlord and alerted Molly that was the last time they could help. "We told her so *Intervention* style," says Patricia, referring to the A&E TV show. "With lots of love and a dose of reality about how she hurt us. Boundaries are firmly in place."

Seeing Molly's path has affected how Patricia and Matthew raise Molly's half siblings. "We do our share of helicopter parenting," says Patricia. "The kids haven't balked much yet, but I worry we'll push them away."

"I don't know about that," says Matthew. "If I'd been around for Molly when she was younger, maybe she wouldn't be in the shape she's in now." Matthew expresses some guilt, but he knows he has done his best under the circumstances.

These parents know they hover over their younger children, but with awareness, they are working to prevent the parenting pendulum from swinging too far in one direction. They don't want to *over*correct. Patricia reminds herself, "Molly's poor choices don't foretell our other kids' futures."

In Chapter Six of *Done With The Crying*, readers are encouraged to visualize their family as a geometric shape. Each section holds them together. A family of three can be a triangle, where each side represents a member. When one person walks away, the family triangle is reduced to two lines, connecting at a single point. If your family were a circle, and one section detaches, the circle is no longer closed. How do you fill the gap, leave it open, or come together in a new form?

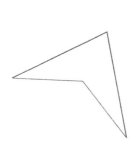

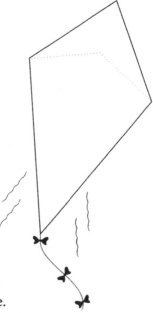

Ruby thinks of herself, Victor, and their two sons as a quadrilateral in the shape of a dart. The idea of a dart fits their purposeful forward momentum. If Martina returns in a meaningful and productive way, the lower lines can drop, forming a kite. Martina can be a new line—perhaps the tail.

For a kite, every part is valuable and works with the rest to provide stability.

Ruby's creative geometric imagery is rich with flexibility, which is so necessary after an adult child's estrangement. As discussed in Chapter One, flexibility is vital to resilience and will help you and your family bounce back.

How Am I Doing?

Now that you have read about these families, consider your own. Perhaps you recognize similarities to your life and circumstances. In these three scenarios, the estranged sibling was older, in families with minors still at home. Your family may be different, so read beyond those specifics. Spend a few moments contemplating your unique situation and family and then write down your thoughts. Use the presented questions as prompts and reword them as needed for your own circumstances.

• Have I been overcompensating for this loss in some way? How?

_____

_____

_____

_____

_____

- Is someone else overcompensating? How can I help?

_____

_____

_____

_____

_____

_____

- Since the estrangement, in what ways have I handled the situation and/or my family life well?

_____

_____

_____

_____

_____

_____

_____

- In what ways can I do better?

_____

_____

_____

_____

_____

_____

_____

- What are some goals I would like to set for myself and my family?

_____

_____

_____

_____

_____

_____

_____

• Write down at least one step to take toward those goals.

_____

_____

_____

_____

_____

_____

_____

Was the Stage Set?

The term "love bombing" was first used in the 1970s to describe the tactics used to convert new members as "Moonies" in the cult of the Unification Church of the Reverend Sun Myung Moon. Today, the term defines a dysfunctional relationship characterized by an intense flooding of affection, attention, and flattery that makes a person feel special and loved. If you've heard the term, it was most likely in the context of romantic relationships where abusers isolate their victims, build immediate companionship that creates dependency, and keeps their target all to themselves.[1,2]

Just as cults use love bombing to trick and trap their recruits, individuals who employ this method may cast a wider net. Parents often tell of a sugary sweet third-party who wooed their entire family and then dropped them when the main target (a son or daughter) married or had a baby with them. If you're looking back at such a history, you're not alone. Here, though, we'll discuss love bombing within the immediate family. But first, let's find out more about this insidious method of control.

When the targeted person objects in any way, the abuser resorts to insults and abandonment and never accepts responsibility. The victim is always to blame. In these abusive relationships, the target may suffer from insecurities, lack confidence, shy away from conflict, or not typically speak up for him- or herself. She or he will do almost anything to win back the "love" that felt so good, even from the abuser who will hurt them again.

Those who seek this sort of control may be insecure themselves, or they may have exploitative natures. They mask their cunning character with charm. Like all bullies, they are adept at singling out the vulnerable.

I often hear from parents who say a son or daughter was bullied by a sibling who later became estranged. In some families, the bullying tactics are a lot like the love bomber's, and it later becomes apparent that siblings may have been primed for their future abuse. Sibling relationships may have been a sort of "training ground" for the abuser.[3]

If you have noted manipulative tactics, narcissistic qualities, or a lack of empathy in the estranged, those tendencies may have developed unnoticed for years. You didn't welcome an evil baby into the world, but somewhere along the way, your wayward son or daughter may have begun the shift toward deliberately manipulating other people. If so, you or other family members may have suffered willful hurt that went unnamed or even unnoticed, maybe for years. Remember single mother Paulette? She looked back at the way she "somehow" always took her abusive son's side. He manipulated her, but the behavior began so insidiously that, in its incremental nature, she was fooled. His bad behavior was interspersed with periods reminiscent of love bombing, during which he charmed her. She was the greatest mom in the world . . . until she wasn't.

Rhonda, a mother of six, has come to believe that her middle daughter's string of bad boyfriends is related to growing up with her now estranged brother. "He was a remarkable boy," Rhonda says of thirty-four-year-old Jeremy, with whom she and her husband have had only sporadic, mostly nasty, contact for nine years. "Looking back, I can see that he used his high IQ, dimples, and stunning green eyes as tools. But I've come to believe that long before he understood he could make women swoon, he practiced by manipulating his sister, Jana, who is two years younger."

Rhonda isn't talking about incest. The siblings played together as all kids do, and for the most part, she felt good about that. "He had a way of doting on his sister," she says. "But a week-long stint of amiably playing teacher, grocery store, or even with dolls, would invariably end with my daughter crying." Jeremy always stopped the game abruptly, often with a destructive act. He would spill the board game and tell Jana she was too stupid to play or call in a friend he'd say was better or smarter.

Rhonda would soothe Jana's tears and have a stern talk with her son, but admits, "Part of me thought the behavior was normal. I grew up with brothers. Sometimes things got rough. Aren't all siblings mean at times?"

I can certainly relate to Rhonda's thinking. Sometimes, siblings are mean. Once when I was four or five, my older brothers, whom I idolized and tagged after, distracted me at the breakfast table. When I looked back, my Barbie doll's dismembered arms and legs were in my breakfast bowl!

Most people who have siblings can tell a story or two of meanness. That's typical. However, Rhonda now looks back and sees a pattern she didn't recognize at the time. One where her son lacked empathy and her daughter would do almost anything to play with him. The pattern continued into their teen years, when socially popular Jeremy would alternately include quiet Jana in his social group and then oust her. Jana was enamored, then hurt, and then forgiving.

"I remember questioning her," says Rhonda. "But she covered for her brother. I can't know for sure, but his repeated abandonment over the years, and later for good, may have set her up for the pattern of lousy relationships she later fell into."

Maybe you recognize a similar scenario among your children. Bullying may have shaped one son or daughter into a follower who joined a sibling in estrangement. Upon reflection, some parents say the unhealthy leader-and-follower relationship started early.

Don't blame yourself for something you wish you'd have identified earlier. Rhonda acknowledged her feelings and then worked to get through them. We're parents, not miracle workers. What once seemed like typical sibling rivalry, teen angst, or the closeness of siblings can appear more sinister in the harsh light of estrangement. Rhonda's commitment to open discussions with her other adult children about how the estrangement and the past may have affected them has worked as an antidote to encourage growth in them and in Rhonda, her husband, and the family unit.

Rhonda and her daughter, Jana, have discussed the possible connection between Jeremy's influence and Jana's subsequent tendency to choose manipulative men. They're hopeful that awareness will be a positive factor in Jana's future. For some, just acknowledging facts is enough. Others find professional assistance productive. Therapy may work as a neutral environment where all can be heard and should not focus solely on the hurt. Moving toward healing and a positive future that honors individuals as well as the whole family should be emphasized.

Whether with a counselor or on your own, honest, loving discussions about changes that have taken place in you and your family can help you all gain awareness and move forward. Choose peaceful, non-rushed times to talk. You may be surprised what comes out of another son or daughter's mouth, and you'll want to be relaxed and open to discussion. We'll talk more about that in a moment.

BEYOND DONE WITH THE CRYING

For the sake of your family's happiness and continued growth as everyone matures, take stock of what you've been through, where you're at, and where you're headed. Rhonda remembers still sitting long-faced around the Thanksgiving table four years after her older son's separation from the family. "We'd been through so much stress with Jeremy's estrangement and the lost years with me crying all the time and hoping to reconcile, that we'd kind of forgotten how to have fun."

Rhonda's thoughts echo that of many parents. It's common to get caught up in thinking they can't be happy unless the estranged adult returns. Don't fall into that trap. It's helpful to laugh and have fun. Give yourself permission.

Families can get so caught up in a wave of brokenness that they no longer know how to relate. In Rhonda's family, estrangement had been the main topic of conversation for years. While communicating had been productive in some ways, Jeremy's absence hung over them like a dark cloud. Everyone tip-toed around Rhonda, fearful of triggering her anguish. When Rhonda realized she'd had enough, she told everyone, "No more letting Jeremy ruin us." Everyone agreed.

Rhonda took the lead in reshaping her family by finding ways for them all to better connect. A group text with a joke or a comical meme that fits something personal to your family can foster togetherness that's rooted in the present. Ten minutes of comedian Brian Regan, whose humor is clean, watched together on YouTube, can be a short time-out to share a laugh. Consider what helped you bond in the past. Rhonda's oldest daughter always shared knock-knock jokes as a kid. The practice continued into adulthood, but Rhonda had been so preoccupied that she barely noticed. When Rhonda remembered that detail, she began looking up new jokes and sharing them. The two soon fell into a bonding pattern that connected to their earlier happy years.

Your techniques will depend on your children's ages and interests. You may need to pen events onto the calendar and fit them to everyone's schedule. At one point, my family frequently attended live events at various venues. Some events supported starving theater groups and opened a new world of entertainment to us. Cultural shows, opera, and plays allowed for togetherness but we didn't always have to talk. Consider sporting events, hiking, biking, indoor rock climbing, or one of those ceramic-painting shops. Institute a game night or do puzzles together.

Especially for families fractured by a serious rift, setting goals for special times and enjoyable connection is vital. Emotional distance and other negative patterns between family members can creep in and begin to stick. Positive times build and strengthen the relationships. Activities forge new connection points and create happy memories for the future.

When parents are distraught and perhaps less emotionally available, their other children may grow quiet, become more self-sufficient, or act out. Earlier we met Madelyn who, in a tense moment, "lumped" her younger daughter, Amy, in with her estranged sister, Nicole. The estrangement set the stage for Madelyn to expect the worst of Amy. "Nicole's leaving tore my heart to pieces," she says. "Maybe I allowed me and Amy to grow apart to protect myself in case she left too."

An apology and a stated commitment to do better can go a long way in forging closeness and cooperation. In opening the lines of communication, be prepared for raw feelings to emerge, possibly at unexpected moments. Conversations about painful times can be fraught with emotion and are rarely a one-and-done. A son or daughter who has felt "lumped in," or sees parents moving forward, may test their love. Just as a young child might act out when things are unsettled at home, anger may erupt from older children or young adults, and may not seem related to the situation.

Madelyn set out to regain Amy's trust. She has worked hard to support and join in with Amy's interests. Things like learning about the vegan lifestyle and purchasing an e-book reader. Amy expressed some resentment, saying she felt as if Nicole took up every ounce of space and energy for a long time. Madelyn apologized, but also stood up for herself. "Life isn't perfect," she says. "Neither are parents."

Madelyn makes a relevant point. Most people can look back at their own childhoods and identify times when their parents were more, or less, available. Financial hardships, an illness, a death in the family . . . These sorts of things drain physical and emotional energy. Discerning adults realize this, recognize their parents' good intentions, and get on with their lives.

As a mother of four children besides our estranged one, I have, at times, apologized, and have also stood up for myself. When Dan cut us off, I was preoccupied and sad. Any loving parent would be. In the next section, we'll hear directly from siblings affected by estrangement. Their distress is real and raw. Parents do well to empathize and work to gain trust, but our sons and daughters can be shown that we also have feelings. We're not robots, able to instantly pivot as if nothing has changed. We require empathy too.

Of her current relationship with Amy, Madelyn says, "It's been two years since our argument that day. We're not as close as I'd like, but Amy isn't all that social anyway." Madelyn realizes that blaming herself serves no purpose. Even if Nicole hadn't left the family or Madelyn hadn't been so torn up over it, Amy is who she is. "Our relationship isn't what I expected and different than the one I had with my mother," Madelyn says. "But we're close on Amy's terms, and I'm fine with that."

When our children are young, we have ideas about what they might do with their lives and how our relationships might evolve. The fact is, they grow up and make their own choices. For the most part, as wise parents with our own lives to lead, we value them for who they are.

When my husband and I set out to start a family, it was import-ant to us to provide stability. We worked at the same business and lived in the same house for their whole childhoods. We never pushed them into interests or careers. Although we never said so (and perhaps weren't fully conscious of this ourselves), Brian and I thought they would marry, start families, and remain in the vicinity—with us and the old homestead a constant. As of this writing, two are in other states and two are in other cities. While we're only estranged from one child, we communicate and visit more often with some of our adult children than others, and even that fluctuates depending on the goings-on. In the years since Dan left the family, there have been a few tense moments and disagreements. That's expected when family members are open and honest. Allowing our adult kids to run their own lives allows my husband and I to move in new directions, too.

Before we move on, I'd like to acknowledge that it's possible that the idea of childhood sibling relationships shaping a person even into adulthood triggers some distressing memories or brings up questions for you. Pause if you feel the need. Revisit the Lifetime Map exercise, pull out a journal, and write out your thoughts or talk with a support figure.

Perhaps you wonder about family patterns that dig deeper into the generations. We'll discuss that further toward the end of the chapter. First, let's build upon the idea of supporting the whole family by hearing from siblings who share their feelings about how the estrangement of a brother or sister has affected them.

Siblings Say

In my online survey of 323 adults with one or more estranged siblings, it's no surprise that 62% said the situation makes them sad. Almost as many (60%) said they were angry. I've listed all of the "feeling" choices and how they stacked up among respondents, who frequently chose more than one answer.

- Sad: 62%
- Angry: 60%
- Confused: 39%
- Hopeful for the estranged one's return to the family: 27%

- Worried: 22%
- Ambivalent: 21%
- Relieved: 15%
- Glad: 4%

In describing their situations, siblings listed additional words including:

- Resentful
- Disgusted
- Embarrassed

- Helpless
- Disappointed
- Drama-free

In this section, siblings offer insight into the burden they often quietly shoulder. After estrangement, the family windchime doesn't make quite the same song, but with awareness, honesty, understanding, and care, you can learn to enjoy a new tune.

More than half of those surveyed said their relationships with their parents had changed since a sibling deserted the family. I use the word "deserted" because that's how siblings often say they feel. Suddenly, they are left with hurting parents they worry about, console, and to whom they feel they must prove their loyalty. Meanwhile, they mourn their own loss. Frequently, they also worry about the sibling who has severed ties.

Thirty-six-year-old Sofia has an estranged brother, Nick, who is thirty-two. Nick has been estranged off and on for over a decade. "I have made the conscious decision to move on," Sofia says. "I love Nick, and I want him to be happy, but I cannot expose myself anymore to his callous disregard for my feelings and my mother's feelings. He is someone I don't even recognize anymore. I need to protect myself. I don't see myself changing my mind on this."

Sofia and her older brother are frustrated that their widowed mother doesn't also move on. "Mom would rather be used by Nick than have him completely fall off the map," says Sofia, whose estranged brother never calls on their mother's birthday, misses every holiday, and doesn't answer his mother's phone calls. Yet if he ever needs a favor, their mother agrees. "And that's the only reason he ever calls," says Sofia.

She and her older brother echo a viewpoint many siblings share: The parent *allows* abuse and manipulation. If the uncaring sibling calls after a year of silence, the parent is sucked right back into the pain cycle. Blind hope overrides the pattern of empty apologies followed by requests for money, babysitting, or some other need. Among the loyal adult children, frustration and even anger sets in toward the sibling and sometimes the parent. Referring to the biblical parable, Sofia says, "The prodigal son learned from his mistakes and came home humble. He didn't return now and then for his own needs and then leave again."

When parents are stuck in an unhealthy, hurtful cycle, their caring sons and daughters can also feel stuck. Although Sofia is determined to protect herself and move on from Nick's "callous disregard," she is repeatedly faced with it because her mother won't let him go. If Nick makes contact, Sofia says her mother imagines him the kind son she once knew—not the self-serving one who exploits her love. Sofia adds, "She will sometimes even make excuses for him." When her mother gives him what he wants, he goes silent.

"It hurts me to see her so hurt," Sofia explains. "Mom cries to me, and I try to tell her he hasn't changed, but she only gets mad at me. She doesn't understand why this bothers me so much." Sofia is determined to be a good daughter no matter what, but even the most caring can find themselves walking a fine line between self-care and respecting their parents.

Tiffanie, a thirty-one-year-old second-born child, says her parents' attitude about the contact she maintains with her brother, who has been estranged for four years, causes friction. As a result, she sees her parents less than she would like. "I'm not close to him," she says, "but he lets me see his two sons once a month or so. My nephews are seven and nine." Tiffanie's other two siblings, younger sisters in their early twenties, don't see their brother or nephews. "It's too stressful for my sisters," she says. "And that's partly because of Mom and Dad."

Tiffanie believed her brother was trying to keep his "high-maintenance wife" happy. She didn't expect the estrangement to last. As a doting aunt to her young nephews, Tiffanie doesn't feel it would be right to just walk out of their lives now. "I love them, and I want my nephews to have some contact with our family, but my parents feel my contact encourages my brother to stay estranged from them."

At one point, Tiffanie says her mother was sobbing. Her father was so upset that he threatened to cut Tiffanie out of the family if she didn't sever ties with her brother for rejecting them. It's been a vicious circle with her in the middle.

Parents are wise to consider how their actions influence the rest of the family. If you recognize similarities in your own circumstances and behavior with those presented here, take a few moments to reflect. Sometimes, families can get so caught up in the chaos caused by a wayward adult child that they sabotage other relationships that are dear to them.

When parents are lost in their own pain or are caught in a cycle of hope and despair, their loyal children may be frustrated and angry. They may hide their own pain so as not to worry their parents. Even parents who do their best to manage their hurt and foster healthy family relationships may not realize the emotional burden their other children can feel.

Siblings may be dealing with their own confusion and sadness. Or they may be managing other issues or ones that stem from dysfunctional sibling relationships. The latter is true of Rhonda's daughter, Jana, whom we met earlier. The mother and daughter speculate that Jana's poor relationship choices are a byproduct of growing up with her manipulative brother.

When manipulation starts in childhood, a cunning sibling knows just how to prompt undue guilt, play the victim for sympathy, or form an alliance. Parents who can face their situations honestly and tend to their own care can better help their other children escape manipulation or codependent tendencies that may have begun early in life. The help isn't necessarily direct, but when parents are open, honest, and work to move beyond their pain, they free the other children to also move forward and grow.

The subject of sibling abuse gets little airtime but research over the last couple of decades is increasing awareness. As with any abusive relationship, the scars may not be visible. Parents may not have recognized the abuse or, as Rhonda explained earlier, one child covers for another.

Siblings who responded to my survey were not asked if they were bullied or suffered any type of abuse, but a few volunteered that they were physically and/or emotionally victimized. Others used language to describe the later-estranged sibling that indicates the possibility: critical, troublemaker, mean, no respect for boundaries, bully, manipulative, controlling, jerk, backstabber.

Sibling abuse has a variety of forms including relational, emotional, sexual, and physical. Sometimes, adults who reject their families cite sibling abuse as a reason. The overall topic is too big for the scope of this book. For those who choose to explore the phenomena further, information is only an Internet search away. Here, we'll get back to a broader look at the experiences of siblings.

To help you better understand how siblings feel and how the estrangement may impact them, read through the quotes below. They were chosen because they reflect the common themes among the siblings polled. Although grouped, the themes often overlap, which demonstrates the depth of emotion siblings feel and the complexity of estrangement situations.

Anger, resentment, responsibility:

- *"I take on more responsibility for my parents as they are getting older. I feel resentful because I have a life, too, and my estranged brother should be sharing family obligations."*
- *"I helped my mother nurse my father when he died from cancer. Now I am assisting my mother as she is dying. I feel as though there is no one else to carry this burden. At times, I feel terribly alone and heartbroken."*
- *"Being the oldest, I feel responsible to try and keep the rest of the family on good terms."*
- *"I worry my estranged brother will be my parents' last conscious thought. They are older and devastated. I try to do everything I can to compensate for him, but I can't succeed. Plus, they lost contact with his daughter, so my son is their only grandchild now."*
- *"I kept trying to fill the void, always trying to make my parents happy. I felt very protective. My mother died before the worst happened. My father got Alzheimer's and my brother reconciled and exploited him. Now, I'm left with guilt because I couldn't stop that from happening."*

Worry about the parents and estrangement's effects:

- *"My mother is struggling, so I don't share anything stressful with her. I don't want her to worry about me too. I think she worries I will also leave her, so I'm always careful what I say. Sometimes, I replay our conversations, fearful something I said accidentally hurt her."*
- *"Mom had always looked younger than her age but not anymore. This has taken a toll on her physically and mentally."*
- *"Our parents have changed. The joy of laughter is missing. We all walk on eggshells because we know how broken and shattered our mom is."*

Worry about the estranged sibling:

- *"Afraid for my estranged brother. Helpless."*
- *"I'm scared for my sister's safety."*

- *"My brother is spiraling into a darker lifestyle and there's nothing I can do but watch."*

Fears about the family and the future:

- *"I know my sister will show up after our mother dies. That scares me, and I don't want anything to do with her."*
- *"My older sister is mentally ill. She has spread so many lies. The minute our younger siblings turn eighteen, she will contact them. I pray they have learned enough from me and my parents that they won't have anything to do with her."*
- *"I worry for my nieces and nephew who can't be a part of the family because of my brother. I worry for my children too. They have lost their uncle and cousins. What will happen when my parents die? I promised to respect their wishes, but how can I not let my brother know?"*
- *"My concern is that she will one day try to patch things up, and then be back to manipulate everyone the way she used to. I'm also concerned about the challenges I will face with her when our parents die."*

Among those polled, 78 percent said the estranged sibling(s) affected their family's well-being prior to the estrangement. Some blamed mental illness and addiction. Others mentioned lies, manipulation, selfishness, and evil. It's no wonder, then, that some spoke of the estrangement in terms of relief.

Here's a sampling:

- *"It's gotten so much better with the rest of my family. I used to listen and agree with my oldest sister's views against my mother. Now I'm grown up and realize how hard my mother had to work to keep a roof over our heads. My other siblings stopped talking to my sister years ago. I couldn't understand why. Now, I do."*
- *"I'm closer to my parents now. I'm glad she's not around to hurt us."*
- *"It's almost easier now, not to have to deal with the highs and lows of having her in our lives."*

- *"At peace. Free of the chaos."*
- *"We no longer have to walk on eggshells or worry about what might happen at family events. We can have fun again."*

One survey question brought particularly concerning comments: *Has estrangement changed you?* Eighty-three percent of those who answered said "yes." Roughly two-thirds of those offered additional comments, which often mirrored those frequently expressed by parents. Many said they felt judged even though their sibling's estrangement was not their fault and expressed how they felt powerless to change the sibling's decision even though they had tried.

Other frequently mentioned issues were mistrust of other people and fear of rejection. The latter extended to people in general as well as to other family members. Respondents also described worries that their own children will one day cut them off.

Some of the siblings mentioned physical complaints such as headaches and stomachaches. Many reported depression and anxiety. They also described walking on eggshells, fearful an innocent comment they make at a family gathering might hurt their parents or other relatives.

Finally, some discussed their feelings of guilt over their inability to bring the family together and their sibling being all alone. Another dimension of the guilt had to do with their own life progress. The typical evolution into adult independence, including moving from the family home, can make them feel as if they are abandoning their parents.

Among the respondents, a few confided occasional doubts as to who was to blame for the estrangement. Darlene was an impressionable thirteen-year-old when her sister, then age twenty-two, left the family. As teens sometimes do, Darlene had a few issues of her own with her mother. When her sister stopped coming around, she thought her mother must have driven her away. As time has passed, though, Darlene realizes her sister made the choice.

Now in her midtwenties, Darlene lives on her own. She and her mother typically get along well and visit often. Even so, occasional doubts surface. Recently, she talked to her mother about these feelings she considers irrational. "They're like a shadow of the teenage me," Darlene says. "I didn't like my mother's rules, and I looked up to my older sister."

Darlene's honesty reveals the "shadow" that can linger in families long after an estranged one breaks contact. Younger siblings, in particular, may not be as aware of history, and perhaps never got to know an older sibling on equal, adult terms. As they grow older, questions may arise. They may ask for details or need you to fill in the stories they overheard but don't fully understand. If the estrangement seemed sudden to them or there were changes in their sibling, they may even worry about their own mental health.

Parents who tend to their own recovery are better prepared to help. Self-awareness is vital. If another of your children comes to you with questions or wants to discuss the estranged sibling, it's important to remain calm. If your emotions are negatively triggered, you may do a disservice to your child who wants to understand something difficult for all of you to comprehend.

If you find yourself reacting, remind yourself to breathe and consider what's at the heart of your reaction. Is fear tightening your chest and causing your voice to rise? It's scary for parents who have been abandoned to think that another child might question who was at fault and how the estrangement happened. Depending on your circumstances and your relationship with the one asking, consider being open about your fears. You may worry another child will cut you off. Or the overall injustice of society's sometimes automatic judgment about what sort of parents get rejected may feel too close to home. While it's unwise to burden your kids with your own emotional fallout, it's fair to peaceably convey why the topic is tough for you.

If you have thought about these possibilities ahead of time, you won't be caught off guard, with fear or anger clawing at your throat.

An honest look at emotions can help. We'll study a few here.

- *Fear.* If you allow fear to rule, you may shut down and refuse to talk at all. You may tiptoe around the subject or even the person asking. Avoidance can spread beyond one conversation and erect a wall that becomes a lasting barrier in your relationship. To a sibling who is trying to understand, you might seem disingenuous or as if you're hiding something. Feel the fear, admit it, and speak honestly anyway.

  Likewise, fear can cause panic. When mothers and fathers believe the estranged sibling is working to turn siblings against them, it's wise to tread lightly. Yet saying nothing lets the pendulum swing too far. If the estranged one asserts that you are an awful parent, your *calm, kind* rebuttal with evidence to the contrary can't hurt.

- *Anger.* A son or daughter who seeks to understand more about a sibling's estrangement can misread your sudden anger. Your clipped responses, rising voice, or defensive posture might be scary. A loyal son or daughter who has come to you for help with their own recovery may feel like a target.

  If you find yourself becoming angry, recognize what's happening. The subject is emotionally triggering for you. Take a few breaths to settle yourself. Speak evenly about what's going on and be sure to make it clear you're not angry at the child who wants to talk about the issue. Take a break if you need to. Admit your anger caught you by surprise if that's true, recognize you need to deal with your feelings—and then do. Turn back to Chapter Three, on emotions, for help. Go back to *Done With The Crying* and its exercises, or consider getting professional support.

- *Love.* With compassion and empathy for yourself and your son or daughter, love provides the most solid ground from which to answer. Counsel yourself that this is your son or daughter whom you dearly love. Wanting to understand more about our lives and about something as confusing as a family member's estrangement is normal. Validate those feelings. Tell them you understand their need to know more. You may have done the emotional work of moving beyond the million-dollar question: *Why?* If so, you're in a good position to help a dear son or daughter.

Estrangement can shadow different family members in different ways and at different times. I know from personal experience, and from families who have shared their stories, that siblings often carry emotional baggage. The quotes in this section make that clear as well. When your other children seek information, parents should give it. However, pressuring siblings to talk about a situation they are uncertain about, have been sheltered from, or that skews family focus onto a wayward sibling that has already stolen the limelight could do more harm than good.

When there are several siblings, they often talk amongst themselves and support one another. One sister related that she and her younger sister had agreed that if their estranged brother ever contacted them, they would never meet with him without first talking it through together. Siblings can reflect upon their family and the estranged one's behavior via their special connection, sometimes with information the parents are not privy to. In fact, 34 percent of respondents said, pre- and post-estrangement, that they knew things about the estranged siblings' life or activities that the parents did not.

Ultimately, adult children don't share with their parents everything they think, feel, or do. Adults make judgments for their own lives. One thing is certain, though. Parents must take care of their own emotional health and recovery. Then, recognizing the pressure, worries, and confusion their other children may feel, they can provide a safe harbor that helps their loved ones step out of estrangement's shadow. When siblings see their parents as resilient, they will feel freer to pursue their own happy, fulfilling lives.

A Sibling's Longing

Sometimes children who remain loyal to parents are the ones hoping for the family to reconcile. Here, we'll look at two scenarios. One where the parents don't trust the estranged one, and one where a non-estranged child wants her mother to "fix" the relationship.

Denise and her husband, Chico, have been repeatedly hurt by their oldest daughter, Leah. They have come to view her as troubled and maybe even dangerous. She's twenty-seven now, and at this point, no longer welcome in their lives.

After six years of estrangement, Leah contacted her sister, then twenty-one, and told her a story that blamed their parents for the separation. "Our younger daughter was angry at us," says Chico. "We were upset she believed Leah's lies and worried because we're afraid Leah will only hurt her. She has caused so many problems, has stolen from us, and even from her grandparents."

The day their younger daughter came to them with twisted facts, Denise and Chico realized how vulnerable she was to Leah's influence. They gently corrected Leah's distorted version of the history. Chico says of their younger daughter, "She seemed to come to her senses." Reminded of the truth, she was embarrassed and apologized to them. Chico and Denise wonder how she was so easily duped.

In the same way the children of divorce often hope their parents will get back together, siblings sometimes long for family unity. Tearfully, their youngest confided that she always expected they would one day reconcile. Similarly, at one point one of my adult children expressed the same longstanding expectation. That feeling is not unusual and can come up in various ways.

Divorced mother, Joyce, says her younger daughter was a busy teenager in high school when her older brother, then twenty-three, cut off the family. "She's in her twenties now and asks me why I can't just fix it," says Joyce, who admits her frustration. "She was there. She saw what happened."

Joyce's ex-husband lured her son away with parental alienation tactics. Joyce doesn't think that's likely with her daughter, who remembers her father's badmouthing of Joyce. "She begged me not to force her to go to the visitations," Joyce says. "Her dad never fought that, and she stopped seeing him."

Still, Joyce worries. "My ex's two sisters, her aunts, have been really nasty to me. I'm not on social media, but my daughter is. Maybe they're talking trash." Recently, Joyce had a cancer scare and adds, "I'm going to be okay now but maybe my daughter's thinking about what it will be like when I'm gone one day. She wants a family, and I'm almost all she's got."

If you're facing a sibling situation, don't let reactionary emotions "prove" any lies about you. Your kind and measured responses reflect wisdom and illustrate the truth. Calmly challenge untruths with facts. Use the other tips in this chapter and respond from a foundation of love. Anger doesn't make your words persuasive.

These conversations can be exhausting and come up when least expected. Don't let them drag on unproductively but make it clear you're willing to discuss the matter again. During tense discussions, remember also to take care of your physical body. Try taking a nourishing snack break. Easy foods such as fruit, yogurt, or toast with butter and honey can prompt good feelings of home while also sustaining energy. You may also need to get up for a few moments or stretch in your chair to relieve physical tension.

Parents can be open, loving, and hope their adult children will be discerning. It's necessary to answer questions and explain as needed. Ultimately, though, parents have only so much influence over the decisions that adult children make.

Family Culture

Dulce didn't think much about how her family and culture influenced how she raised her son, Luis. That is until he began a series of episodic estrangements. Luis is the oldest of Dulce's four children. He was twenty-five when his father died and, at that time, became increasingly overbearing. "He left his brother alone," Dulce explains. "But he tried to run me and his sisters' lives."

Dulce herself comes from a family of nine children. Her oldest brother, Francisco, was always in charge. "It's how our family worked," she says. During her marriage, she escaped her brother's domination, but when her husband died, Francisco became a father figure to Luis. The more time Luis spent with her brother, the more he acted like him. If Dulce and her daughters didn't do what Luis suggested, he would fly into a rage. Eventually he'd storm out, and they wouldn't see him for weeks. In the meantime, he would go to his Uncle Francisco and complain. Then Francisco would "badger" Dulce into reaching out to her son.

"I thought Francisco should be telling Luis to treat me better," says Dulce. "But he would go on about a mother's unconditional love." Eventually, Dulce would relent, call Luis, and apologize. "Luis only came back bossier," she says.

The last time Luis went no-contact, a friend gave Dulce *Done With The Crying*, and she did the exercises. "Something inside me changed," she says. Exhausted by the family turmoil, she asked herself the question many parents caught in these tumultuous relationships with adult children ponder: *How do I want to spend my remaining years?*

Francisco started in on her, but Dulce took a stand. She told Francisco she had been a good mother, that she didn't deserve to be treated badly by her son *or* him, and that if Luis wanted to reconcile, it would be with the help of a counselor. She then sent Luis a short e-mail telling him the same thing.

Dulce's other children supported her decision. They believed that Luis had been spoiled, saying Dulce had always put his interests first. Upon reflection, Dulce realized they were right. She also began to see that she had been acting on an existing family pattern. Dulce's oldest brother had been given preferential treatment and made the leader over his siblings. What is more, she could see that her uncle, her father's older brother, had enjoyed a similar role. In her family, the oldest boy's dominance had been a right. Dulce's daughters rejected the notion.

"They're smart young women," says Dulce. "They don't have to live under the cultural rules that grant men dominance because of gender and birth order." Dulce adds, "Neither do I." She is also rais-ing her younger son (now thirteen) to recognize that women have the right to make their own decisions and contribute to society.

Since I first began speaking out about and studying parent-and-adult-child estrangement, I have gained insight from thousands of families from around the world. Dulce's family culture isn't rare. Mothers with indigenous ties in Australia, as well as those from New Zealand, South American countries, India, and even a few from the U.S., have conveyed similar situations where a prominent male figure wields family power.

In some families, it's a female relative who dominates and dic-tates. Regardless, those who move beyond intransigent family mem-bers adhering to rules (whether traditional or dysfunctional), may pay a price. The situations often include enabling of the estrangement by other relatives, which spotlights familial roles and negative patterns.

Painful realizations about one's place in the family of origin can be emotionally devastating. This book cannot cover every sce-nario. Readers who relate to something said here are urged to find empowering ways to view their circumstances, such as how Dulce saw women's changing roles and how that helped her daughters.

Let's turn now to Mei, who emigrated to the U.S. in her twen-ties. Her husband Xudong, who is eleven years older, emigrated at age thirty. They met in graduate school, wed, and later had a son. Unfortunately, their son began disconnecting with them soon after he married.

Mei believes his mother-in-law, Qiu, who holds a powerful position in their community, contributed to the estrangement. To explain, Mei shared that Qiu came to America as a baby. In nav-igating between the two cultures, Qiu had a long head start over Mei and Xudong. She is an astute businesswoman whom Mei says pulls the financial strings of relatives still emigrating to the U.S. "Qiu also triggers cultural guilt to demand that people adhere to traditional values when it suits her," Mei explains.

Of course, Mei and Xudong didn't see this at first. They were just happy that their son had finally found a mate, which wasn't easy since he held a non-professional degree. Mei says this made him less desirable among traditional parents who steer their daughters to marry doctors and engineers, who are seen as having brighter futures. Mei's son had remained single and lived with his parents until he was nearly forty. Qiu's daughter was in her thirties but also unmatched. Both families were happy when they hit it off.

In Mei's culture, it is customary for parents to help their son get a suitable home for his family. Mei and Xudong paid high city rent prices for an apartment near their daughter-in-law's mother, Qiu. That way the kids would have a place to stay while they looked for a home.

Mei and Xudong spent many weekends on the hunt. Their daughter-in-law wanted to continue living close to her mother in the city, which made finding the right residence difficult. Tension spiked when several deals fell through. Their daughter-in-law became pregnant, which added additional pressure. Xudong suggested they move to his and Mei's neighborhood, where bigger homes with yards were plentiful—and less expensive. Their daughter-in-law refused, so her in-laws scraped together every penny they could, and continued looking.

Xudong, then in his early eighties, grew weary of traipsing around the crowded city, in and out of overpriced homes. Mei did her best to keep the peace between her outspoken daughter-in-law and her husband. Meanwhile, her son plugged in ear buds and kept quiet.

Eventually, they did secure a deal for a home with some problems but in the right location. The couple moved in and broke all contact with Mei and Xudong—except for the needed repairs! Because Mei and Xudong had spent their life savings, they asked Qiu if she could pitch in. She wouldn't and reminded Mei of their traditional culture, and parents' responsibility to help a son. In their close-knit community, Mei and Xudong did their best to comply. Maintaining tradition brings them honor.

To many, the idea that these parents must hold fast to traditional values while their son does not, will seem ludicrous. Some would consider this an example of a cultural divide or clash. Those are glossy academic terms for what really took place: the selfish exploitation of cultural values.

In Dulce's situation, she was able to reduce the negative impact of all that has happened by focusing on what she sees as positive outcomes. Dulce took a stand. Her siblings have joined with Francisco in seeing Luis, and even in keeping secrets about him. She was hurt when she saw her son's wedding announcement on social media a year ago and no one had told her. Also, one sister recently let it slip that he and his wife are expecting. Despite feeling like an outsider in her own family, Dulce sees the rewards as worth the price. "I have more freedom than my siblings who still follow our brother's rules," says Dulce. "My oldest son is just like him. Maybe he's not around, but at least I get to think for myself. So do my daughters."

The Straw that Breaks the Camel's Back

In Chapter One, you read *The Boat*. What I left out of that illustration of swim-to-shore resilience are the people so often poised to push parents back into a toxic sea. Frequently, when parents get their land legs and walk forward, someone important to them stirs up doubt. Well-meaning people may fan a flame of hope that parents may have thought was long extinguished. Sometimes, their estranged children even lure them back in.

The term "growing a backbone" implies standing firm. The trouble is that even after many years, a parent's most carefully cultivated backbone can grow tender. Standing firm can be difficult—especially when people we care about have a Hallmark ending in mind.

Over the years, relatives have asked, "Have you heard from Dan?" Usually, I had nothing to report. If there was some bit of news, I told the truth, simply and without much detail.

Around nine years into the estrangement, I had a short conversation with Dan. I told Dan of our good memories of him, asked him if the separation was to continue, and reminded him that his father and I were getting older. He replied that people do die, and that we'd die too.

Any hope that we would reconcile turned a gloomy corner that night. So, not long after, when my brother asked if I'd heard anything, I related Dan's words. Then I shrugged and changed the subject. There was no need to talk about something so futile. Besides, Brian and I had other issues to contend with. One of Dan's siblings had moved home after ending a bad relationship. Also, we were working to close up our family business of more than three decades. Brian was retiring, partly because he wasn't well. When Dan made the "you'll die too" comment, I realized reaching out to him had been inspired by the emotional tumult that accompanied those life changes—and it had been a mistake.

A year after that, Dan sent me a text. This time he wrote that we were great parents and that he had failed us time and again. Seeing his words, my heart didn't leap for joy. I knew from the seesaw of experience that this didn't mean we would reconcile. Although these texts seemed genuine, he had been absent from our lives so long that we weren't sure what motivated them. His last contact had been unkind. To trust would require a leap of faith and, in the past, we had been down the road to nowhere.

That previous year of transition and Brian's declining health had been hellish but, with the help of doctors, his health had improved. The issue was under control. Dan's sibling who had moved back in with us was progressing. Our business was closed. We were heading in a new direction. Why did Dan apologize now? Caught off guard, I thanked him for saying what he did and told him these friendly texts surprised me after his previous words. I also said that I forgave him, as I had since the beginning, and told him he was off the hook. My backbone was strong—or so I thought.

Months later, one of my brothers asked me a hypothetical question: *If Dan said he'd been wrong, said he was getting counseling, and told you he wanted to make things right, would you be willing?* The question surprised me. We were long past the early, confused daze when we couldn't believe the distance would last. My immediate family wasn't sitting around worrying about Dan anymore. He was no longer a part of our lives. Some family members had died. Others had been born. Dan had walked away from us, and we had gone on. A big chunk of history existed that didn't include him. To answer that hypothetical question required stepping onto the slippery slope of hope.

Although I've imagined my share of tearful reunions, hope has only led to more hurt. Even so, every birthday since Dan left us, I had blown out my candles with a silent wish: *Please let my family be complete.* Yet, on my birthday following Dan's apology texts, I stood over the glowing candles as the wax melted into the cake and wondered if my wish had become a habit, detached from any faith. So far, to "reconcile" had referred to a solo pursuit. Was I done with him? My husband assured me that he was. It had been too long and too hard. Life was too short to entertain people who had a track record of doing us wrong. I agreed with his reasoning.

Even so, a couple of months later, when an older family member asked if we'd heard from Dan, I choked up. Tears sprang to my eyes as I related Dan's apologies. Surprised by my sudden emotions, I then laughed and explained the only thing that made sense, "I guess those words were good to hear."

My family member folded his hands on the tabletop. "Well, he's maturing."

His words struck a nerve. "Maybe," I conceded. "Or maybe there's another reason." *Had a church group suggested Dan apologize?*

Was his apology part of a twelve-step program where you need to make amends? Had someone in his wife's family convinced him to contact us? There was no reason to state the list of possibilities. Loved ones want a happy ending—and I can't blame them. In that moment, I realized that no one *fully* understands. And I don't need to try and explain. People may genuinely empathize, but even those who are closest to us do so from their own experiences. They don't walk in our shoes.

A few months later, Dan's name came up with family again. My brother reported that he'd seen him on social media. "His hair is longer," he related, saying that one of his children, Dan's cousin who lives in another state, had shown him a picture. *Hmm.* So, Dan was reaching out to extended family. I tucked that nugget away and changed the subject.

In the summer, my young grandson pulled out an old photo and identified the uncle he didn't know. He couldn't remember Dan's name, so I told him and asked him what he did know about his uncle. He shrugged. "He doesn't talk to you." My grandson hugged me, said he loved me, and then ran off to the table to draw. A few minutes later, he called me into the kitchen where he had written each of my adult children's names on a separate sheet. With magnets, he had affixed the sheets to the refrigerator by birth order. Happy faces smiled from every O. Hearts dotted every *i*. My grandson's sweetness cut through my resolve. I snapped a photo of all the names and texted it to Dan: *Just so you know, you're thought of by someone who has never met you.* He immediately texted back: *Awe, very sweet.*

I set down my phone. I had dared to hope. He had replied in kind. So why did I have a sinking feeling that I had made a mistake?

A few months later, my answer arrived. Early one morning, a series of unkind texts began. Arrows of meanness that hit their marks: The fragile hope of a mother's heart. The tender backbone I had allowed to wobble. Eyes stinging, I replied: *As always, I wish you well.*

When the meanness continued in sporadic, name-calling texts over a three-week period, the truth glared. Dan was a stranger. Not the boy I once knew. Not the young adult I once imagined had the world at his feet. He was a man in his thirties, bullying his aging mother. Unwilling to allow him to verbally abuse me, I enforced a boundary that derives from self-respect. I told him he would be blocked.

The very next day, my back went out. I could barely move or walk. As I knuckled through the pain, I imagined my tender spine. When Dan rejected us, I had developed the backbone required to get on with my life. I had faced the reality of how he'd changed, which required that I change, too. Even so, my heart held a tiny ember. His apology sparked a delicate flame, but it was the Hallmark hope of extended family and my grandson's innocence that weakened my resolve.

Maybe it was a coincidence that my back went out, but I don't think so. More like my physical spine was illustrating its tenderness, telling me with no uncertainty that my figurative spine needed tending. The pain centered in the same spot that plagued me when the estrangement began—only back then, I didn't make the connection.

Hope itself is a beautiful expression of human nature. Just as the pain of childbirth fades behind the joy of welcoming a newborn baby, a parent's heart (and backbone!) can soften over time and with distance. Hope is not a mistake, but it's also no guarantee of a happily reconciled family. Temper your hope with reason. Weigh the history. Examine what else is happening in your life and who may be influencing you.

If you dare to hope, and then are the recipient of renewed cruelty, consider the painful reminder a gift. Revisiting reality allows for reasoning that erases self-doubt. You know why you had to swim to shore.

Healing in the Family Tree

Years ago, as a thirty-eight-year-old mother of five and a "non-traditional" student in an undergraduate psychology class, I proposed a theory to the professor: I believed the anxiety I had often experienced derived from my ancestry. My father also suffered panicky bouts. I deduced that the nervous feelings which, at times, had drenched me in sweat and caused my heart to race with fear, were in my genetic makeup. I thought the panic attacks could be a throwback to some stress response that originated when my Muscogee Creek Indian ancestors were driven from their homelands on the Trail of Tears.

The professor laughed, saying, "Probably a learned behavior."

I hadn't *learned* the episodes that gripped my physical body with very real panic, often for no apparent reason. Dismissed by an authority figure, I didn't argue, but years later, scientific research reflected my theory. As it turns out, our ancestors' traumatic experiences *are* passed along through the genes. At least that's what some evidence we'll discuss here indicates.

For some of you, what follows in this section may seem a little "out there." Bear with me as we dig into the family tree and the shadows it can cast. The science of our DNA and how epigenetics work supports this section. You may gain insights that lead to healing answers.

Family secrets can have profound effects. When events or people aren't discussed, or are viewed as taboo subjects, they can take on greater significance. Unclear history gets filled in with guesses or assumptions that make it worse. Or, family members get mythologized in a heroic light. People such as a long-lost father or an ex-spouse who abandoned the family can exert influence on family members without that impact being recognized. The same is true of past violence or concealed wrongdoing. In part, the therapeutic art known as "family constellations," founded by German therapist Bert Hellinger, is based on such family history. Family constellations facilitators say that clients' complaints can at first seem nonsensical and rootless. Yet, with the discovery and acknowledgment of a family secret or traumatic history, their clients can make sense of their issues and resolve them.

Hellinger's work speaks to a sort of family conscience or soul. Each member holds an idea or image of their family, but suppressed or unresolved elements may exist. People who are not discussed, situations that hurt others, that sort of thing, remain whether talked about or not. In families with an estranged adult child, the missing persons are often thought about at family events. Though the estranged ones are physically absent, their psychological presence may loom. That's why it's important to allow your other children and family members to express their thoughts and feelings. When it's safe to express themselves, they feel supported, which dilutes the possibility of negative effects.

Native Americans and other indigenous peoples have long acknowledged the influence of ancestors on family members' present lives. This may seem mystical or magical, but scientific research demonstrates the connection. The language is different, but the words can mean the same. Intergenerational trauma is real.

In our bodies, biological markers show that trauma does pass from one generation to the next. The children of parents with PTSD, for example, are three times more likely to experience PTSD symptoms. They also have an increased likelihood for depression and anxiety. Prominent researchers in this area of study believe, as I do, that this can be inherited as well as learned.[4,5,6]

Maybe you can relate to this phenomenon. Much has been researched and written about those who survived the Jewish Holocaust and their descendants. Though not directly involved, their heirs can carry related emotional and physical symptoms. Today, that knowledge is being extended to other, less studied, groups who have experienced similar injury, as well as to trauma in general.

Recently, one of my sons surprised me by sharing what he knew about inherited stress. He talked about a study I was familiar with, wherein mice were exposed to a scent like that of cherries while also receiving small electric shocks. The mice soon shuddered at the scent, even in the absence of shocks. These mice were conditioned to react to the smell. What is relevant here is that this fearful response was passed along to their pups and their grandpups even though these generations were not previously exposed to the smell or shocks. Even offspring produced through in vitro fertilization from the sperm of sensitized males shuddered at the scent.[7]

That day, my son told his dad and me that he had always been sensitive to father-son relationships in movies, books, and on TV. He said, "I think I inherited some father angst."

My husband, Brian, and I were not surprised. Brian's father left his family when Brian was just a toddler. My husband also has no memory or knowledge of his paternal grandfather. On my side, my mother was estranged from her father since her early teens. She spoke of him only enough for us to know that he was not a good man. Despite my son's positive relationship with his own father, when you consider this family history with intergenerational trauma in mind, the "angst" my son describes makes sense.

It felt good to then tell him about what I've come to see as my own inherited angst. I get anxious in situations where someone else speaks for me. Also, I have always been distressed when pushed to hurry or to agree. I don't like surprises and loathe being driven to unknown destinations. Connecting this to my ancestors being denied a voice, pushed off and driven from their homeland, has helped me make sense of and manage my responses. Making the connection freed me to move past the feelings that previously had no explanation. Panic attacks and anxiety no longer have a hold. With a bit of reflection, you may have similar pieces that fall into place.

Some of you will be familiar with the idea of humanity's collective conscience through studies about Carl Jung. Others may connect these ideas with spiritual learning, using terminology such as "generational curse" or "sins of the father" that pass through one's lineage and continue. Even karma, by some definitions, fits. These ideas are expressed differently, but they mesh with today's scientific research and growing knowledge of epigenetics. While our DNA remains stable, epigenetic tags on our genes are more flexible. That means that our non-coding DNA is affected by lifestyle, behavior, and what we're exposed to. These then influence us and are perhaps passed on to heirs. Is it possible, then, that some of our offspring are acting on influences even they can't identify?

Earlier, I mentioned the psychological presence of an estranged adult child at family events. The estranged one will likely have similar feelings about severed family ties. Unresolved issues have a way of exerting pressure and, according to family constellations theory, will repeat and present opportunities to resolve. With insight into family situations and history, healing can occur. According to many who practice some form of family constellations, when children blame their parents rather than accept them, they set themselves up for continued opportunities to play the victim, which impedes or even halts growth. Or, if they choose wisely, they can resolve issues for their own growth as well as the positive evolution of their family conscience and, as some believe, all humankind.

This goes for parents, too. Don't let self-blame imprison you. Recognize your own failings and then hold yourself to a higher standard. Acknowledge your own influences, history, and limitations—and forgive. Self-compassion is freeing.

Over the years, some parents of estranged adults have expressed the idea that there is some vast shift causing the epidemic of family rifts. Given the countless numbers of kind, caring parents who did their best and are disowned anyway, perhaps there is some truth in this theory. A "toxic parent" culture exists today. Sometimes, adults are encouraged to blame, rather than honor, the parents who gave them life. Whether epigenetics, the zeitgeist of an entitlement or victim-playing culture, or a combination, it's obvious that some adult children are influenced.

The subjects of family constellations, epigenetics, and the effects of past generations on future ones are vast and complex. While I don't proscribe to everything I've heard, read, or seen in this realm, it's certainly fascinating and much makes sense. If you're interested in this growing field of science, you'll find a few reading suggestions in the box. The list is by no means exhaustive. Books focusing on specific culture/ethnicity might be of particular interest to you. Online booksellers are the easiest way to browse based on niches of this interest area.

You may not have an opportunity to ask an estranged family member pertinent questions or persuade them to explore family history that could possibly motivate the feelings that led them to cut ties, but this knowledge may help you minimize harm to the rest of the family. Don't allow the estrangement to become a taboo subject or to cast an unchecked shadow over your loved ones. Work to become comfortable with the subject of your estranged adult's split, honestly discuss the matter, and perhaps avoid future influence.

Earlier, I shared how my young grandson who has never met Dan wrote the names of each of my five adult children on individual sheets of paper he attached with magnets to the fridge. On a subsequent visit, his colorful chalk art out on the walkway listed the same names, complete with happy faces and hearts. Later, he pointed to Dan's photograph and said in an ominous tone, "The one of whom we do not speak." I was taken aback by his statement and its dramatic delivery. Gently, I replied, "We can talk about him anytime you'd like." My answer satisfied him. He skipped off without needing more, but if or when he ever wants to talk about it, I'll be ready.

Related Reading

- *Connecting to Our Ancestral Past: Healing through Family Constellations, Ceremony, and Ritual* by Francesca Mason Boring. This Native American author fits Shoshone and other indigenous beliefs and rituals in with Hellinger's theories.

- *Family and Other Constellations Revealed* by Indra Torsten Preiss. A comprehensive guide to the theory and practice of family constellations. Easy to read, with insightful case studies and research.

- *It Didn't Start with You: How Inherited Family Trauma Shapes Who We Are and How to End the Cycle* by Mark Wolynn. Emotional inheritance explained, with case studies and exercises. Note: Some of the case studies deal directly with the subject of rejected parents. Wolynn recommends making peace within familial relationships. Even so, be forewarned that the tone of some of the examples may seem harsh to some parents.

Warning! Genograms Can Be Addicting.

When I first learned about genograms, the freedom of applying my family tree for self-discovery fascinated me. A genogram *is* a family tree you create (on paper, as a poster, or on a computer) that encompasses much more than names and dates. It can account for people's lives and how they lived them. By highlighting details and identifying patterns within families, a genogram can also provide insight into your own life. My first genogram focused on occupations. I learned that my entrepreneurial spirit goes back several generations. No wonder I have almost always worked independently. Entrepreneurism is also in my husband's family tree. *Hmm.* No surprise then that we ran a business together!

In Chapter One, you completed your Lifetime Map. With a genogram, you can expand gained awareness and explore it however you choose. Track estrangements throughout the family tree if you'd like. Recognize missing father figures, children who strayed from the fold, a history of substance abuse, violence, or trouble with the law. A genogram can reveal patterns or give clues to possible personality issues or mental illness. You can also use a genogram for health history and discover tendencies that can help you make wise lifestyle choices. Track relatives who were natural entertainers, those in similar occupational fields, women who broke conventional molds, or relatives who fought injustice or took in strays. Who among your relatives faced hardships yet were resilient? Going back just a couple of generations can be revealing. Examining ancestors' strengths can enhance your own.

Genograms do not have to be all serious either. Looking for the fun in your family tree can prove as enlightening as any tragedy. Who often told a joke to cut tension, looked on the bright side, or always prevailed with a smile? How you use your genogram is up to you.

As an example, I've included a simple genogram that highlights estrangements in my family and my husband's family. My genogram here only goes back as far as our grandparents. If I had included siblings and prior generations, you'd see more estrangements— although until Dan chose this, I wasn't familiar with the term.

I've followed a standard model, which uses circles for women (always on the right in a couple) and squares for men (always on the left in a couple). Variations in the lines that connect people indicate relational elements such as estrangement or divorce. In the legend, I've added a few more of the standard genogram symbols, but these can become much more detailed, depending on how many generations are included or your theme. You could come up with your own symbols if that makes more sense to you. Because estrangement is the focus of my sample genogram, I chose a wavy outline for those individuals. Typically, an opening in a split connection between people would indicate the disconnect. So, in the example, I have also added that detail to my own estranged child's symbol stem.

On my example, you will note that my estranged child is included beneath the marriage line that connects me to Brian. Here, I've excluded Dan's four siblings, but you would add each of your children by birth order. Ideally, the marriage line that connects my parents would show my siblings beneath it. Brian's parents' marriage line would show his siblings. The siblings' marriages and families could also be included, but you can see how things could get crowded. For purposes of illustration, and for privacy, I excluded these details. If you wish to explore your family more fully, one option is to use separate sheets of paper to allow more room for detail.

Genograms can be done simply or with much complexity and can offer insights into your family you might not have previously considered. Some in the helping fields swear by genograms and have seen them work a sort of magic in getting people to open up and to connect family members in surprising and healing ways.

To get started:

1. First, decide on a focus theme. Health/Mental health? Marital relationships? Education? Estrangement? Occupation? The choice is yours.

2. Next, consider how many generations you will explore and who will be included. Will you include relatives' spouses, adoptees, or only blood relations? Your answers may depend on your focus.

3. Then, gather your information. Make a list of your relatives. Note your focus detail and any relevant specifics. In my genogram, I noted Brian's mother's divorce from his biological father, her marriage, divorce, remarriage, and second divorce from the man who raised him. You will note that the square representing his stepfather has a dotted line next to its solid stem, which I've used to indicate that he adopted Brian. My mother-in-law's marriage to a third husband is also shown. Your genogram's focus, combined with your family members, will contain its own particulars. In gathering your data, you may need to consult family members or records.

4. Finally, construct your genogram on paper. Enclose relatives in circles or squares, add connection lines to indicate relationships, and note relevant details by using the shorthand symbols from

Estrangements

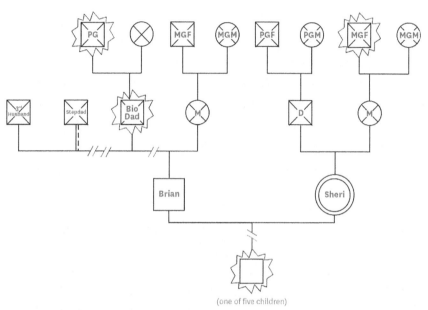

(one of five children)

Legend

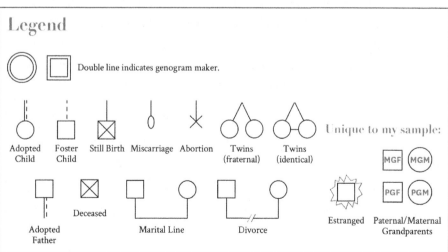

the legend. Or devise your own symbols. Make notes next to each person. Here, I haven't added dates of birth, death, or marriage, but those may be important details to you or for your focused theme.

Throughout the process of gathering information and completing your genogram, look for patterns. Use the lines at the end to reflect on any gained insight or questions for further study.

Genograms can be addicting. You can recreate one for a different focus, or combine themes, as many times as you'd like. As is shown in the example, title your genogram for its focus and organize individual genograms for reference (your own and/or for sharing with other family members).

Options:

- Use a white board to really spread out. That also makes it easy to erase and redo. Or expand your genogram to poster size.
- Get creative or make it a piece of art. Add photographs or symbols to represent family members and how you feel about them. For the basic structure, consider adding a background element such as a tree, or perhaps a river with meandering tributaries.
- Your genogram is your own, but if you ever want to share, send me a note. Tell me what you learned or include a photograph. Your journeys fascinate me, and I learn from you.

_____

_____

_____

_____

CHAPTER FIVE

The Wider Family

*"Though aging reduces speed,
it increases experience and understanding."*
—Ernest Agyemang Yeboah

A t the home where my husband and I raised our children, a
small pond sports goldfish, pink and yellow lilies, and bright
red dragonflies that dip and dart. It's a peaceful spot. The water's
glassy surface reflects blue skies and puffy clouds, but in the hot,
inland California summers, the water quickly evaporates. The pond
requires frequent refilling, which stirs up mud for a murky mess.
That's how it is when estrangement hits. Even in the most peaceful
of families, expect a little mud to surface.

This chapter digs deeper into the mire of estrangement and
how it spreads, sending ripples (or waves) across the wider family. Topics include information for committed couples, and more
about extended family, stepfamily, and grandparenting concerns.
In reading the examples, consider how the experiences, discussions, and solutions may apply to you. Advice from the trenches
helps you cut through the muck, regain your peace, and find a
clear way forward.

For the Grandparents

For most of us, becoming a grandparent is pure joy. When we snuggle a newborn and feel those tiny, strong fingers grip one of ours, every trouble slips away. From that first hiccup or smile, we're captivated. As our grandchildren grow, they adore us (we really are grand!) and spending time with them can have positive effects on our well-being.[1,2]

Grandchildren provide an excuse for us to play like kids again. In them, we can touch both our past and our future. Yet, a grandchild's presence has a way of rooting us firmly in the moment.

Children grow and change so quickly. One day they're sitting on a lap, pointing to the pictures while a doting grandparent reads. The next, they're running to share the book they can read aloud themselves. Grandparents whose special bond is severed lament the time lost and describe the sorrow as deep and cutting. Yet they worry more for their precious grands than they do for themselves.

How does the disconnection affect innocent grandchildren? Are they told the loving Gigi or adoring Gramps no longer cares? Are they fed lies about a much-loved Mamaw's sanity or intent? Imagine the potential harm to a child who is told their good opinions about a loving Poppa have been all wrong. Could this lay the groundwork for future self-doubt? If their sweet grandparent doesn't love them anymore, who can they trust?

It's enough to drive a grandparent crazy with worry. That's one reason some will do almost anything to stay in touch. Others must weigh the connection against the reality of their own ability, and the guilt they feel for not doing more. In the chapter sections that follow, we'll explore some common scenarios and ways to cope. First, let's hear the perspective of a grandchild who loves the grandmother her mother loves to hate.

From a Grandchild's Point of View

Cynthia, now fifty-two, knows what it's like to be a child caught between a grandparent and a parent. She'd been close with her grandmother and maternal aunts because she and her unwed mother lived with them until she was three. Her mother eventually married, and they moved out. That's when the episodic estrangements began, and Cynthia didn't see her "Mamaw" for weeks or even months at a time.

The extended family tried to help but their efforts sometimes aggravated the problems. An aunt hosted Cynthia's fifth birthday party and made sure Mamaw's gift was there even though she wasn't. When Cynthia opened the wrapping to find an Etch-a-Sketch, she was over the moon. "My mother bought me a gift, too," she says. "But Mamaw always listened. She knew the thing I most wanted."

Throughout the party, Cynthia oohed and aahed over the Etch-a-Sketch. "On the way home, my mom was livid," she recalls. "I was just a little girl going on about my gift from my grandma, but in the car, she berated me." Cynthia's mother took the precious gift away. That's when she learned not to speak well of her grandmother. Even during times when her mother was friendly to her grandmother, Cynthia knew her happiness about seeing Mamaw could ignite her mother's temper.

Whenever her mother was angry, Cynthia would overhear her talking badly about Mamaw on the phone. "I knew my mom was wrong," Cynthia says. "My mother would say to whoever's ear she had on the line, 'I'll show her. She won't get to see her granddaughter.' Mom was being mean to Mamaw, and I knew it was a form of punishment." Cynthia says she felt "flattened" and describes the episodic breaking of her bond with her grandmother as repeated trauma. "We were both being punished."

During the months-long separations, an aunt or other relative would occasionally arrange a visit for Cynthia and her grandmother. "But Mamaw would just cry and cry," says Cynthia. "And

I'd be her comforter." When those short, mournful visits ended, the need for secrecy was always stressed. "I wasn't to tell."

Cynthia was just a little girl, trapped in a cruel situation for which she blamed her mom. "As I got older, I was angry at my grandmother too," she says. "I used to wish Mamaw would just stand up to Mom rather than keep me in the middle. I needed a strong figure who could make me feel more secure. Seeing Mamaw reduced to tears only made my mother seem more powerful."

Cynthia's advice for grandparents in similar situations is to make any such visits fun. A grandparent's stable influence can provide security, as well as an example of stability and resilience. Cynthia didn't want her mamaw to talk badly about her mother or make promises she couldn't keep, but she would have liked her grandmother to make the few minutes they had together fun—like the times they shared when she was very young.

When Cynthia grew up and started her own family, she thought she would finally be in control. She tried bringing her mother and grandmother together. "By then, Mamaw had suffered too much," Cynthia says. "She couldn't subject herself to any association with my mother. I think she had PTSD from all the years of upset and abuse."

Over the years, Cynthia has sought help for her sadness and distress with a few different therapists. Of the complex relational layers that can exist within families, she says, "They call it 'trauma,' but they don't know much about estrangement. How to heal the bullying and abuse that goes on over lifetimes is a mystery to many in the mental health field. They don't understand, and they just aren't equipped to help."

Cynthia wishes her grandmother would have taken care of herself all those years. Instead, she let her daughter's meanness ruin her life. She explains, "Mamaw was the matriarch of the family, but she gave her power away. If she had insisted on better treatment, I think my mother would have backed down, even if only because she needed a babysitter. That's why she made up with my grandmother whenever she did." Cynthia believes that if her grandmother had refused to put up with her daughter's bullying, things would have been different and better.

Cynthia believes grandmothers in these situations feel a lot of guilt. "But even if my mother hadn't let me see mine for years, the bond was already there. I wouldn't have forgotten her."

What's a Grandparent to Do?

When sixty-four-year-old Dee refused to tolerate her daughter's verbal abuse any longer, she also lost her connection with her grandchildren, who were then eight and seven. "I didn't see or talk to them for ten years," says Dee. "But one day the doorbell rang and there stood the oldest. My granddaughter was nineteen." Soon after, she brought her younger brother. "Since then, they come regularly and have become a delight."

Dee's grandchildren attempted to bring their mother into the family picture. When that didn't work out, Dee worried what would happen to her newly rekindled relationships, but the grandchildren returned. "They said, 'Oh, you know Mom,' and then we got on to the things we do or share together," Dee explains. "We don't make it about her. Our time is always positive."

Dee goes on: "When the children were young, my daughter used them as pawns. If my opinions didn't match hers, she kept them away for weeks at a time." If Dee groveled, they'd eventually be in touch again—at huge cost to Dee's well-being. The verbal abuse was escalating. "The kids would cling to me," says Dee. "I remember their tummy aches and crying jags. The discord was hurting them, and when I finally told my daughter no more abuse, I knew a court battle would hurt the kids even more. I had to let them go."

For holidays or birthdays, she at first sent gifts, but her daughter intercepted them with thinly veiled coercion tactics. "She would tell me how much the kids missed me and add that if she only had money for something or another . . ." Dee ignored her and stopped sending presents. Instead, she put cash into a savings account, and when the time is right, will give her grandchildren the money.

Dee's advice for grandparents? "Get on with living!" She refused to focus on her pain or let anger and anguish rule her life. She's like another grandmother who made sure she was up and dressed early every day. One morning her grown grandchildren showed up. She had long since decided that if they came looking, she'd be ready—and she was. "On that day, I was even wearing lipstick!" she recalls with a laugh.

These grandparents got their wish but even if the grandchildren had never sought them out, there would be no downside to living well despite estrangement. Every day, they were up and ready—*for life*.

For some, the prospect of being out of touch causes grave concerns. Laura's adult daughter is a drug addict, which is a constant worry. Right now, she and her children live with Laura's ex-husband (their grandfather), who Laura says is retired and a recovering alcoholic. At times, Laura feels guilty and worries she isn't doing enough. Currently, she sees the children every weekend and two nights after school.

"I'm the one making sure they have shoes, clothes, and go to the dentist regularly," she says. "Their granddad keeps food in the house and makes sure they're up for school and catch the bus every day. I don't think our daughter will upset the boat, but I've told her that if she ever tried to break my contact or move the kids out of her dad's home, I would seek guardianship. With her history, which includes a criminal record, and my steady influence in the children's lives, I think I'd win." For now, though, Laura can't bring herself to step in.

Sometimes, her daughter curses Laura when she drops off or picks up the children. At those times, Laura suffers guilt and contemplates whether she should be fighting for guardianship now. "The children would probably be better off with me," she says. "But

I'm on my own and still work full time. Also, I have an auto-immune disorder that's exacerbated by stress. I need my downtime." Laura is like many grandparents who must weigh their own capabilities against reality and what they believe would be best. "I'm just across town," reasons Laura. "I can be there in ten minutes if I'm needed, and my grandchildren know they can call."

Meanwhile, she says, "I do have a plan for if the situation were to get worse." Laura has consulted with an attorney and is prepared. She documents every disruptive encounter with her daughter, as well as keeps notes of her visits with the children that include how they are or anything they report about their mom. "It's a paper trail," she explains.

In addition to having a plan, Laura suggests keeping the situation in perspective. "Time is passing," she says. "Things will change. My grandchildren are thirteen and fourteen. Almost adults."

Some grandparents get to bond with their young grandbabies, and then endure tremendous grief when the connection is severed. If the children are very young, the grandparents have little hope of ever seeing them again.

You may recall Julia and her husband, whose story was related in *Done With The Crying*. Their only son married into a well-to-do family with a pattern of alienating their adult children's spouses from their own families. Julia recently contacted me with an update. When her son and his wife had a baby, they apologized for being "selfish" and asked to reconnect. For two years, they visited most weekends, and everything seemed fine. Then, when Julia's precious grandbaby was two, the parents stopped contact again. "We're still trying to understand it," says Julia. "The pain of missing our granddaughter is palpable." As time passes, Julia has no illusions about the baby even remembering her.

Julia holds out hope that, one day, her son will see that his wife and her family are wrong, and that he will stand up to them. "But it's just a hope," she says. "I won't let it consume me."

Julia's advice? Stay busy with things you find meaningful—and cultivate a sense of humor. She laughs. "I started an apology memo to my son. When I'm feeling down, I pull out my laptop and add new items. You know, like how sorry I am for making sure he brushed his teeth and had clean underwear."

Although Julia and her husband are devastated by the renewed loss that now includes their precious granddaughter, they are getting on with their lives. Julia's husband is retired and has begun researching locations for a downsizing move. Julia finds meaning in her work with senior citizens. "They sometimes tell me about adult children who neglect them," she says. "And I can help." In helping them, Julia helps herself.

Can Someone Facilitate Visits?

Yolanda and Tom see their estranged daughter's children through the kids' father, David, who moved back to Southern California when he and their daughter, Patricia, divorced. Patricia stayed in Texas with the kids. "On holidays or over the summer, he makes sure we see them," Yolanda explains. "But I don't know if that would have happened if we hadn't asked."

Patricia first cutoff her parents when she was still married to David. A year later, when Yolanda heard that the couple had divorced, she reached out to him. After much discussion, David agreed to help.

"At first, Patricia threatened to ban us through the court system," says Yolanda. "But her ex told her we had the right. Since he stood up to her, she hasn't protested. We've been seeing our grandchildren regularly now for four years. Even David's mother sometimes drops them off, and we're invited to their family's events. In a way, David's family has adopted us."

The grandchildren say they don't talk much to their mom about the visits, and to avoid stirring conflict, Yolanda and Tom don't post photos on social media. After a trip to Disneyland and California Adventure in 2019, they printed the photos and tucked them into a physical album rather than posting online as other grandparents might. "When the kids headed back to their mom's in Texas, they left their souvenirs here," Yolanda says. "That's not unusual for them, and they don't say why, but I imagine they've learned to sidestep conflict too."

For the first couple of summers, the children were concerned they wouldn't get to see their grandparents again. Yolanda says, "The older they get, the easier this all becomes. We are so fortunate."

Tom adds, "We were worried when the COVID-19 pandemic hit, but David kept the kids with him the first two weeks of summer. Kind of a quarantine period. Then they stayed with us for two weeks."

It's not unusual for grandparents to maintain contact through an ex-spouse who exercises parental rights. In *Done With The Crying*, I shared Sondra's story. Her son's ex-wife kept her involved with the kids. Sondra even sees her son at their school events, but he never speaks to her.

These are just two of many examples where ex-spouses facilitate continued contact with loving grandparents despite estrangement. If the exes remarry and have other children, they frequently include the grandparents as extras for the new baby, too. Obviously, this requires negotiating boundaries with the new baby's other grandparents and not stepping on toes. I often hear that these situations are loving, inclusive, and even easy.

Grandparents who see their grandchildren through an ex-spouse offer those in similar situations this basic advice: *Don't be afraid to ask.* When you succeed, keep the visits with the grandchildren fun, as Yolanda and Tom do, and as little Cynthia wished her mamaw would have done.

Yolanda and Tom offer a few more suggestions:

- *Be respectful and kind.* "Acknowledge that facilitating visits could create conflict with the ex, your estranged adult child," says Yolanda. "It can and probably will. We made sure David knew we understood his concerns."

- *Be patient yet be persistent.* "Our estranged daughter has remarried and is a part-time stepmother to two children," says Yolanda. "I reasoned very softly with David that she probably wouldn't want to make waves in her new relationship by making untrue accusations in court. David said he'd think about it, and we gave him a few weeks before asking again."

- *Don't give up hope.* "I have a friend with an estranged daughter who took a more demanding attitude," says Yolanda. "Her ex-son-in-law hung up on her and then ignored her for a couple of years. Last year, though, he put the kids on a Zoom call with her at Christmas and mentioned maybe getting her together with them soon. So, even if it doesn't work out at first, there may still be hope."

If you decide to contact an ex-son- or -daughter-in-law, empathize with his or her possible concerns, such as fears about losing joint custody or worries about effects on the children if the estranged parent is miffed. Also, recognize that an ex may be eager for post-divorce peace, therefore leery of adding more stress. "If David had been really resistant, we'd have had no choice but to back off," says Tom.

Estrangement with one's adult child and, by association, one's grandchildren, can occur in a variety of situations. Some adults lose custody of their children due to incarceration or because they abandoned them for such things as addiction. In these cases, it is not uncommon for a custodial parent to exclude the in-laws from their children's lives. This also sometimes happens to one set of grandparents when both parents are missing or incapacitated, and the other grandparents have been granted guardianship of their children.

Some grandparents fight for visitation rights. Others conclude that the conflict would likely be more hurtful to the kids than allowing the parents to keep the children from them. To help you explore whether this is right in your situation, consult the box, "Grandparents' Rights Suits: The Hidden Costs." Laws vary by locale and are subject to change. Gaining legal rights to see your grandchildren is difficult, but not always impossible. See the "Grandparents' Rights Resources" box to connect with other people and information for your unique situation and in your area.

Grandparents' Rights Suits: The Hidden Costs

Grandparents seek visitation rights for the best interests of their grandchildren and believe parents' actions to break their bond is hurtful—to them and to the children. They're right. Reciprocal relationships between grandparents and grandchildren can be good for both generations, as children grow[3] and when they become adults.[4] Also, a close relationship with older family members exposes children to what it's like to grow old. That can provide a buffer against the ageist attitudes prevalent in modern society. At a time when the number of people in the older population is growing so quickly, letting young people form bonds with the elderly, learn from and understand them, is a plus for society.

There are lots of reasons why it's healthy for loving grandparents and their grandchildren to interact. Unfortunately, when court battles ensue, the children can suffer. Even if rights to visit are legally obtained, the fight can have side effects. The stress of a court battle on parents might make them irritable and less emotionally available to the children. The financial impact of expensive attorney's fees may draw from resources needed to raise the child.

Visitation is not the same as custody. State law varies but, with some caveats, grandparents' *visitation* rights are widely recognized. That doesn't mean visitation is always awarded or that gaining legally sanctioned visitation will be easy. An ongoing relationship and the best interests of the child are important factors under the law. When relations with the parents are contentious, proving these requires documentation . . . and stamina.

In suits where custody is the aim, you should know that proving the parents unfit may be required. Extreme, dangerous situations might call for such an argument. Individual situations require individual analysis. In general, such a course is likely to cause unintended problems. To prove a parent unfit may require investigations and psychiatric evaluations that will stoke parents' anger. Additionally, the children's lives may be similarly disrupted by questioning and assessments.

If your grandchildren have been removed from your life, keep your wits about you. Don't let emotions reduce you to irrational words and actions you will regret. It goes almost without saying that if you want to reconcile with the parents, filing a lawsuit diminishes the chance. Also, the children may feel torn between all the people they love.

Grandparents' Rights Resources

- *The Canadian Grandparents Story* by Daphne Jennings (2019), written by the president of the Canadian Grandparents Rights Association (https://canadiangrandparentsrightsassociation.com) This book covers the history of CGRA and its inroads in the government and legal system. Elder abuse in its many forms is discussed from a variety of perspectives.

- Grandparent Rights Advocates National Delegation (https://www.grand-usa.org/) Legislative news, resources, and support in fifty states.

- Bristol Grandparents Support Group (www.bristolgrandparentssupportgroup.co.uk/). Championing grandparents' rights in the UK.

- Alienated Grandparents Anonymous, Inc. (http://www.aga-fl.org/) Offers telephone support calls, news of legal efforts, and groups in fifty states and twenty-two countries.

A Grandparent's Legacy

Some grandparents save mementos from earlier happy times, write letters, gather gifts, and keep diaries so that someday, if the grandchild comes looking, they will have those to give. Such offerings can serve as tangible evidence of the love they felt during the years of separation, as well as characterize a loving relationship that existed too early for the child to remember.

Many hope to hand these items over personally, but at some point, make these part of a will or trust. To protect your wishes when an estranged adult child is expressly disinherited, attorneys often suggest that a letter of explanation be held with the legal documents. But asking an estate attorney to hold numerous letters or gifts isn't practical. A safety deposit box can be useful for the purpose and access made a part of the will or trust. Some grandparents enlist the help of a reliable, carefully chosen person to pass items along.

Frequently, grandparents conclude that writing letters and gathering items served their own well-being, but after years of separation, rethink the idea. One grandmother asked, "Could hearing from me after my death disrupt the relationship between my grandchildren and their parents?" Though hurt by her adult child's decision to go no-contact, she decided to leave her precious grandchildren a monetary gift only. Like she did, most grandparents deliberate over any decision of what to leave and, ultimately, base their actions on what they believe will be best for the children who are innocent in the rift.

Today, when genealogy sites are all the rage, some grandparents open accounts that will make them easily found by their grandchildren. A few keep blogs, complete with photographs, and letters of love. I have also seen YouTube tributes. Social media and other online and public channels require caution. Public postings could be viewed as invasions of privacy. A legal professional can offer specific advice. You will need to weigh any possible repercussions to everyone involved.

If you do decide to write letters for grandchildren, consider what you want them to convey. In Pat Hanson's book *Invisible Grandparenting*, she talks candidly about some letters she has written that weren't for sharing. Consider what words would be well-received and helpful, reveal you as you truly are, or even debunk a tall tale about you.

One grandmother explained that she first wrote letters to tell her side of the story. Years later, she decided that writing the letters had been for her. She'd dispelled a lot of grief and anger in them. She'd said her piece, but the harsh words were for her eyes only. She destroyed those letters and wrote a single one instead, and in it, told the grandchildren she had loved them and that it had not been her choice to sever ties. She included some photographs that told about her history, her parents, and extended family. "In case they needed maiden names or other information to make connections someday," she says. "If I do ever get to see them, then it's here for them. As time goes on, it will be left for them with my estate. Everything will go to my grandchildren."

Along these lines, I favor the idea of leaving what's called an "ethical will" (sometimes called a "legacy letter"). The idea has value for any grandparent, not only estranged ones. An ethical will conveys your values, beliefs, wisdom, and personality to all your family. The tradition has roots in Jewish culture, but ethical wills are much more widely used. These documents can consist of simple lists about such things as what you love, important life lessons, instructions for relationships, or general happiness. Or an ethical will can be something more elaborate. A book with photographs, recipes, family stories, or personal statements about any knowledge and wisdom you'd like to impart.

If this idea appeals to you, do some further study. Start with Wikipedia. The site includes a decent history about ethical wills from their origins to more modern times.

Maybe you can't communicate directly with a grandchild just now, but a well-planned written representation of who you are, your values, and some family history could offer hope that you can touch a precious grandchild's life someday.

When Adult Grandchildren Don't Reach Out

To try and stay in touch despite the separation, many grandparents send cards and gifts. Others wait to reach out until the grandchildren are older teens or legal adults. Sometimes a heartwarming reunion occurs. Other times, their tries are met with silence or the reception is lukewarm or even hostile.

When Jane and Peter reached their seventies and faced medical problems, they began to worry that time might run out. For six years, there had been no contact with their son, their only child, and his daughter, their only granddaughter. In the past, their son had been difficult. Jane and Peter had remained patient with his rants and accusations. They tried to understand and reason with him when he called them worthless and said they'd never done a thing for him. The opposite was true. They also adored their granddaughter and had barely been introduced to very young twin grandsons.

After a series of particularly vicious verbal attacks, they knew they could no longer tolerate their son's meanness. Worn down and suffering physical effects, they told him they were done with his abuse. That's when he refused to let them see their granddaughter, who was then age ten. Jane and Peter continued to reach out to her. They knew from postal receipts that their cards and gifts reached their destination in the neighboring city, but they were never sure who opened them or if they were discarded by their son.

For their granddaughter's sixteenth birthday, they shopped for just the right card. They packaged the beautiful greeting with a special necklace they had put away when she was young. The jewelry matched a necklace with a ruby heart surrounded by pearls that Jane wore, and that her granddaughter had always loved. They had planned to one day wear the necklaces together. Jane and Peter sealed the envelope and sent their gift on its way.

A few days later, their granddaughter replied with several hostile texts. She accused them of missing the last several years with her by choice. She said her father was blameless and asked them if they would ever admit that. The grandparents did not reply. They believed their granddaughter had been coached, but they were heartbroken. What had she been told about them?

Earlier in this chapter, we met Cynthia, who shared what it was like to overhear her mother talking badly about her grandmother. Despite her mother's animosity, when she needed a babysitter, she would call on Cynthia's grandmother. So, Cynthia was always reunited with her. Those periods of loving contact counteracted her mother's accusations and hate. A child without contact may believe any information they are given.

That's especially true if a child never knew the grandparents or if contact was lost very early. The child may not even ask about an absentee grandparent. As a kid growing up, I had an absentee grandfather. Although no one used the word "estranged," my mother hadn't seen her father since her early teens. At that time, her mother had moved her and her siblings to California. Although Mom didn't talk about her father much, what little she did say showed him in an abusive light. Her siblings had no contact with him either. I never questioned whether my mother was telling the truth. To me, her father was a bad man they had all escaped. Even when I was an adult, seeking him out never crossed my mind. He was a figure I didn't know, rarely thought about, and had no desire to meet.

When my estranged grandfather died, my siblings and I received notice of his estate. Apparently, he had gone on to have another family. My mother (who predeceased him) wasn't an inheritor, and neither were we. Obviously, this letter from a legal firm thousands of miles away caused curiosity. It was concrete evidence of our biological grandfather and blood relatives we had never met. Even so, our discussions never rose beyond vague speculation. My mother had closed the door on the man she had called a "monster." Why would we open it?

Has the Role of Grandparents Changed?

In a 2016 letter to an advice columnist, a young mother complained about her in-laws, saying they didn't help enough with her children. The responses from grandparents were telling. Those who wrote in were proud they had raised their own children without their parents' or in-laws' day-to-day involvement. They themselves helped with homework, fixed meals, and carted their children to school events. Readers who wrote in said that, during their own upbringing, their grandparents had a secondary, though much beloved, role. Some were incensed the woman expected her in-laws to act as caregivers while she and her husband worked. The basic consensus among grandparents was that they had already done their fair share of childrearing.

I've been a fly on the wall in online discussions where rejected parents said much the same. They remembered Sunday family gatherings at the grandparents' home. The older generation was revered, but grandparents lived their own lives separate from a second round at parenting.

Nowadays, it's not unusual to see grandparents picking up the tots at preschool, volunteering in elementary school, or carting them to extra-curricular activities. A friend who gives horseback riding lessons says that, in the last decade, her interactions with grandparents have become far more common. They often bring the children, schedule lessons, and even pay.

Increased life expectancy, changing societal attitudes, and familial commitment of the older generation all play a part. Grandparents often want to help, enjoy being with their grandchildren, and derive meaning in providing intergenerational glue. This is all good when their adult children appreciate them. Unfortunately, that's not always the case.

Grandparents aren't robots that a person can add oil to or plug in for a recharge. Yet, they tell me that they're treated with disdain or are ruthlessly cast aside when their health fails or they need time off. It's heartbreakingly cruel that the threat of estrangement is used to keep them in line, especially when they're physically suffering. Grandparents are torn between their own needs and their love for their grandchildren. When they are manipulated or underappreciated, they can begin to feel like servants, commissioned to serve first their own children and then their grands. Some wonder, "When is it *my* time to enjoy life?"

It's equally sad when the responsibility of family connection is put on the older generation. Authorities in the fields of familial estrangement sometimes counsel grandparents to hang on in one-sided relationships. They reason that, with time and patience, the relationship will eventually change for the better. It's a rosy theory. Meanwhile, the continued distress takes a toll on the older folks' health and well-being. They wonder: *How much time do I have left?* Some people who say they were led to keep trying with cold-hearted adult children later wonder about the motivation for such counsel. From time to time, I get an earful about all the money spent on a pipe dream about reconciling that left rejected parents and grandparents with emptier pockets and feeling like fools.

Counseling older persons to accept unkind treatment—from anyone—is harmful to a vulnerable population and subjects them to further abuse. Suggesting they continue to try and cultivate these hurtful relationships because the adult children don't care as much about family ties—a nicer way to say they don't care about their parents—calls for special words. Here, I'll settle for the famous line of Michael Turko, whose work I enjoyed over his two decades at San Diego's KUSI-TV, fighting authority overreach and abuse: *It ain't right!*

Perhaps these counselors don't comprehend the level of cruelty that exists in some of these relationships. Or perhaps they aren't told. It's a known fact that victims of abuse (whether verbal, psychological, financial, physical, or sexual) frequently don't tell. Older people may worry about upsetting the family, disrupting their grandchildren's lives, getting their adult child in trouble, or even losing their independence. They may feel utter shame that their own child treats them so horribly. Even with a therapist or doctor, the specifics may be minimized, or the language softened, to protect their adult child or themselves.

Disclosing the raw facts of your own child's meanness can be painful or embarrassing. Sufferers feel isolated. Yet, according to a recent study, elder abuse, defined by the subtypes above (and described more fully to include, among other things, not letting an elder see family), affects approximately one in six older adults worldwide. The same study reveals that, despite its prevalence, elder abuse is not prioritized via public health as abuse to other groups is.[5]

Negative stereotyping could also be a factor. Ageism permeates culture in the U.S. and many other countries. Relatively few mental health professionals have specific training for working with older adults. Also, on an individual client-to-therapist basis, clinicians have rated older people as less suited to therapy. There's a gap in educational opportunities in this area, which makes no sense given the rising numbers of the aged.[6] Some clinicians may see older folks who seek help for intergenerational conflicts as rigid, dependent, or set in their ways, and therefore discount their accounts of family turmoil (even unintentionally). If true, it's a shameful disservice. Negative, ageist stereotypes such as being inflexible, bumbling, sick, cognitively impaired, frail, and boring are largely myths.[7]

Could You Be a Surrogate Grandparent?

Some estranged grandparents find heart-lifting, zestful vigor in other relationships involving children, such as working with kids in the community or becoming an extra grandparent to a young neighbor family. Routinely, grandparents share these joys and encourage their fellow estranged parents and grandparents to look for opportunities. Do an Internet search for "foster grandparents" or "surrogate grandparents." You'll find organizations at national and local levels. Senior centers or grandparents support groups may also offer information.

Around the holidays, churches and community organizations pair needy families with benefactors. The holiday focus allows for a short-term commitment without continued pressure. This lets those who worry about overextending themselves more readily participate and gain benefits.

One grandmother was given the names, ages, and wish lists of two sisters whose parents needed help. She was over the moon about the fun of shopping for those girls. Like most grandmas, she chose toys they wanted but added necessities, too. Giving pajamas and new toothbrushes felt right, she said, and boosted her sense of worthiness and self-esteem.

Even your choice in a hobby could put you in touch with children. In the last few years, my friend who teaches horseback riding has seen an influx of students in their 50s, 60s, and 70s. She notes how the youngsters and oldsters in her programs are often drawn to each other. The briefest of exchanges bring kids' smiles and wipe the years off older wranglers' faces. These interchanges between old and young may work to dispel myths about old people and aging, and thus help society form more positive and more accurate views about aging.

People are living longer and so they have more years to enjoy their lives. This means they are also around to help in times of crisis—which is a boon for grandchildren whose parents aren't up to the task. In the U.S., largely in response to the opioid crisis that has destroyed millions of lives, the *Supporting Grandparents Raising Grandchildren Act* was signed into law in 2018. This act helps grandparents in the caregiver role find needed resources and support. That's good, but at a time when estrangement, the stories of grandparents denied contact with their grandchildren, and the opioid crisis with its numerous innocent victims are so often in the headlines, I see an opportunity.

Perhaps some energetic, estranged grandparents can organize, form an alliance, connect with grandparents who are in guardianship roles, and offer support. Acting as surrogate grandparents could give older folks who have stepped in as primary caregivers a break, while also filling the hearts—and arms—of displaced grandparents.

When Others Interfere

Earlier, we discussed familial patterns that may exert pressure in a variety of ways. In Chapter Four, we met Dulce, whose older brother interfered in her relationship with her son. In her family and culture, the oldest male sibling was given much authority. With the help of her daughters, she saw that her son had similar role expectations—and he wasn't nice about it. In reading her story, you may have considered how your own family and culture have influenced your estrangement experience.

Especially if your extended family has interfered, excused, or ignored the behavior, reflect upon your response to the Lifetime Map exercise in Chapter One. It was designed for you to gain more insight into your personal history, including your place in the family. This may be of help when considering family interference and how to deal with it.

Let's look at a couple of examples, beginning with sixty-two-year-old Margaret, whose only son is estranged. Margaret believes growing up with "controlling types" contributed to her becoming a people pleaser. She also married a controlling man. "When Raoul left me for another woman, my mother blamed me," says Margaret, who had been ill after her son's birth. She endured three surgeries and gained weight. "My mother said I'd let myself go." With a sigh, Margaret adds, "If I'm honest, I've never lived up to my mother's standards." Margaret was a successful businesswoman, but says, "My mother was disappointed I didn't pursue graduate degrees and go into something more civic minded."

Margaret was twelve when her father had an affair and left the family. "I woke up one day and he was gone." Margaret's mother leaned on her for emotional support and required her loyalty. For the most part, Margaret complied. Looking back, she is surprised she pursued her chosen career path, but is glad she did, because doing that allowed her to see herself in new ways, apart from her mother's view of her.

Despite this, in her midthirties, Margaret married a man who didn't treat her well, but that her mother adored. "Raoul was distant like my father," she says. "I was always trying to please him." She also sees her mother's traits in her ex. "Raoul created triangles with our son and other family members. He and my mother both."

Margaret is speaking of emotional triangulation, a situation in which one person comes between two or more other people, carrying tales or interpreting and influencing the others' relationships. Triangulation sometimes occurs innocently, as when one person is frustrated with another's behavior and tells a third party. The first person may only be blowing off steam, but upon hearing, the third party may develop negative feelings about the second. It is often problematic, regardless of intention. In narcissistic relationships, triangulation is used intentionally, to set up competition for attention or control.

"After my divorce, my mother wove stories for our son and created a sort of lore around my ex." With a small laugh, Margaret adds, "Raoul is no dummy, either. For her birthday and on Mother's Day, he still sends her a lavish gift with a handwritten card that proves his loyalty."

Margaret knows the situation is dysfunctional but until her midforties, was too caught up in her own need for approval to understand. "My son was helped to look down on me from the time he was very young," she says.

With the support of one good friend from her business days, as well as a caring pastor who encouraged her to look more closely at her history, Margaret began to recognize some strong narcissistic traits in her mother, her grandparents, and some other relatives. At that time, she sold the home where she raised her son and moved to a smaller community an hour away. Putting a little distance between herself and the rest of her family has been good for her. She says, "I can't go back and change anything, but I can have a different future." She laughs. "Even though I'm in my sixties."

In the last nine years, Margaret's mother has insisted she visit for the holidays when Margaret's son is in town. "I used to go to please her," says Margaret, who didn't attend the two most recent times. "It's too painful. My son would hug me and act like everything was fine, but when the holiday was over, he'd be back to ignoring me or telling me why I'm not good enough."

Margaret's mother stirs up the family, then other relatives start in. "They tell me a son should love his mother," says Margaret. "But their compassion always turns to blame. If I had only done this, or if I would just do that . . . They tell me to keep trying, but I know I can't change my son."

Despite all of this, Margaret can see the good in her mother. "She has always been devoted to helping people in need, and she taught me to recognize my blessings." Margaret organizes her mother's household help and visits her once or twice a week. "Sometimes, I think she really does see the truth," says Margaret. "But it's much too late to try and hold her accountable. I realized that in my forties, when I first saw the light about my family and my codependency. Mom was in her sixties then. Now, she's almost ninety. This started eons ago and is probably even in the genes. I forgive her because it frees me. I have a clean conscience."

In her new town, Margaret walks on the greenbelt, is involved in her church, and has a few friends she sees regularly. "I live a mostly peaceful life," she says. "Getting this far has been a battle but I'm starting to trust myself. Not second-guessing every interaction, worrying I'm trying too hard to please someone or gain their approval."

Let's turn to Sukie, who lost a daughter and son to the parental alienation her ex-husband started even before her divorce was initiated. At one point, Sukie felt like her older sister had joined her ex's team. When her children were in their midteens, they wanted nothing more to do with Sukie, yet her sister arranged to see them through their father. "She said she wasn't about to let her son miss out on his cousins because of me," Sukie says of a heated moment. "Because of *me*? My ex poisoned them against me. My sister's complacency helped."

Sukie's daughter and son, now in their late twenties, still see her sister for their cousin's birthday and at holidays. "I'm invited too," says Sukie, "but my adult children give me an air kiss and don't look me in the eye. They're all over my sister and our aunt and uncle who are getting up in years. Our folks are gone now, and our family is small. I'm not willing to bow out completely and be left with no one. Besides, deep down, I know this wasn't my kids' fault."

Sukie has worked hard to get past her anger. "At my ex and at my sister. In the beginning, she probably thought if she rocked the boat, my ex would turn my kids against her, too. Her son had already lost his dad." Those are guesses because Sukie's sister has never explained any of this to her. "My sister is seven years older than me. Who knows? Maybe she resented me coming along." Sukie believes it's possible there are underlying motives of which even her sister isn't fully aware. Her reasoning allows her to remain friendly with her sister.

"Sis developed agoraphobia after her husband's death," says Sukie. "Her life is narrow, but I'm a nurse with a full-time job. My life is full. Most days, I don't think much of my son and daughter. They were influenced by my ex. I fell for him once. I know how persuasive he is."

Sukie hasn't given up hope. "I still reach out on the kids' birthdays, but my e-mails aren't answered. I don't expect things to change, but I'm here if they do. And I'm here for my sister. She's my family, and amazingly, her son takes me to lunch every month or so. I'd never push him, so we don't talk about his mom or my kids, but I have a feeling he *gets* all of this."

Margaret and Sukie have come to conclusions that explain family members' behavior yet allow them to maintain a connection. Dulce has concluded that the values from her upbringing don't mesh with who she has become and interfere with her having a good relationship with her capable, independent daughters.

"Having a strong family figure that everyone turns to and leans on is not necessarily bad," Dulce says. "But that person should be wise, loving, and fair. Not chosen because of birth order and gender and allowed to lord over everyone like a tyrant." Letting go of her son and brother has complicated other familial relationships, but Dulce says, "I can't fit back into the expected slot."

Each of these mothers has made difficult choices they believe are right for them. You may or may not agree with their chosen course of action. Regardless, your response to their situations can help you shape how you handle your own.

In talking with thousands of parents, I've learned that meddling relatives are not uncommon. However, not every parent whose relatives interfere, or enable estrangement, identifies corresponding family patterns. Sometimes, relatives are misguided. Some have independent motives you may never understand. How you respond comes down to your unique situation. Weigh carefully whether any action you take will make a positive difference or exacerbate the problem.

Triage

As a nurse, Sukie is familiar with the practice of "triage." It's a French word that means "to sift" and was first used to sort through injuries on battlefields. Today, triage is used in clinical settings to prioritize level of need and urgency. Triage involves asking smart questions to determine what's most important, and then developing care goals toward diagnosis and even prognosis.

In family situations, a similar method of sifting through what's most important and finding immediate solutions can work. When it comes to enduring estrangements, the family changes and needs change. As time goes on, a fresh "triage" may be required. The basic method is in the bulleted list below. Read on for how this might look in real life.

- *First, determine what's most important to you.* For years, Margaret's subconscious goal was to please other people, particularly her mother. When she began to understand this about herself, she balanced her personal peace with her values. "I wanted to be a good daughter," she says.

- *Make decisions and put solutions into practice.* Seeing her mother as part of a bigger family and recognizing their traits and how they may have affected herself and her mother were part of Margaret's solutions. She maintained her self-image as a "good daughter," not only by helping her aging mother, but by attending the holiday events where her son was present.

- *Recognize that needs can change.* Margaret's need to move away from the home where she'd raised her son, as well as to no longer see him, supported her changing needs over time. She could no longer reconcile maintaining that home, or enduring the painful meetings, with her need for peace.

- *Reevaluate what's important.* For Margaret, that meant coming to terms about what it means to be a "good daughter." She continues her once- to twice-a-week visits and still helps her mother. Bowing out of the holiday events didn't change her self-image. Yet a more urgent need had also emerged.

- *Put new solutions into practice.* "Missing the holiday events with my son meant standing up to Mom," Margaret says. "That's been part of my growth." Margaret maintained her self-image as a respectful daughter by explaining her position, silently recognizing her mother's inability (or unwillingness) to express empathy, and then holding fast to her decision. She could do that, yet still be kind—a "good daughter" in her own eyes. "I still order food and help organize Mom's events," she says. "She needs that help, and I can give it."

Next, let's look at Sukie's example. When Sukie explored what was most important to her, it was staying in touch with her small family and maintaining hope that her children will one day see how their father negatively affected their judgment of her. That meant recognizing her ex's persuasive powers, forgiving her sister for her clumsy words, and looking beyond them to understand her sister's pain.

Even so, Sukie realizes that as time moves forward, what is most important to her may change, and other needs could grow more urgent. "I'm tired of being alone," she says. "In the next two years, my kids will reach their thirties, and I'm going to date again. I'd like a partner to grow old with."

As a nurse, Sukie is getting at another goal of triage, which is to move toward the future. Clinicians aim for diagnosis, treatment, and a good prognosis. As conditions change, people must alter their goals to fit reality. Nurses work in a range of clinical settings. In emergency care, the goals are different from those who work in continuing treatment and health maintenance. Situations go from life and death to a patient's acceptance of change, a need for comfort and fulfillment despite pain or debility. Expectations change. It can work the same for parents.

Sukie plans to reevaluate in a year or so. She is preparing for the possibility that if she does join with a partner, his needs, and "maybe even his family," will take precedence in her life. She plans to remain open to what's best for her in the future.

As you navigate difficult relationships, "triage" can help. If you're troubled by extended family's expectations, how your interaction shapes your self-image, or are hurt by interference, consider the bulleted list and the examples provided in this chapter and the overall book. How do your story, your feelings, and your experiences fit? What's most important to you right now, and will that always be true? Take a few moments to reflect. Then use this form of triage for the best possible care and outcome given the circumstances.

Estrangement: It's Catching

Estrangements can spread in ways you might not imagine. Mitch's older son moved in with a new girlfriend and then he rejected the family. Mitch was surprised when his younger son, who still lives with him, reported that a cousin in an online video gaming group had dropped out. The gamer said he would not participate after knowing the truth. The "truth" was actually lies told by Mitch's older son, but that's sometimes how estrangements spread.

Mitch's younger son also lost some in-person friends shared between the two brothers. The loss was difficult for Mitch's younger son. In time, though, the changes in others motivated him to find new activities that freed him from his brother's social circles. He attends college, works, and has made new friends.

Like a loose thread that's tugged, a rift can unravel other relationships. You'll recall Myrna from Chapter Two, whose daughter-in-law managed to alienate her from longstanding friends in her town. Even religious congregations can suffer the spread. Parents tell me they switch to a new church or will attend services at a different time to avoid certain people or gossip.

In families, existing relational problems or entrenched patterns may get spotlighted. Affected members must reflect upon what's important to them and then manage their distress and the threat of rippling rifts in ways that support their values. Not everyone chooses to remain in contact with meddling relatives.

Wallace's only child, a son, has been estranged for seven years. Wallace always felt like the "black sheep" of his family. He inherited his dark coloring from his biracial Pacific Islander father, who abandoned the family when Wallace was young. His half-brother, on the other hand, had the fair skin and blue eyes of his own father, their mother, and the rest of their family. The brother's father ran off while she was pregnant.

"I'm a hard worker and steady, but my little brother, with his quick temper and inflated ego, was always the family favorite." Neither of the boys' fathers took responsibility for their sons, yet it was only Wallace's father the family ever talked badly about. Wallace remembers hearing relatives call his father a "bad seed," often mingled with remarks about his dark skin. As a teen, when Wallace spent summer days in the sun, the family commented on how dark his skin became, too.

When Wallace's son rejected him, his brother, who has no children, interfered. "He got together with my son, and then he told me I needed to look within." Wallace did try. To his son, he apologized for whatever he might have done and asked questions to try and find out where he went wrong. He also requested for them to go to counseling together. Nothing worked.

Wallace was hurt when his brother and his two elderly aunts continued to see his son. "My brother condoned the estrangement," he says. "My aunts are in their late eighties. I didn't bother them with my feelings, but I tried to talk to my brother. True to form, he lost his temper."

That day, Wallace's brother called him a racial slur. He said the family had never approved of Wallace's father. He also told Wallace they didn't approve of *him*.

Wallace still occasionally checks in with his elderly aunts, his only living blood relatives besides his brother, whom he doesn't plan to contact again. He closed his social media accounts as well, because it hurt to see his brother playing father to his son. That his son inherited the family's fair features also isn't lost on Wallace.

Not every family has such deeply woven strings that may unravel, but meddlers are common and hurt feelings abound. Sometimes, discussions and empathy can bring understanding and maintain family ties. Other times, allowing rifts to spread is the easiest or most sensible choice.

In his early sixties, Wallace believes trying to set right ingrained patterns would be painful, and probably impossible. He thinks that one day his son will realize his mistake. Meanwhile, he isn't waiting for someday to enjoy his life. He is thankful for the moment, living each day with integrity, and hoping for the best.

Advice: Be Discerning, Not Desperate

In the shock of rejection, parents are sometimes desperate for help and too quick to take advice. Weigh any advice for its merit particular to your situation, reflect on possible motives belonging to its source, and learn to trust yourself.

First, consider whether the advisor really understands the situation. Friends and family may not understand the dynamics. They say things like, "She'll come around." Or, "Just say you're sorry." Or, "I would never let my daughter treat us that way." These statements minimize the situation or assume you have more control over the relationship than you really do. For rejected parents whose children have schooled them with blocked contact points, raging threats, character assassination, blame, or a litany of complaints, the situation's severity is clear. Recognizing their inability to control their adult child's behavior is Estrangement 101.

Unfortunately, even people in authority or supposed experts don't always recognize this truth. Also, "estrangement" doesn't mean the same thing to every researcher, therapist, psychologist, spiritual leader, or counselor—and they're not always patient enough to hear the whole story. Some liken it to a typical phase when young adults move out, go off to college, and grow independent in their decision-making. Others assume the parents have done something wrong, and in putting the responsibility to reconnect on the parents, validate the child's decision to sever ties. Some put too much emphasis on the child's motives, minimize (or don't recognize) abuse, and neglect the parents' pain.

No matter its source, ask yourself, *Is the advice:*

- *idealistic?* (Clichés about motherhood and unconditional love.)

- *simplistic or minimizing?* ("Just apologize." Or, "He'll come around.")

- *too narrow?* (Scaled to situations in which your estrangement doesn't fit?)

- *hurtful?* (Watch for "should" phrases, or assumptions you are in the wrong.)

If you feel misunderstood or dismissed, pay attention. The advice may not be right for you.

Second, consider the source. Even the nicest people sometimes offer advice to support their own agenda, even inadvertently. Family members may wish things could be easy again. Estrangement has a way of touching the lives of those in your circle. Consider what motivates whoever is offering advice.

Relatives can feel forced to take sides or worry that inviting the estranged ones will result in a confrontation. Do they hurt someone's feelings? Or risk ruining a special family event? They may advise you to reach out again. "Maybe she's come to her senses," they say. "She's more mature now. She has a child of her own." You, on the other hand, may be finally healing from the last emotional bruising. You view more contact as putting yourself in the line of fire.

Someone in an unhealthy relationship where they enable bad behavior, or make excuses for and cover abuse, is probably invested in believing what they do makes sense. Advising you to act similarly helps prove themselves right (even without them recognizing this motive). A similar example would be a friend who is also a rejected parent. Let's say this parent is a mom who sends gifts for every birthday and holiday to her estranged grandchildren. If you decide to stop sending gifts to your estranged grandchildren, your change may *feel* invalidating to her. The reality is that person's decision may be the right one—*for her*. There is no "one size fits all" advice for something as complex as estrangement with its many nuances unique to families and the people within them.

Third, listen to your gut. Begin to listen to your physical body. Does what someone tells you make your chest tight or your shoulders ache? Maybe there's a gnawing sensation in the pit of your stomach when you listen to something you don't really want to hear. It's not always easy to understand what these bodily messages mean, but checking in, physically, helps to register discomfort of any kind. It's there for a purpose: to get your attention.

- How does the advice make you feel?

- Do you feel uncomfortable with the advice because it isn't quite right for you?

- Does it make you feel inferior or guilty in some way?

When advice puts you on the defensive, it may be way off the mark for you. Or, when advice triggers a strong emotional response, it may help you to stretch, grow, and learn. The lesson isn't always that the advice is right or that you've been wrong. Sometimes, what is emotionally provocative holds lessons about your past and the need to learn now what you didn't learn then. It's possible that you need to be more flexible, learn to let go of what you can't control, or perhaps stand up for yourself.

If you feel upset by or torn about advice, consider past instances when you took advice and later regretted it.

- How did you feel at the time?

- What compelled you to follow the advice?

- What wisdom can you pull forward to the current situation?

Also, look at any advice that you immediately knew wasn't right for you. How and why was that decision easier?

Whether estrangement is new to you or you've grown long in the tooth with it and are considering whether to try again, are making end-of-life decisions, or for some other reason are receiving advice, don't be too hasty. Spend some time with your thoughts and feelings as you consider any advice. Calmly weigh your situation against the advisor's understanding of the overall problem and your goal in your unique situation. In your circumstances, *you* may be the best expert. What's your best advice for yourself?

Supporting Your Marriage and Your Spouse

When Vera divorced, her twenty-six-year-old daughter sided with her dad. After more than a year of trying to win her daughter over to no avail, Vera surrendered to her daughter's decision and began working on her own happiness. Three years later, a widower, Sergio, entered Vera's life. His two adult daughters accepted Vera with open arms. They had young children, and at age fifty-two, Vera stepped into a grandmotherly role she "just loved."

Sergio's daughters and their families visited most every Sunday. Vera and her husband attended the grandchildren's school events, and the family found every excuse to celebrate together. The extended family of his daughters' husbands were also welcomed, and Sergio's brother and sister, along with their spouses and children, were close. It was one big happy family. Then Sergio's younger daughter divorced and remarried in the space of eighteen months, and everything changed. She began to distance herself and eventually estranged from them all.

Cut off by his daughter and not allowed to see his grandchildren, Sergio was heartbroken. Having been through the pain of estrangement, Vera wanted to support him, but her mind wandered to her own daughter. She began to doubt herself and the situation. *Had she tried enough? Did her daughter miss her but not know how to reach out? Maybe her daughter was ashamed. Could that be what held her back?* To complicate matters, Vera worried that Sergio's extended family must figure she was to blame for *his* daughter's estrangement. Maybe they thought she had caused the rift with her own daughter and now with Sergio's.

When someone as close as a child rejects you, it shakes you to the core. Hypersensitivity about what other people may think of you is common. Social situations hold weight, and parents may see rejection where it doesn't really exist. A declined invitation or unanswered e-mail may be interpreted as evidence of another rejection rather than a reflection of someone's busy calendar. Even when you know better, doubt can creep in. *Be aware.* Then you can challenge your thinking for its accuracy and move beyond it.

Vera understood that the new estrangement was triggering her old self-doubt. She realized she had a choice to make. Allow the distress to consume her or get a handle on her emotions so she could help her husband through the crisis. She consciously chose the latter and sat down to come up with a plan.

First, Vera dug out her old copy of *Done With The Crying* and went over key areas that had helped her before. To put her questions about her own daughter's estrangement aside, she decided to reach out. She did so in a short e-mail from the heart, telling her daughter she still missed her and asking her if they could talk. Her daughter didn't reply in e-mail but did "friend" Vera on social media. Once connected, she publicly mocked her mother. Although the reality hurt, Vera could see that nothing had changed. Her daughter was a grown woman, making a conscious decision to hurt her mother. Vera had tried. Once again, she concluded that she would not waste her life continuing to try. Her daughter knew how to find her.

One thing down, Vera then confronted her worries about what Sergio's family might be thinking about her. When her daughter first cut her off, Vera felt like most parents, who worry people will automatically believe they are to blame. Thinking Sergio's family might also blame her was a new dimension to the same old theme, and she realized Sergio might be suffering the same feelings, thinking people were speculating about what he must have done to cause the estrangement. While he was embarrassed to tell friends and associates, he didn't feel that way with his family at all. "He told me they knew of other parents whose adult children had cut them out of their lives," says Vera. "They didn't blame those parents. If anything, they blamed it on the times."

After that, Vera spoke with his sister directly. "Having it out in the open was better for the whole family," says Vera. "Everyone had been tiptoeing around me because they knew about my daughter and knew this new estrangement was hurting me, too." Vera says that Sergio's sister told her she knew Vera loved her brother. "She said God must have known what was coming up and had put me into Sergio's life because He knew I'd understand and could support him."

More than a year has passed since his daughter cut all contact. Vera says, "I think I've been able to smooth things over for my husband and by taking charge of family events. I also occupy his other daughter's little ones when their mom needs to talk about her sister with her dad."

Now, let's look at a different situation. Here, we'll meet sixty-one-year-old Catriona, who divorced when her sons were teens. Nowadays, they're men in their late thirties who rarely speak to her. Catriona remarried six years ago and is candid about what brought her and her seventy-four-year-old husband, Patrick, close: "Problems with adult children."

"My husband's son is a narcissist," she says. "He has been diagnosed with Narcissistic Personality Disorder." Catriona characterizes her own sons as having "narcissistic tendencies like their father." Catriona says she learned years ago that they only reached out to her when they wanted something. "When I stopped giving, they stopped calling," she says. "It was tough, but for my own survival, I've detached. My husband, though, can't cut the cord."

Catriona has spent the last several years vacillating between anger and empathy. When Patrick's son calls or comes by, her husband gets excited, believing everything has changed. "Patrick gives him money, then his son disappears again, and then my husband is sad. It's a vicious cycle."

Catriona has spent countless hours cheering Patrick up when he's down and then trying to convince him that his son is using him. She says that intellectually, he gets it, but emotionally, he won't let go. Unfortunately, his wallet is attached to his heart. At times, he has given large sums. This has hurt his and Catriona's finances.

"At one point, he gave money that was earmarked to pay off my car," says Catriona. "We're not rich." Even so, Catriona says that she has come to terms with her husband's inability to act sensibly on the truth. "I've let it go because I can't change it. It's up to him whether he gives money."

A year ago, Catriona opened her own bank account. "I ask my husband to contribute three quarters of his pension, and I pay the bills with our pooled money. He doesn't have access to my account." So far, the arrangement has worked, but Catriona admits to fear, asking, "What if he can't contribute one month because he's given his son too much?"

What do you think of this arrangement? I couldn't live with the uncertainty and distress caused by a narcissistic son talking my husband out of money we both need, and then abandoning him until the next time. The son is manipulating his father, who has forked over thousands of dollars to try and win his love. It's emotional extortion and elder abuse.

Catriona worries her husband will give too much. She is moving toward taking full charge of the couple's finances to protect them both. It's not unusual for one spouse to manage the money, and Patrick is getting up in years. Catriona must think of their circumstances and weigh all possible consequences. If her husband is so easily duped by his narcissist son, could the abuse worsen?

Financial coercion can take many forms. If adult children are added to a bank account, they could then clear out all the cash. Some parents are persuaded to change their will, alter their beneficiary on life insurance, or sign over real estate.

Catriona says her husband is of sound mind. Yet, he continually gives money to his manipulative son, despite the problem it has caused in his marriage. That's cause for concern. The financial abuse of elders in the family is more common than most people realize. It's important that married partners protect one another and themselves.

The Cheese Stands Alone

In the first or second grade, I remember standing in a circle with classmates to play a game as we sang "The Farmer in the Dell." The teacher chose which kid would be the farmer for the accompanying game. Then the farmer picked a fellow student to take as his wife, the wife took a child, the child took a nurse, and so on. At the end of the song, there was always the cheese, and according to the lyrics, the cheese stands alone. As the song drew near its end, hopeful, pained expressions pinched the remaining kids' faces. Everyone wondered: *Who will be left as the stinky cheese?*

None of us had a clue about any historical or literary meanings attributed to the song. To us, the game that got us out into the sunshine was supposed to be fun. In actuality, the game became an exercise in popularity, humiliation, belonging, and exile. It always ended the same: The unchosen kid was left as the cheese, and the cheese stood alone.

In my class, another girl and I were in a puppy love triangle over a boy we'll call Johnny. Playing that game made a spectacle out of us. Invariably, the teacher chose Johnny as the farmer. Laughter and tension filled the playground circle as Johnny looked from me to the other girl, to his friends who goaded him on, and then to whichever one of us he chose. On any given day, I might be his wife . . . or the stinky cheese.

As the parent of an adult child who has been estranged for double-digit years, I have sometimes felt like that cheese. I suspect many of you have, too. You're the odd bird who adds complexity to a family reunion, or dreads questions about your son or daughter. You sit quietly, perhaps holding back tears in a group of friends talking about their grandchildren, or you're the usually steady employee who calls in sick the Monday after Mother's or Father's Day.

Rejected parents need people who understand. Yet in everyday life, you're faced with people who don't. That's why it's important to grow your emotional muscles, participate in activities that build your confidence, and recognize your self-worth. You can learn how to stand alone when necessary.

My elementary school experience forced me to stand alone. It taught me to laugh at myself along with my peers. I also learned that while things wouldn't always go my way, I would survive, and the next day, situations might change. Finally, it taught me something about authority figures. My little love triangle was a well-known dynamic in that class, yet the teacher instigated more drama by making Johnny the farmer. The lesson? Not all authority figures have their subjects' best interests at heart.

Countless parents say their son or daughter was encouraged to go no-contact with them by a therapist, church leader, or someone else in a position of authority. For parents seeking help, the opposite is often true: Someone we trust or look up to encourages us to remain engaged. Some mean well. Others don't. It's up to you to weigh the advice no matter who gives it and determine whether it's right for you and your situation. (See "Advice: Be Discerning, Not Desperate," earlier in this chapter.)

Remembering my grade school experience, as the year progressed, my affection for little Johnny waned. I didn't like competing for him and wouldn't allow him to choose my fate. One day, when he picked me as his farmer's wife, I refused. The entire class looked on as Johnny's face grew beet red and crestfallen. That's when the teacher stepped up to force my hand into his.

In my blue dress with the rickrack trim, I pulled my hand away. Brave yet fearful, I looked down at my lacy ankle socks folded neatly above my patent leather shoes as I stepped away. The teacher didn't force me any further. Johnny chose the other girl, and the game went on. I was left as the cheese.

Our class didn't play the game again. I felt kind of bad for Johnny, who later got a nasty skin condition on his face. A lot of kids made fun of Johnny, and even the other girl stopped liking him. I don't know what eventually happened to the teacher, the other girl, or Johnny. I'd like to think they learned lessons as I did. People who exert authority don't always do what's right. And you can stand up for yourself.

That year, I got another chance to choose my own fate, but failed. I let my cousin, who was my best friend, talk me out of continuing the free, afterschool dance lessons. When the teachers bumped me up to a higher level without her, she no longer wanted to go—and didn't want me to either. So, I quit with her. It's a decision I regretted, even years later, when the 1980s TV dancing show, *Solid Gold*, was a hit. The opportunity for free dance lessons never presented itself again. Looking back, I see another lesson: It can be difficult to follow your own compass when faced with opposition from someone who means a lot to you. Through these and other experiences, I grew emotional muscles and learned that I can stand alone and still be okay.

The truth is, nearly everyone has something in their history, family, or beliefs that, at times, makes them the cheese. That's why there are so many songs about loneliness. Even among close friends and supportive family, there are times when I don't fit, feel misunderstood, or figure I'm the subject of speculation. I can't fix that. But what I can do is recognize my own worth, cultivate healthy relationships, forgive the ones who unintentionally hurt me, and be grateful for the ones who don't. I can also stand up for myself.

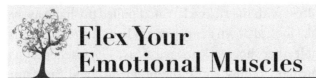

Flex Your Emotional Muscles

Without overthinking this or censoring yourself, write down the names of relatives, friends, or authority figures who trigger your anxiety or make you feel insecure or angry. Next to the name, jot down a word or phrase to describe the feelings they bring out in you. To illustrate, I've added two examples from Marta, a mother whose three daughters are estranged from her. You can name anyone—even societal influencers, experts, or authors whose beliefs unsettle you.

NAME	YOUR FEELINGS
Marta's Auntie Jo	*Worried she'll ask about the daughters*
Luella (Marta's older sister)	*Angry*

Some of you will instantly identify your feelings and know why you wrote who and what you did. Others may require more reflection. There may be more to mine from your feelings than you originally think. Let's look at Marta's examples. She worries that her aged aunt, her late mother's sister, will ask about her girls. "I don't want to upset her in any way," says Marta. "To hear that they are still not talking to me distresses her." That one is straightforward. However, when it comes to Marta's older sister, Luella, the anger runs deep.

Luella helped raise Marta because their mother was sick. Their mother eventually died when Luella was twenty-two and Marta was fifteen. A year later, Marta became pregnant. She didn't want to marry the father. "Luella talked me into it," she says. "For the baby and because of our faith." Two more babies soon followed. Marta eventually divorced, and the father had little to do with their daughters, who by then were aged eight, seven, and five. Eventually, he stopped coming around entirely. Marta worked two jobs to support the girls. When they grew up, he contacted the daughters on social media, and over time, he made Marta out as the bad parent. The girls began distancing themselves and making accusations Marta knew he'd concocted.

Now, at twenty-eight, twenty-seven, and twenty-five, they are estranged from Marta. She tried to convince them of the truth, but after two years, she has backed off. "At least for now," she says. "But Luella thinks I should keep trying. In her eyes, that's what a good mother would do." For Marta, her sister's opinion brings up the past. She regrets marrying at Luella's insistence all those years ago, but knows Luella sacrificed a lot to help raise Marta and their younger sister. "Luella took care of our father until he died. Me and my sister had families and were busy working."

Now, turn to your own list. Certain people may trigger emotions that stem from long-ago events. Use the lines here to jot down your initial thoughts. If you need more room, use paper.

Remember, what you write is for your eyes only. No need to censor yourself, but you also don't need to get too detailed—yet. We're warming up.

_____

_____

_____

_____

_____

Now might also be a good time to return to your Lifetime Map from Chapter One and review people and events that have made you stronger. Don't overlook trying people and tough situations. Some of the most difficult life passages likely formed the basis for your biggest triumphs. Reflecting on past challenges helps to identify unconscious triggers or admit to ones you struggle with— and allows you to finally move beyond them. Things like seeking approval, proving yourself worthy, or always being the one to bend.

Maybe your "perfect" sibling still makes you feel a little lesser-than, especially since the estrangement. Did you move around a lot as a kid? It's possible you've never found a place to really belong. Were you ever bullied? New situations may trigger anxiety. Louder people or those with aggressive personalities may make you feel "wrong," even when their two-cents advice is overpriced.

Consider whether there's an old story you've been telling yourself. Or maybe there's a family story with a hold over you. Are these stories still accurate and helpful? Now may be the time to lose them.

Here are a few examples of such stories and how they can hinder you:

- *No matter how hard I try, I can never get ahead.* This one might be the result of some Negative Nellie from your past taking up residence in your head. Most of us have times of struggle, but this waiting-for-the-other-shoe-to-drop outlook puts getting ahead beyond reach. The psychological term "locus of control" refers to your beliefs about how much you can affect your own life and destiny. If you have an external locus of control, you believe you have very little control over your life, your successes, and your future. An internal locus of control means you believe your efforts and actions influence your successes or failures. A person's locus of control develops as part of cultural, familial, and life experiences. It's not innate—which means you can change yours. Don't give yourself defeatist messages. Create your own destiny. Start by adopting a new motto. *If I try, I might succeed.*

- *If you want something done right, do it yourself.* This belief might be the result of living with a doer. My mother was a whirlwind of activity—and so am I. My dad called us both "efficient." I basked in the warmth of his praise, and I bet my mom did, too. The trouble is that none of us can do everything ourselves. My mother could never ask for help. I believe that attitude contributed to her early grave. For my own well-being, I've had to learn to delegate. All work is no fun. Besides, sometimes "done right" is a relative term.

- *I'm a giver.* Being a giver is a wonderful quality but not if you give too much or give to those who underappreciate and always ask for more. Sometimes, it's your turn to be on the receiving end. Any good quality, taken to extremes, is self-defeating. Give yourself permission to let someone else do the giving sometimes.

SHERI McGREGOR

We all have our stories. What do you tell yourself? One life coaching client told me her mother had instilled in her the pursuit of excellence with an emphasis on working fast. Overall, her good work ethic favorably shaped her life. However, in estrangement, there was no swift fix or excellent result.

The full term coined to name people's internal/external sense of power was "locus of control of reinforcement." That's because the results of our behavior, rewards or punishments, reinforce our beliefs and shape our outlook. The term has been shortened over the years, which makes it seem static, but it is not.

Very often, parents who have suffered emotional abuse, manipulation, and estrangement lose their sense of having power over their own lives. It's as if their adult children hobble their will. They reason that if something they've worked so hard for, and believed was forever, can fail, then what is safe? That's where knowledge of another psychological term can be of help: *contingency*. Even those who strongly believe their actions influence their successes or failures, and have seen that at work in their lives, cannot control everything or everyone.

To illustrate, consider the COVID-19 pandemic and the government-mandated restrictions. Many small businesses that belonged to hardworking people with successful track records failed. Their downfall was contingent on external circumstances. It wasn't a personal failure. Just because your adult child is unkind and/or walked away from you doesn't mean you failed. Your good work and intentions were contingent on external circumstances, which, as it turns out, you couldn't control.

My coaching client had a strong internal locus of control that began in childhood and positively affected her life. With her son's estrangement, her thinking needed to shift to a pursuit of contentment with things as they were. That meant recognizing where she truly had control and where she didn't. Consider your own personal and family stories. Reflect upon how they may influence your

196

thoughts and actions around the estrangement. Lose them altogether or alter them to better fit.

Let's get back to Marta. On his deathbed, her father told Marta and her younger sister that Luella was an angel on Earth. After he died, Luella stayed on in their family home. Marta and her sister, guided by their father's words and the knowledge that Luella had sacrificed so much to care for him, relinquished any interest in the home. Luella inherited his meager savings, never married, and has lived a quiet life of volunteer work in their community and church.

Luella has always had advice for Marta and her sister. The family lore about her, enhanced by their father's dying words and the knowledge of how much of her own life she has sacrificed, makes Marta feel as if she can never argue with Luella's advice or even defend herself. "I'm indebted to Luella," she says. "When I finally stood up to her and told her I had to let my girls go, she refused to speak to me." Marta describes the way Luella clamped her lips so tightly together and held her chin so high that it reminded Marta of an obstinate child.

After that day, Marta kept going by the house, attempting to make Luella understand. "The more I tried, the more she resisted." One evening, Marta took her sister a loaf of homemade traditional sweet bread. "But she refused it," says Marta. "I stood in her kitchen, thinking, *Okay, I'll have to give in and keep trying with my girls.*"

Marta remembers that her feet would not move. She says, "My chest was tight. I could barely breathe, and in that instant, I knew giving in would kill me." She looked at her sister, who sat on the sofa with her long neck ramrod straight, and suddenly realized how weak Luella really was. "For once, I had to stick fast to what I knew was right."

That's when Marta's feet did move. "I went around to face her and very calmly told her that I'd spent my life doing what she said was right. I told her I loved her but that I was an adult and had been for a very long time. I told her I appreciated everything she'd done for me, and I would always love her, and I hoped she could accept my decision and still love me."

Since that time, Luella hasn't spoken more than a few words to Marta. Their younger sister has pled her case to Luella, but Luella badmouths Marta, saying she's blaming Luella for her own past mistakes. Marta hopes she will come around, but in the meantime, she says, "I can't change my feelings to please her. That she can't see the truth of what my daughters are doing to me, and that I have wasted years of my life and deserve my own happiness, is very sad. But I can't help that."

Marta is standing in her own truth. She is working on herself and her life by eating for better health and vitality, as well as exercising. She joined an adult education writing class via Zoom where she has started to make new friends that she looks forward to meeting in person. This isn't the place she'd thought she'd be at this point in her life, and she doesn't know where any of her new pursuits will lead, but she's enjoying the moment and the journey.

Marta is like most of us. When faced with opposition from someone who means a lot to us, we may cave. We may fear losing the relationship, the other person's approval, or even the approval of the family. Long-held family or personal stories we've told ourselves may further complicate things. Marta stood in her truth anyway and knows in her heart that to finally do so was a huge step for herself and her life.

Earlier in this chapter we met Margaret. She finally told her mother she could not attend the holiday gatherings where her estranged son would play nice, and then cut her to pieces in later e-mails and texts. One reason she continued to attend the events for so many years was because of her need to maintain her self-image as a good daughter. For her own benefit, she had to recognize that she could refuse to comply with some demands and keep up with other, more important activities that took care of her mother and proved her worthy as a daughter.

Marta dared to see beyond the family lore and recognize Luella as a human being instead of a saint. Luella's life experiences don't give her the wisdom to rule Marta's life or judge her as less than a good mother for letting her daughters go.

Do you face similar situations in the shadow of authority figures, whether in your family, church, work, or social groups? Can you see beyond yours or your family's story and stand in your own truth? How can you strengthen your emotional muscles? Return to your list and your initial notes if you need to. Use the lines below to write down some of your thoughts.

Notes

CHAPTER SIX

There Are No Perfect Parents

"If your compassion does not include yourself, it is incomplete."
—JACK KORNFIELD

I sometimes receive e-mails from parents with guilt and regrets. They tell me they made mistakes that they believe are beyond the typical ones every parent makes. They abused substances, for example, or remembered some form of neglect. The dynamics can be different when parents know they're culpable in such ways. Yet, in interviewing these parents, I discovered their stories of shame and strength, of love and letting go, hold lessons for us all.

Most parents of estranged adult children put their history under the microscope, and at least for a while, wonder if they're at fault. While you might not relate to some of the parents in this chapter, you may see a bit of yourself in the others, and therefore gain insight. After hearing from these parents, I began to wonder:

- How long must a parent pay penance?
- How many times must a parent's contrition be proven to a son or daughter?
- Do some parents, in their anguish and guilt, become gluttons for punishment?

- Do some adult children recognize the parent's vulnerability and, deplorably, exploit it?
- Are these parents easy targets for blame that (wrongly) absolve adult children of their own mistakes?
- Are parents seeing the whole story?

This chapter aims to answer those questions, and others, that parents may have grappled with. As you read the parents' varied experiences, consider how you feel about them, what you may have in common, and what you can discern for your own life. Later in the chapter, we'll more closely examine their observations, along with additional tips and information that can help any parent come to terms with mistakes and shape a better future.

A Stranger in the Cradle

When Sylvie held her newborn daughter, she didn't feel like a mother. No love, no connection, just despair that she didn't feel the way she should. Yet, if her own mother phoned to see how she was getting on, Sylvie would say that all was well. When her husband came home from work, she put on a smile and told him her day was great. How could she admit the truth to them? She had begged her husband to have a child, and for a long time, he had resisted. Sylvie's mother had worried she wasn't mature enough for motherhood and had also been against the idea.

Sylvie didn't know she was suffering from postpartum depression. The condition is thought to be triggered by the rapid shift in hormones after birth and, according to statistics at www.postpartumdepression.org, may affect as many as one in seven new mothers in the U.S. each year. These days, heightened awareness and screening are more commonplace, but Sylvie was alone in her distress.

When her daughter turned one, Sylvie and her husband separated. For a time, they shared custody. "Everyone thought he was a good father," says Sylvie. "He was so stable and mature." Sylvie, on the other hand, could look at her daughter for hours and feel only a void. She couldn't seem to connect, and because of that, felt she had no place even being a mother. When she accepted a good work opportunity several hours away, she felt safe leaving her daughter in the father's care. He was a responsible and loving parent.

Sylvie visited, of course. She would arrive bearing gifts and try to connect with her little girl, but admits, "I felt like a stranger."

Sylvie now characterizes her decision to move away as "selfish" and "only thinking about myself," but at the time, she felt pushed away. "I had no place as a mother. I felt her father would fulfill all her needs." Her family also believed her daughter would be fine with him. Now, of her decision to move, she says, "It was the biggest mistake of my life."

When her daughter turned fourteen, Sylvie got a call from the police. "That was the day my world collapsed," she says. "My daughter told them she was sexually abused for many years. On that day, her father had tried to rape her." Her teenage daughter had fled and asked for help.

Sylvie boarded a bus, and on the long ride, a shameful refrain hiccupped in her mind. "I'm a monster. The mother who left her daughter alone all those years with a pedophile. And what is worse, I begged him to have her with me. He hadn't even wanted a child."

After that, Sylvie became a full-time mother again. They settled into an apartment together, and in the day-to-day act of being a mother, Sylvie was flooded with maternal feelings. The two were alike in many ways. They were finally together and connected but at a price. Sylvie says, "Me loving her came too late. I imagined my daughter crying alone, asking for her mother while her father abused her."

During the "four beautiful years" they lived together, Sylvie says her daughter sometimes expressed anger. She also hung out with friends and began smoking pot. Sylvie wanted to keep her daughter safe, but when she was eighteen, she moved in with her boyfriend. "I didn't want her to, but she was an adult." Sylvie consoled herself with her daughter's promise to stay in touch. "Now, I was loving her and wanted her in my life." But her daughter didn't stay in touch. She didn't return Sylvie's messages, and finally, also blocked her on social media.

Upset, Sylvie went to the shopping center where her daughter worked. Quietly, she asked her why she wasn't returning her calls. Her daughter grabbed her hand, said she was grateful for all that she had done, but added, "I don't see you as my mother. I don't feel anything for you. I never have." Her daughter said that Sylvie should go on, live her life, and be happy. She had a new family and there was no place for Sylvie in her life.

"I knew why," says Sylvie. "I was not there for her when she was a child."

In tears, but not wanting to make a scene at her daughter's workplace, Sylvie headed for the exit. As she approached the door, there was a tap on her shoulder, a security guard. He said, "Your daughter doesn't want to see you here. I was told that when she is working, you can't come." Humiliated and shaking, Sylvie left.

Feeling as if she didn't deserve to live, Sylvie isolated herself and suffered anorexia. At one point, she got down to sixty-three pounds. A walking skeleton, she began to ask herself how she could possibly still be alive. In her own way, Sylvie began to connect with God. She started to think maybe her life had a purpose, even if she didn't understand what that might be.

During her struggle with anorexia, five-days-per-week therapy, eighteen months in a group home with other women, and frequent contact with social workers, Sylvie never once mentioned having a daughter. All the therapy focused on her disorder. Even in her family, the subject of her daughter became taboo. Sylvie didn't want to talk about the source of her pain. Recently, though, she saw her gynecologist, the same physician who'd delivered her daughter.

"He asked about her," says Sylvie, "and I thought I might as well take the opportunity since he opened the door."

Sylvie told him about her disconnection from her newborn all those years ago. For the first time, she related the horrible feeling of her daughter crying and not knowing what to do. She confided her horrendous confusion and guilt at the time. How painful and scary it had been to consider putting her helpless daughter in the trash bin. "My doctor said I'd had postpartum depression," says Sylvie, crying softly. "He was sad I hadn't told him back then. It's useless to know about this now. It's too late."

During our conversation, Sylvie said she couldn't forgive herself. I listened with tears in my eyes, imagining the horror of a young, inexperienced mother, believing she was evil and afraid to tell a single soul. She didn't understand how or why she could have so wanted a baby yet then feel so disconnected.

Sylvie is making progress. A couple of years ago, she didn't believe she had a right to walk on this earth. Now, she gives herself that right. One thing that helps her is to avoid isolation. Sylvie has forced herself to try new things and has found meaning in her volunteer work as a cook at a homeless shelter. She says, "Love that was trapped inside of me flows out to those people. It's been lifesaving work, and I feel human again." For Sylvie, seeing people who were involuntarily starving also helped with her anorexia. "It triggered a new consciousness for me. I could not go hungry on purpose again."

Setting short-term goals to socialize and stay busy has led to long-term goals to find work again and get her own apartment. She's looking forward to that but also fears she'll slide back. "If I see someone who looks like my daughter, the self-loathing can start up again," she says. Her continuing progress requires diligence about her every thought or action.

In helping others and in telling her physician about her feelings from all those years ago, Sylvie is feeling more in charge of her life, useful, and accepting of herself. Sharing her story for this book is another measure of her progress. She has also made an appointment with a therapist to talk specifically about what happened with her daughter and the estrangement.

"I can live with guilt," says Sylvie. "My guilt is valid. I'm partly responsible, and I cannot take my actions back. I believe in second chances. My guilt won't kill me. I can go out and do fun stuff. I can enjoy the mundane pleasures of life. I have recently started taking care of myself again, coloring my hair that had gone completely white. This thing really aged me, but I do have a right to live."

Sylvie maintains hope that her daughter will return to her life but knows she can't wait for that to happen to take action for her own well-being. Even so, she says, "I don't know how yet to forgive myself. That may come from someone else loving me, or that may be a gift from God, a grace."

Clarity in Hindsight

"We weren't there for our son when he needed us most," laments Eileen, a fifty-two-year-old mother from Canada, whose mentally ill son, Bobby, may be living on the streets.

Bobby's history is like many children who exhibit symptoms on the cusp of adulthood. By the time the school or parents understand the roots of what's happening, the child is an adult, and their options to help are limited.

Eileen looks back at Bobby's senior year of high school with regret and confusion. He had become anxious about school and life. She tried to help, and set up doctor appointments because she was worried, but Bobby didn't keep them. His school focused on his disruptive behavior and punished him. To complicate matters, Eileen and her husband, George, were in turmoil themselves. George had shifted from sales into management and began to struggle. He was drinking more, full of nervous energy, sometimes angry, and unable to sleep. George was eventually diagnosed with bipolar disorder.

Over three years, Eileen and George worked through George's diagnosis and treatment amidst a sea of change. With George unable to work, the family lost their home and moved to a small apartment. Their older son went off to college, and Eileen became the breadwinner.

During those difficult years, Bobby managed to graduate from high school. Then he began to travel, trying different jobs. He didn't last long any one place, and a few times, needed rescuing. "We'd send him a bus or plane ticket home," says Eileen.

Once home, Bobby was irritable and sometimes flew into rages over the tiniest things. George and Eileen encouraged him to eat meals with them and interact, but he isolated himself. Eileen showed him job advertisements, but he'd yell at her and tell her not to talk to him at all.

"He was drinking and drugging," says Eileen. After George's diagnosis, she and George suspected bipolar disorder, but Bobby blew them off. He was of legal age. They couldn't force him to listen and seek help. One evening, their son was ranting and throwing things around. Eileen says, "He was out of his mind." In desperation and frightened, Eileen called authorities. "We thought they would keep him, and he would finally get help, but they just let him go."

After that night, Bobby moved into his older brother's spare room in a nearby city. He wouldn't talk to his parents, but his brother gave them updates. "Bobby got the idea we were all gossiping about him, and left," says Eileen, who assumed he would eventually turn up as he always had.

Eileen did reach out via e-mail, but Bobby never replied. His occasional social media postings reassured the family. An old friend of his did hear from him occasionally and would pass along the news that he was doing fine and was sober. He never said where he was, but they knew he was alive.

Eileen and George slowly rebounded financially and settled into a little house. Eileen tried more diligently to contact Bobby, but he blocked her on e-mail and social media. Six years have passed since she and George have seen or spoken to Bobby. He also stopped calling his old friend.

Eileen reflects on her regrets amid the chaos that descended upon their lives. "We wanted to help, but we were going about it the wrong way. He must feel like we let him down, and we didn't provide the help he needed. He must not have felt loved."

Two Christmases ago, their older son was downtown and bumped into Bobby on the street. When Bobby saw him, he bolted. After that, Eileen hired a private detective, but he couldn't find Bobby. Eileen and George still occasionally drive into the city and circle the streets, eyes peeled for their son.

Eileen opened a new e-mail account to avoid Bobby's blocks. She wrote a heartfelt letter, telling him how much the family misses and loves him, apologizing, and asking him to get in touch. "I told him we're willing to let him stay with us and heal," says Eileen. "I wouldn't suggest he get a job. He could have all the time he needs." Not knowing whether he will receive it, she also printed the letter, and if she gets the chance, will hand it directly to him.

"The thought of him out there on his own . . ." Crying, Eileen says, "I've forgiven myself. I know we had a lot going on. I didn't understand what was happening to my husband, let alone my son. We know more about how the health system works now and could help him navigate it." In a stronger voice, Eileen adds, "Bobby's thirty-two now. He might not want treatment. He might still be angry and difficult to live with. Still, I'd like the chance to try."

Sending the e-mail to apologize and offer help was a proactive step that counteracted her feelings of powerlessness. Still, late at night, when the house is quiet, Eileen's thoughts stray to her son, out there somewhere, all alone. "It's been excruciatingly difficult since I've tried to find him and hit walls," she says. "But I know I need to get on with my life."

Not All Bad

Sixty-three-year-old Camille looks back on marrying at age twenty and wishes she'd waited until she was older. Her parents were married for more than six decades and had an idyllic relationship. "I think I wanted to re-create that sweet home," says Camille, who quickly became pregnant with her daughter, Allison. Camille divorced when her daughter was ten. "Allison's father remarried, and Allison would come home from visits in tears, saying her father never stuck up for her." When Allison turned thirteen, she was old enough to legally shut off visitation rights. Her father didn't try to stay in touch.

Camille remarried and, at least for a while, she and Allison did have a happy home. Her new husband was a hard worker, and Camille also worked full time, but family was at the center of their lives. Those were busy, contented years. Camille stayed involved in her daughter's activities and was dedicated to being a good wife and mother.

The marriage began to sour when Camille's husband began staying up late and drinking. "He could still get up for his job the next day," says Camille. "I was falling off to sleep after a full day's work, and he'd be mad that I was a party pooper. Sometimes, he'd go out. I was so afraid I'd lose him." Her husband confided that his secret to energy was crystal meth and suggested she try it, too. Desperate to save her marriage, Camille gave in. "At first it was like a miracle," she says. "I could do everything. Go to work, clean the house, attend all of Allison's high school events, and still feel good." After a pause, Camille adds, "But there was a downside. I knew I had to stop."

Camille divorced and got clean. Within two years, she fell for a man she believed was her soulmate. They had met at an addiction recovery meeting and were on the same, more wholesome path. Wary of marrying again, they began living together. Even her daughter loved her boyfriend. Eventually, though, her daughter grew envious of the couple's closeness. At twenty, she moved out to live with some fellow college students. "But we still saw each other," says Camille. "We did our nails together. We'd shop, and Allison would pick out my clothes. I thought we were close."

Years passed, and Camille's soulmate started using again. When he wouldn't stop, Camille gave him the boot and got a place with her daughter. Allison was nearing thirty, had finished school, and was doing well financially. "She wanted me to go out with her every night, and I couldn't afford to eat out at restaurants all the time," says Camille, whose physical health was also suffering. With chronic asthma and arthritis pain, Camille found comfort through her church, but says, "Allison accused me of choosing God and my friends over her."

Soon after, Camille's daughter moved more than 2,000 miles away to join a boyfriend she'd met online. She married him there and, for almost a decade, went silent. Even when Camille's parents died within two months of one another, Allison stayed away. Overwhelmed by grief, Camille was diagnosed with depression.

When Allison's husband divorced her, she got in touch, and Camille welcomed her into her home. Although Allison never brought up her mother's past drug use, Camille had a lot of guilt about it, and her daughter's volatile personality seemed to bring that out. She apologized to Allison for everything she'd ever done wrong as a parent. "Allison was my life," says Camille. "When she walked in, the room just lit up."

Despite those feelings, having her daughter home created chaos. Allison was argumentative, and Camille found herself trying to please her daughter, often unsuccessfully. "She was judgmental and selfish," says Camille. "Allison even disowned her best friend who had become like an adopted daughter to me. Allison's ex-husband says she's like an overgrown infant, and I see that. She wants everything her way." Unhappy, Camille began to realize that her daughter's approval may be too important to her.

When her daughter met a new man and moved to another state, she urged Camille to also relocate, but Camille's life was more peaceful with Allison gone. At fifty-eight, and in increasingly fragile health, she told Allison she couldn't move. Allison was angry. "She told me she was tired of being hurt by me," says Camille. Allison blocked her phone, social media, and e-mail. Camille had no choice but to accept her daughter's second estrangement, but she never thought it would be permanent. Two years ago, she underwent open heart surgery and got word to her daughter. "Allison never called," says Camille. "That really hurt me. I don't try to reach out anymore because it's fruitless."

Medication helps Camille with her depression. "My emotions took a big hit when my parents died. If I'm not on medication, I get suicidal. After they passed away, Allison was my reason to stay alive. Since she cut me off, I've had to find other reasons."

Camille has worked hard to overcome her regrets, forgive herself, and build a good life. "I go to the gym and have friends who care about me. My 'man picker' doesn't work well, so I won't remarry. I have my church, and I love to see live music on the weekends. It's a full life, but there's a big piece missing. I still want my baby girl with me."

Tears flowing, Camille quickly adds with determination, "But I can't live my life based on her approval. I spent years trying to please her and apologizing. I regret my mistakes, but I wasn't all bad. I'm not about to guilt myself out over the past anymore. I can't change that, but I can control what I do now and in the future." Her voice growing stronger, Camille says, "Every day, you get to start over. That's what I do."

Definition of "Wrong"?

"Look up 'wrong' in the dictionary and you'll see a picture of me." That's how Marcella felt about herself when her two adult daughters stopped speaking to her.

A stay-at-home mom, Marcella's life revolved around her daughters. She was overweight and unhappy in her marriage, but the girls were her life. When they were teenagers, she had gastric bypass surgery and began taking better care of herself. Then one day, as she was vacuuming the stairs, she fell and broke her tailbone.

"My physical pain outlasted my thirty-day supply of Vicodin," she says. "That's when I discovered that a glass of wine not only eased my pain but also my mind and unhappiness." Due to altered metabolism combined with lower food intake, blood alcohol levels rise faster and take longer to return to normal in someone who has had gastric bypass surgery. So, it didn't take much to make Marcella drunk.

Over the next two years, Marcella's wine intake increased from a glass a day to a whole bottle. When drinking, she could escape the pain of her husband's insults, which had begun after her bypass surgery. With the weight loss, she had changed her style of dress and cut her hair, but instead of being happy and proud of his wife, Marcella's husband of twenty years criticized her. "His family had never liked me," she says. "When I lost weight, he joined in their negative appraisals."

At that time, Marcella realized her overeating had stemmed from stuffing down her feelings. Many years earlier, her husband had an affair. With the help of church counseling, she forgave him—even when he cheated again. "We had both been unhappy for a long time," says Marcella. "My husband wanted out, too, and I think my drinking provided the excuse."

When the divorce was finalized, Marcella quit drinking and remained nearby for her children. Then, her oldest daughter embarked on an exciting career for which she frequently traveled, and her younger daughter graduated high school and moved away to attend college. With her girls grown and gone, Marcella moved to another state with a lower cost of living. That's when her ex-husband began badmouthing her to their daughters. "I was made out to be the bad guy," Marcella says. "By moving, I had abandoned my family."

The parental alienation tactics worked. For six years now, Marcella's daughters haven't spoken to her. Their cutoff also extends to Marcella's family. Even when her father had a heart attack and was in the hospital, her daughters didn't respond to phone calls or reach out to their granddad in any way. "It hurts my family," says Marcella. "Their cousins, their uncle, even the grandparents the girls used to spend summer with . . . Erased."

These days, Marcella is remarried to a man she calls "fun-loving." Her second husband has six children, and their thirteen youngsters call Marcella "Grandma." She says, "I'm happy, but then along comes my daughters' birthdays, and it's like losing my right and left arms." On days like those, Marcella's two years of drinking haunt her. "Honestly, the estrangement has more to do with my husband making me out to be a bad mother than me being one. But my drinking led to divorce, and divorce takes its toll on families."

When the raw ache of rejection and regret plagues her, Marcella tries to focus on others who need help or prayers. Her door is always open for her daughters to reconnect. She sends them occasional e-mails and honors their birthdays, even though they never reply. She has no physical addresses for them. "I gave my girls a wonderful life," she says. "For two years, I was that picture next to 'wrong' in the dictionary, but I can't keep punishing myself."

Doing Her Best

Nola and Ray waited a dozen years for a baby to adopt. When their oldest, Jessica, came to them as an infant, Nola says, "We were over the moon." The baby grew into a smart and sociable, well-spoken toddler, but by the age of eight, she grew defiant and frequently lied. "About even the stupidest stuff," says Nola. As a teen, Jessica was sexually promiscuous.

The parents did their best to provide a loving home and guidance for Jessica, as well as two younger daughters they subsequently adopted. Nola says her depression sometimes got in the way. She did seek help and was given medication, but says, "At times, I'd get frustrated. I'd be angry everyone was making us late to somewhere important and be yelling at them all to hurry up and get in the car. Even the dog would run and hide." Later, Nola would feel bad and apologize.

At age eighteen, Jessica was diagnosed with borderline personality disorder. She had been seeing a therapist because of her difficulty maintaining friendships, her general recklessness, anger, and wild mood swings. Now, Nola and Ray had a name for Jessica's behavior. They stuck by their daughter through two unplanned pregnancies. With counseling, Jessica began to get her life in order. Her parents helped her with a car and offered reduced rent on a condominium they owned. They began to enjoy a more peaceful relationship with Jessica, who had moved into an adult life of work and motherhood. They doted on their grandchildren who adored their Nan and Pop.

Just as things with Jessica settled down, their youngest daughter, Beth, began abusing drugs and alcohol at age fourteen. The partying worsened over the next year. One morning before dawn, Beth came dragging in and admitted to having been out using drugs. The teenager went off to bed but Nola sat up, worrying how to help her. The next day, the morning passed while Beth snored in her bed. Nola finally prompted Beth to rise and dress, and then she took Beth into town to work with her dad at their store. When Nola went back later to check in on Beth, she found her scowling at customers and being generally disagreeable as she bagged their orders. Concerned for their business, Nola asked Beth to get her things to go home.

In the car, Nola yelled at her, grabbed her arm, and even spit in Beth's direction at one point. "It was bad," says Nola, mortified at the memory. Swallowing a sob, she goes on: "I was just so frustrated. Worried about her drinking and using drugs. I was mad at my husband because I thought he should have been watching her better at the store. And I was exhausted."

When they got home, Beth left the house, saying she would go stay with Jessica and the children. Ashamed of her own behavior, Nola let Beth go.

During the two weeks she stayed at her sister's, Beth kept her appointment with the counselor she'd been seeing. When she confided that Nola had lost her temper and spit at her, the counselor reported it to authorities. Soon after, Child Protective Services (CPS) came knocking. Nola felt like a criminal, but she and Ray were honest about all that had been going on. They knew they needed help with Beth, and CPS intervened to secure the family services. Nola was relieved.

Unfortunately, the family stress negatively affected their older daughter. "Jessica began to spiral again," says Nola. "Suddenly she made up all sorts of crazy lies about us, saying we'd abused her for her whole life. She thought she should get legal custody of fifteen-year-old Beth, too." CPS didn't agree.

Beth and Nola began attending a program for Dialectical Behavior Therapy (DBT), which, in part, focuses on responding calmly to the stresses of life. "*I* benefitted," says Nola, who had sought therapy and had taken medication for her depression much of her adult life. "The DBT was the first time I received a good set of tools to help, like how to be present and prepare for things ahead of time." The DBT also helped Beth. She graduated high school and began working.

Meanwhile, Jessica refused to let Nola and Ray see their grandchildren. "We were so close," says Nola. "Ripping us out of our grandchildren's lives must be horrible for them, too." Eventually, Jessica took her children and moved out of their condominium as well.

At that time, their younger daughters confessed relief that Jessica was out of their lives. They said she had a bullied them and having her around created chaos. "Ray and I and our two younger girls forged a new bond together," says Nola. "We all went to therapy and seemed to heal after that."

Nola and Ray haven't seen Jessica or their grandchildren for more than five years. When Beth turned eighteen, she moved out with a boyfriend whom Nola and Ray believe is kind and good. Up until last spring, Beth stayed in touch. She and her boyfriend would come for dinners at the family home, and Beth would go to the discount movie day with her dad. But over time, the contact devolved to a texting relationship.

Then, one day when Nola texted that she was going by the store where Beth works, everything changed. "I needed a nice dessert for a guest," she says. "Beth texted me not to come. I offered to go when she wasn't there, but she got mad." Nola was also surprised when Beth stopped answering texts. They have had no contact for almost a year.

Nola and Ray are thankful they still have a healthy relationship with their middle daughter. Their estranged daughters have also cut contact with her. She assures Nola that she is a good mother. Even so, Nola has looked back on the times she got frustrated and wishes she'd been more patient. In her mind, the one big blowup loomed, the impetus for the visit from CPS that triggered the return of Jessica's mental health issues and chiseled fissures into the family.

Recently, Nola did the exercises from *Done With The Crying*. "Not to be melodramatic," she says, "but it has changed my life." Rather than solely focusing on her mistakes, Nola was able to measure any downfalls against her overall parenting. "You know, I was a pretty good mom," she says, expounding on the things she did right. "The good outweighs the bad. I was given a set of circumstances, and I did the best I could. What else could I do?"

Sins of the Father?

Six years ago, Graham's marriage hit a rough patch while he was working on a graduate degree to garner a higher salary. He says,

"I neglected my wife, Jillian, and she got pretty close to a neighbor who worked from home. He was around to make her laugh when I wasn't." When Jillian asked for a separation, Graham moved out to a nearby apartment. "I saw it as temporary. Even when I went by the house one morning to put the trash out for her and saw the neighbor leaving at the crack of dawn." Graham didn't confront his wife. "I was too humiliated," he explains. "And scared she might ask for a divorce."

The couple told their daughter, Marcia, they were taking some space. She was twenty-eight at the time and living a busy life an hour away. One day, while Graham was using the apartment complex's gym, his daughter stopped by unannounced. From his treadmill vantage point through the full-length gym windows, he saw her let herself into his apartment. He wiped the sweat from his brow and rushed out, but a neighbor waylaid him with chatter about someone having parked in his space. "When I finally walked in, Marcia was standing there with her arms crossed. My laptop was on the coffee table, opened to a naked woman." His daughter had snooped through his browsing history.

Married for twenty-nine years at the time, Graham says, "My head may have turned when an attractive woman walked by, but until my wife slept with another man, I never looked at porn." Graham blames his bruised ego for the misstep. His daughter reamed him out that day and has held it over his head ever since.

Two months later, Jillian realized the neighbor wasn't right for her. Graham moved back into the family home.

Over the next several years, Marcia remained aloof with Graham. She met with her mother, mostly without him. Despite this, Graham says, "I paid for her graduate schooling, bought her a car, and financed her destination wedding. The marriage didn't last a year."

Thirteen months ago, on a rare visit with her father alone, Marcia asked him to help her buy a house. Graham explained that he and Jillian needed to save for retirement. Marcia became angry and brought up the porn. "When I told her how stupid that had been, and just a dumb ego response to her mom kicking me out, she threatened to tell her mom about it," Graham says. "Apparently, she'd taken a picture of my laptop open to the site, next to my keyring and a bill with my name on it. Hearing that, I was pissed." Graham came close to telling her he'd seen another man carrying his shoes out of the family home at daybreak. "But I didn't want her to know what her mother did. Our marriage isn't her business."

When Graham refused to let his daughter blackmail him, she started to cry. "She said her ex-husband had always looked at other women, and that all men were the same. Even me."

That day at lunch, Graham's daughter named off all the things he had done for her the last few years. In her eyes, she had been blackmailing him all along. "When I think about it, she's right," says Graham. "I did spoil her, and maybe partly to keep her quiet. I had my wife back and didn't want to rock the boat." Graham regrets that fact more than his dalliance to a porn site. "I've been a good husband and dad. I feel guilt, but I'm not a bad person. I should have defended myself better, even to Jillian."

Until recently, Graham had never told Jillian he saw the neighbor man leaving their house either. The revelation was unsettling, but Jillian was later relieved Graham knew about her affair. The parents hope to reconnect with Marcia, but she has blocked all communication with them.

A couple of months ago, Marcia's ex-husband paid them a visit. He'd seen Marcia on social media and was troubled. She had moved 700 miles away to a bigger city, which was news to Graham and Jillian, too. He also said she was in a lesbian relationship with a woman he recognized. He believed Marcia may have divorced him for the woman.

"We were surprised," says Graham. "But Marcia's love life is her business."

Graham and Jillian sent a card to Marcia's prior address, hoping it would be forwarded. In it, they offered to meet with her on her terms, even with a family counselor of her choice in her city. She mailed the card back with a nasty letter in which she called her mother a fool for staying with her father. With a groan, Graham asks, "How do we unravel all of this? It's up to Marcia at this point."

Lost Years

Anita rose above her childhood with a timid mother and an alcoholic father to become an upstanding, outspoken citizen in their small, Christian community. She married and eventually had a daughter of her own. When Brianna was ten, Anita's husband died in a car accident. Within a year, Anita's mother also died.

Grieving horribly, Anita now had another emotion to deal with: anger. "I had always expected my father to die first," she says. "My mother suffered in the marriage. She enabled my father. She was a devoted wife who was like so many of her era who would never break their vows. My father had quit drinking by then, but he had health problems. I had assumed that one day, she'd be free." Instead, Anita was left with an ailing father she loved and hated all at once.

One evening, Anita's new neighbor saw her cursing under her breath as she took the garbage cans to the curb. When she then slammed down the lid, he called out, "Yeah, give it a kick, too." Startled, Anita tried to smile at his joke but began to cry instead. When he apologized and offered her some chocolate and a talk, she joined him on his porch. He also offered her a drink to calm her nerves. "I took it," says Anita. "And then I took another." Anita describes the way her distress lifted that night, "As if a bird came along and plucked up all my sadness in its talons and flew off."

After that night, Anita began turning to liquor regularly. "First it was just a drink every other day or so with my neighbor," she says. "Then I'd stop my car in the driveway and sneak a glug from a bottle before going inside the house. Eventually, I was drinking most of the evening in front of the television."

Anita managed to function enough to keep her business afloat, but the nighttime drinking took its toll. She would nod off in her chair each night and awaken later just enough to stumble off to bed. "I missed a lot of time with my daughter," she says. "When she started high school, my father moved in with us. He needed oxygen and wasn't well, but he was sober. It was me who had the problem, and drinking wouldn't bring my husband or mother back."

Anita struggled for two years, quitting alcohol for weeks or months at a time, and then returning to it with a vengeance. When her daughter started her senior year of high school, Anita began counseling. It was through a church group that Anita eventually came to terms with the injustice of her husband's death, her anger toward her father, and her mother's years of simmering resentment while enabling him that, Anita believes, led to her mother's early death. She quit using alcohol for good and threw herself into her life.

"I sometimes felt horrible for those years I spent in a stupor each night," says Anita. "I had missed so much, but my daughter forgave me. I'd apologize, and she'd just hug me and tell me not to worry. That we were okay now. And we really were okay. She graduated high school with honors, went to college, moved to a bigger city three hours away for a job, married, and started a family. When my father died, I remarried too. We all got along fine. I was busy and so was Brianna, but we talked on the phone almost every day, and we saw each other every couple of months. In the summer, my grandchildren would come stay with me and their grandpa, my second husband who everybody loves. My daughter would join for a couple of weeks, and then her husband would come for a few days too. We were good. I thought things were good."

Twenty-five years after Anita took her last drink, her daughter lost control of her car one night and ended up in the ICU. Anita rushed to her daughter's side and discovered she had been driving drunk. "Thankfully, no other cars were involved," says Anita. "But as she lay there in an induced coma, all my demons came back to roost."

BEYOND DONE WITH THE CRYING

Two days later, when her daughter woke up, Anita was still at her side. "By then, I'd heard from her husband that she'd been drinking for a couple of years," says Anita. "It had recently gotten worse. I was ready to help."

But as nurses tended to Brianna's needs and changed the bed sheets, Anita's daughter shot her an icy stare. When the medical personnel left the room, and Anita tried to talk to her, she told her to go away. Anita left but remained nearby. That afternoon, she returned, and her daughter was tearful. Squeezing at a wad of Kleenex, she cried, telling Anita about a variety of problems in her life. Her marriage was rocky, one of her kids was struggling in school, she had no confidence, liked to shop, casino gamble, and drink.

"I took her hand," Anita says, "but she shook it off and screamed for me to just leave. She said everything wrong in her life was my fault." Her daughter also called Anita a slew of bad names: bitch, slut, cunt, drunk, low life. "She said I was a crap mom, *always*, and that she'd spent the last twenty-five years trying to please me just so I'd love her." Anita's daughter also said the last thing she had ever wanted was to be like her, yet here she was, a drunken slut like her mom, only worse.

In tears, Anita said she was sorry over and over. Her daughter continued to rail, and Anita fled the room. She spent an hour in her car sobbing before pulling herself together enough to make the drive back home to her husband's arms.

From subsequent, heated conversations, Anita gleaned from her daughter the reason she called her a slut. The idea was connected, somehow, to the time Anita had spent with her neighbor when she first began to drink. "She imagines we slept together," says Anita. "In fact, she concocted a big story about me sleeping with him *before* my husband died, and that his accident was somehow related. I never slept with my neighbor." Anita's daughter, as it turns out, had engaged in two affairs during her marriage.

When her daughter had recovered from the crash, her husband divorced her.

Anita's efforts to communicate have mostly been met with silence. Anita talks to her grandchildren on the phone or via video chat occasionally, when their mother will let them, but says, "They're growing up, and I can feel them drifting. They barely know me anymore."

After those calls, Anita cries. "I've sent money to my daughter," she says. "I know she's not drinking anymore but she's struggling with her husband gone." Lately, though, her daughter has initiated the money sending. "She *will* text me for that," says Anita.

The last time, when her daughter asked for a large sum to get herself out of debt, Anita's husband intervened and said "no." Her daughter texted him that her mother's money was none of his business, and that Anita owed her after such a "fucked up" life. She also called him a nasty name.

"The hurt that fell over my husband's face . . ." Anita's voice trails off. "I made mistakes, yes, but he shouldn't be paying for them, and haven't I paid enough yet?"

More to the Story

The parents presented in this chapter aren't so different from any who look inward and soul search for the cause of their estrangement. Often, there is no clear-cut or sensible answer. You may or may not relate to their experiences, but you probably felt for these parents as I did.

Were you mortified for Sylvie? Painfully isolated in the confusion of undiagnosed postpartum depression, she saw her lack of motherly feelings as a personal defect. Sylvie also misjudged her child's father. Years passed before she discovered her mistake about him. Sylvie blames herself for her daughter's suffering, but she is also a victim.

Did you empathize with Eileen? During a maelstrom of distress and change related to her husband's newly diagnosed bipolar disorder, she struggled to find a way forward and didn't know how to help her son. Eileen is too hard on herself. Even in the calmest of circumstances, mental illness can be confusing and difficult to identify or alleviate. Their son's abuse of booze and drugs complicated everything and blurred his need for help behind his bouts of rage.

Some parents who blame themselves were the victims of circumstances beyond their control. Others made choices that hold them hostage to guilt, and their own self-recriminating reminders that they caused the rift. Sometimes, their choices are only partly responsible, or perhaps not at all. I hope that in these parents' stories, and in how they interpret and feel about them, you have gleaned insights into your own experience.

We'll close this chapter with answers to the questions listed at the outset. As you read, consider how these parents' thoughts help or hurt them. Contemplate how their experiences might apply to you. Later, you'll use the provided space to write your own answers and make plans to utilize what you've discerned.

How long must a parent pay penance?

Camille says, "For years, I thought if only I'd done something differently, Allison would still be in my life. If only I'd tried harder with her dad. If only I hadn't gotten into meth. If only I hadn't yelled at her when she broke my mother's dish. If only I'd spent more, done more, or even done less."

After a breath, Camille continues, "Then there are the *should* thoughts. I should have worried less about money and run up my credit cards to go out with her when she was living back at home. I should have stopped going to church like she asked. I should have moved when she wanted me to, styled my hair how she said, eaten the foods she thought were right . . . Then maybe Allison would love me. The truth is, I can't keep chastising myself. I can't live my life for her approval. I tried that, and it didn't work."

Anita can relate. She and her daughter, Brianna, had grown emotionally close and remained that way for two decades. They talked almost daily, visited often, and vacationed together with Anita's grandchildren. Anita had put her years of dogged self-reproach behind her. Yet when her daughter had a meltdown and let loose with a boatload of blame, Anita nearly drowned in regret.

Unwilling to wallow in self-pity, Anita sought support. She reminded herself that she had acknowledged and apologized for her wrongdoing (many times). She had taken responsibility for her actions and had gotten her life in order.

"I've been clean and sober for twenty-five years," she says, describing her character as a steady employee and a good citizen. "Every once in a while, something will trigger those guilt feelings, and then I have to work hard to put them behind me again."

How many times must a parent's contrition be proven to a son or daughter?

One of the last things Sylvie's daughter said to her was a directive. "She told me to go find my happiness. She said I should forgive myself and get on with my life." Upon reflection, Sylvie realizes that her constant apologies and guilt only made her daughter sad.

Sylvie holds herself accountable, but she is progressing toward her daughter's wish. By opening up about her feelings, accessing further support, and taking charge of her life, she is extending to herself the compassion her daughter did. It's an ongoing process.

Do some parents, in their anguish and guilt, become gluttons for punishment?

Camille sought her daughter's approval for many years. She remembers posting a Facebook meme that honored her Christian beliefs. Allison railed against her—both online and in private. "I could never be myself. I was afraid to do anything she didn't like; afraid I might lose her." Allison only grew bolder in expressing her opinions about her mother's life. For a long time, Camille complied, believing, "I'm a recovering addict. Didn't I owe her?"

After writing up Marcella's story of breaking her tailbone and, for two years, using wine to dull the pain, I shared a draft with a writer friend who helps me edit. She stopped at Marcella's statement: "My drinking led to my divorce, and *divorce takes its toll on families.*" Referring to Marcella's unfaithful husband, my friend asked, "And cheaters don't?"

She makes a good point. Marcella gives herself credit for the good she did in her children's lives. Even so, in the shadow of estrangement, does she shoulder more than her share of blame for the divorce?

Do some adult children recognize their parent's vulnerability and, deplorably, exploit it?

In Chapter 4, we talked about overcompensating. Even if guilt isn't the motivator, fears about losing touch can set up an imbalanced relationship. Camille's daughter used her mother's guilt to control her. Graham's situation is a bit more complex.

"I used money to win her approval back," Graham says. He admits to spoiling Marcia, not just to keep her quiet, but to avoid confrontation. "I couldn't even confront my wife when another man came creeping out of the house. After this whole thing went down, and Marcia cut us off, I realized I've avoided confrontation for my whole life. I'm working on that now."

Are these parents easy targets for blame that (wrongly) absolves adult children of their own mistakes?

"This is purely speculation," says Graham. "But Marcia's ex-husband thinks she left him for the woman she's with now. Maybe me and Allison separating, and Marcia finding porn on my laptop, triggered her own guilt. Maybe she cheated on her husband." With a groan, Graham adds, "I don't know if that's true, but it helps me feel a little better. If she's just an evil blackmailer who hates her folks, then that's worse."

Anita doesn't have to guess. When her daughter wrecked her car, Anita rushed to her hospital bedside. "She told me how much she hated me. She said she'd always hated me and that she had spent her whole life trying not to be like me. But she's in her forties. She made her own choices. I was just an easy target to blame."

Are parents seeing the whole story?

Nola says, "My daughters did this for reasons that go far beyond any mistakes I made. I may never understand the reasons, but their leaving says more about them than it does me."

Your Turn

If you haven't done the prior exercises in the book, I strongly suggest you return to them. They set the stage for revelations about you and your history on which this exercise builds. If you avoided some of those exercises, contemplate why that is. If you're troubled by them, consider what support you may need. Make healing a gift to yourself.

As you contemplate and answer the questions that follow, reflect upon the chapter's stories of regret, what you thought or felt as you read about these parents, their feelings, and how they have coped. Consider any insights you may have gained, either in reading this chapter or prior ones. Did any of these stories strike a nerve? Be honest with yourself. There's no need to feel guilty about stating the truth. Clarity is a lot like sunshine. It can spotlight the way forward.

- How long must a parent pay penance?

_____

_____

_____

_____

_____

_____

_____

- How many times must a parent's contrition be proven to a son or daughter?

_____

_____

_____

_____

_____

_____

- Some parents, in their anguish and guilt, become gluttons for punishment. Have you? How?

_____

_____

_____

_____

_____

_____

- Some adult children recognize a parent's vulnerability and exploit it. In any way, to any degree, has this happened to you? How?

_____

_____

_____

_____

_____

_____

- Sometimes, parents become easy targets for blame that (wrongly) absolves adult children of their own mistakes. Does this apply to your situation? How?

- Parents don't always see the whole story. Graham speculated about the possibility that his daughter's own guilt contributed to their estrangement. How might you be missing something? Is it possible there are blind spots?

Now, let's take what you learned and apply it to your life moving forward. Here, we'll see examples taken from the lives of the parents in the chapter.

- Certain dates, events, or situations can be triggers for parents' regret and guilt. Camille is active in her church but allows herself to skip some of the family-oriented events. She knows these are triggers that will set her back. *What sorts of things can trigger you?*

_____

_____

_____

_____

- Plan ahead to cope with setbacks. Camille may not always attend family-oriented church events, but often contributes a food dish or volunteers to set up. These activities raise her self-esteem, and act as a ballast to any emotional triggers. For Anita, it helps to remind herself of her success: a sober, productive life. With your identified triggers in mind, consider how best to cope. *How can you pull yourself back from the edge of despair and into the present?* Don't be too hard on yourself. Baby steps go in the right direction.

_____

_____

_____

_____

- Self-compassion is important, yet people may not have been taught to treat themselves well. Regarding ourselves with empathy and kindness is known to raise spirits, aid in healing, and help us to cope. *If a friend told you your own story, would you offer compassion?* Be your own friend. Nola takes short vacations she can enjoy in the moment and savor later. Camille calls herself a "gym rat." Graham can relate. With their fitness routines, they are kind to themselves. Sylvie recently cut and colored her hair. Like the old L'Oreal commercial, she deems herself worth it! *How can you take care and be compassionate and kind to yourself?* Write down a few ideas and implement them. You're worth it.

SHERI McGREGOR

Notes

CHAPTER SEVEN

Is Reconciliation Possible?

"True reconciliation does not consist in merely forgetting the past."
—Nelson Mandela

Frequently, when a child cuts ties, reconciliation is the stuff parental dreams are made of. Upon reflection, in the shadow of false starts, repeated stops, and continued conflict and/or distress, the imagined ideal may be traded for a starker prospect: a cordial relationship or at least one without animosity.

Reconciliation is not as easy as it sounds. "Be careful what you wish for," is a phrase I have heard often. Reconciling often comes at a price. For some, the cost is too high, and they must come to terms with changes in how they feel and what they want—or don't want. For others, reconciling is not what they dreamt it would be, but the reality becomes acceptable.

Reconciliation *is* possible (sometimes). Don't look here for flowery language and false hope. This chapter takes a real look at reconciling, which isn't always as pretty as a (family) picture.

Bend . . . Or Break?

Imagine receiving a phone call from a stranger who tells you he is a therapist. He verifies your identity and says your adult child asked him to convey a message: Your relationship with your son or daughter is over.

One mother remembers receiving a call like this. Faint, she gripped the phone in one hand and steadied herself against the kitchen counter with the other. The voice of a licensed stranger said he'd been working with her daughter and son-in-law. He had called to provide her with their rules: There would be no more contact. They would not accept her cards, gifts, or written communication. If she came to their door, they would call the police on her.

She remembers her nervous laugh. *This must be a prank.*

Nancy Lee Klune, author of the book *Banished: A Grand-mother Alone* (2018), describes a similar call as the introduction to her estrangement nightmare. More commonly, a therapist or other advisor helps a son or daughter craft an e-mail to initiate the no-contact rules, but the calls do happen.

Therapists also make calls to adult children whose parents want to reconcile. Earlier, we met Mei and her husband, Xudong, whose son became estranged after marrying. Unsuccessful at reconciling and feeling at her wit's end, Mei consulted with a psychologist who specializes in estrangement. "I paid him a lot of money," says Mei. "His call to my son did no good."

I'm not surprised. Imagine hearing a mental health profes-sional say your parents have been talking about you. That's where the walls go up. Your parent has been talking to a mental health professional—*about you*. How many estranged children would hear anything more?

Although this contact-by-a-mediator method of reconciliation is said to be effective, I'm not convinced. I'm not suggesting dishon-esty but, as was discussed in Chapter One, the term "estrangement" is variably defined. So is "reconciliation." Mediating profession-als may believe an amicable phone call or two constitutes success. When the relationship falls apart again—and it often does—the parents may not return to the professional with the failure. The therapist doesn't necessarily get to learn how it all turned out. On the other hand, I frequently hear from disgruntled parents who, in retrospect, believe they were sold methods or programs for recon-ciliation that amount to snake oil. Like Mei, in their desperation, they paid "a lot of money" for help they later see as exploitative.

Others describe a measure of success, which very often includes a hefty dose of eggshell walking to maintain the contact. Parents are frequently given the how-to of such a walk. They're instructed to speak using "cloying tones," be "always listening and sympathiz-ing," and are told to "always praise."

On the one hand, all of us learn to moderate our language. We behave differently in different settings all the time. Parents may consider the generational trends and the social environment of our children's growing up years, and how that is different than our own. That's not necessarily wrong. On the other hand, there's a point where all the patience and understanding shifts to enabling or treating adult children like babies. Where do/would/will you draw the line? Also, how real is a relationship where one adult always caters to the other?

Many parents have been told that the responsibility for any "rela-tionship" is on them, that their children aren't as invested as they are and lack any sense of duty to them. That's different than parents who hail from a generation that includes gratitude and due respect toward those who brought them up. Their sense of duty, loyalty, and family devotion then extends to their children, which is problematic when the children treat them poorly or are abusive. Let's look at one mother, Patty, whose situation is representative of many I hear.

Patty and her daughter have been estranged periodically "for years." Currently, they have been "reconciled" for less than a year.

Patty describes the situation as "always delicate." Prior to the current connection phase, Patty sought the help of a psychologist who taught her about generational differences and, as she says, "advised treating my daughter like a toddler."

At face value, this makes sense. Different generation equals different upbringing and social beliefs, which equates to different treatment. The trouble is, at some point, the parent will mess up in the child's eyes, and the "child," who is trained to get her way, will demand that her parent comply. How is this different from a toddler who screams for candy in the supermarket check-out's impulse-buy zone? The parent gives in, and the child learns to cry to get their way.

Here's how Patty explains the "reconciliation" technique she's been taught: "In order to be accepted by my daughter, I need to give her what she needs or wants from me. Nothing more, nothing less. I know this is totally unfair, but if I want a relationship with my daughter and grandchildren, it is pretty much her way." She goes on to say, "I should always be smiling and always accepting."

Patty knows it won't take much for her daughter to run off and avoid her again—kind of like a toddler who tells Mom he'll hold his breath unless she gives him what he wants. This isn't reconciling. Reconnection? Yes, but this "on" period follows the same pattern that has occurred with her daughter for years. Patty walks on the proverbial eggshells until her daughter deems some behavior is wrong. Then she holds her breath again. So does Patty, waiting for her daughter to allow her back into her life.

Patty hopes that one day her daughter will mature, that she will understand and appreciate Patty's efforts, and that their relationship will change. Will it happen? Possibly, but at what cost to Patty's well-being?

Through the generations, new knowledge debunks old. Maybe some of the silly "always be . . ." type advice will go the way of other antiquated parenting methods. Recommendations such as putting infants to sleep on their tummies (now associated with Sudden Infant Death Syndrome) and supplemental bottle feeding for tired new moms (when less suckling decreases milk production) proves that experts' suggestions have not always been right. In my opinion, all the cloying tones, subservience, and babying may be training adults with difficult personalities they can get away with bad behavior and even be rewarded for it—which is a disservice to these individuals, and to society as a whole.

A Shared Delusion?

The psychological term, *shared delusion*, describes two or more people who share delusional beliefs, despite evidence that refutes the faulty notions. This joint, altered reality is most often seen in close, long-term relationships where one person has a mental disorder and convinces the partner of untrue beliefs. Here, I use the term to describe how, in the shock of rejection, even the kindest, most loving parents can doubt their true history and accept the skewed reality of the child who rejects them.

Too often, hurting parents seek help and find advisors who join the adult child's version of reality. They recommend apologies and amends letters that don't reconcile with reality. When parents have already apologized (as most do) or share their proposed letters, their words are picked apart as demanding, negative, or an attempt to "guilt" a child back into the relationship. For many parents, the advice continues a *never-good-enough* message they have repeatedly received from their kids. In minefield relationships, the parents learned to consider every word, hoping to avoid the inevitable cold shoulder or explosion.

In caring relationships between kind people who want to get along, apologizing opens communication lines and can pave the way to deeper understanding and closer ties. When relationships are inequitable or uncaring, and the complaints are untruthful thus unjustified, apologizing can make things worse. Some may say that if another person has a beef with you, their perspective is their "truth." That's one way to look at it, but what if their perspective is untrue?

Take a hard look at the evidence. In *Done With The Crying*, there's an exercise: "The Good You Did." Parents are asked to reflect upon the role they played in their estranged child's life. They review the most basic of necessities such as changing diapers, to remembering more elaborate support such as sewing school play costumes or putting a young adult through college. This helps parents see through the self-doubt triggered by their child's rejection of them. Reflecting with an eye toward the good they did helps parents reclaim reality. Most did their best. The evidence is irrefutable.

Your adult child's "truth" may be revisionist history or exaggerations devised for unknown reasons or to justify their own behavior. A persuasive third party may convince your son or daughter you're no good, you have never been there for them, are too controlling, or some other fill-in-the-blank offense. Regardless, what isn't true, isn't true. Let me say that again. If an adult child accuses you of things that are not true, then your child's "truth" is incorrect. You don't have to buy into the delusion your child has manufactured or been brainwashed to believe.

Attempting to understand, parents often try on their adult children's possible perspectives. The ability to step into another person's shoes fosters empathy, which is necessary for understanding, forgiveness, and any reconciliation—but it must go both ways. If parents can try to understand their adult children's perspectives, then the "children" can be guided to understand their parents' perspectives as well. What good can come from infantilizing adult children? As with any adults, estranged adult children can, and should, be led to see other people, including their parents, as individuals with their own cultural influences, stressors, and opinions. Yet, in a society that routinely sanctions parent-blaming by adult children, parents are advised to prostrate themselves and remain one-dimensional, servant-figures. In situations such as Patty's, parents can never achieve the pinnacle of perfection their children expect of them.

I see too many parents who, in desperation, apologize for accusations that make no sense. Often, these parents find that as soon as they agree to whatever condition or admission is required of them, the adult child moves the goal post anyway, and they remain estranged. That's one reason I find it nonsensical that parents are advised to enter the realm of fantasy and apologize for things they didn't do.

Parents, you know if your adult child is hurt by some real circumstance. Maybe you were too busy during a child's senior year of high school. Maybe your son felt unsupported and missed you at his basketball games when your mother died, and you were a mess. Maybe your daughter wished you would have waited another year to restart your career because she felt abandoned when, in her eyes, she needed you most. Perhaps during an acrimonious divorce, you were preoccupied with trying to maintain peace or to keep your child safe, yet your actions weren't explained or were misunderstood. Those difficulties and hurts are real. They qualify for an apology, or at least a sincere explanation and assurance that you were doing your best at the time but that you wish you could have done more or had handled situations differently.

We all have incidents or phases in our history where we could have done better—and our children can learn that even though we're parents, we're also human. That's different from a child inventing a history you don't recognize. Those very real complaints about circumstances when you were not as attentive as usual are different from a history that paints you as evil *and that simply is not true.*

It is unwise and counterproductive to share in a delusion. Even when it belongs to a child you love so much that you'd do almost anything to regain a relationship.

Are You "Guilting" Your Adult Child?

Earlier, I wrote about a time when my health was at an all-time low. After the first year of silence, my son, Dan, had phoned. We had a friendly talk, and he said he wanted us to have a relationship. He assured me he would call again "soon." That talk sparked hope, but when he didn't call again, the fragile peace I had worked so hard to gain dissolved. Scary visual disturbances led me to the doctor who was mortified by my symptoms and bloodwork. The stress of the estrangement was hurting me. I had to take charge. So, instead of waiting in a sort of limbo as more months passed, I called my son.

When I explained that I'd been waiting for his call, that I'd been emotional, and that my health had suffered, my son put me off. He was gruff and dismissive, yet later, I wondered if he might have viewed my words as an attempt to "guilt" him. That hadn't been my intention, but the conversation haunted me.

There was no hidden plan behind my words. I'd been as direct as always. I had laid out my thoughts and feelings to him. In all of Dan's twenty-five years, I had never tried to motivate him with guilt. My son knew how I spoke. He also knew *me*. Him thinking I was trying to "guilt" him made no sense. *So, why did I ever think he might?*

When Dan rejected me, my self-esteem dipped so low that I second-guessed *everything*. I searched for help and came across a mental health professional who dissected the parents' language in the letters they wrote to their estranged adult children. Their words were analyzed for how they might be received as an intention to trigger feelings of guilt. In desperation, I took the guidance to heart.

After an adult child's estrangement, distraught parents flail in the murky waters of their own identity. They may grasp at almost anything to stay afloat, on a wave of hope that they can repair the relationship.

If you're a parent who used guilt to motivate your estranged adult child, you know who you are. Admit it. Then work on more than your language. Work on yourself and how you interact with the people you love. However, if you're not guilty of this behavior, then don't let your anguish and desperation to reconnect stir self-doubt. Don't take advice that doesn't fit. Your child knows you. Why would your speech suddenly be construed as an attempt to "guilt"?

Here's another thought: If your words trigger adult children's guilt, maybe it's their conscience knocking. Maybe your son feels guilty because he has treated you badly or the guilt your daughter feels is her inner wisdom, confirming that her behavior is wrong. Don't make yourself responsible for another adult's feelings or behavior.

If you're not a "guilter," then guidance that assumes you are is nothing more than Olympic level training to walk on eggshells. There's an acronym for that: W.O.E. Walking. On. Eggshells: *Woe!* It's a fitting term for any relationship where one party lives in fear, believing they may be one word away from another estrangement.

For more information about advice, consult the box in Chapter Five, "Advice: Be Discerning, Not Desperate."

Can *Some* Contact Work for You?

Some parents believe almost any contact is better than none. So, while they don't necessarily define the superficial or infrequent contact as "reconciliation," they reason that at least they are no longer estranged. If the connection is non-hostile, this can sometimes be acceptable.

One holiday weekend, a father and mother were feeling down while they listened to music to pass the time. One song reminded them of their son. After some discussion, the mother sent the link to him with a short and sweet text: "I miss our history," she wrote. "Can we share our future?" After many years of silence, he replied, saying that he also loved that song. He has since visited them and brought along their granddaughter. He was pleasant to them, and their interaction was positive. The parents view his visit, and meeting their granddaughter, as a gift. They're cautiously optimistic, have decided they will not press him about the past or future, and are hopeful for continued contact. How that takes shape will be on their son's terms. In the meantime, these parents are getting on with their own lives as they have always done.

That's how it is for Wayne and Betty, a couple in their early six-ties who continued to reach out lovingly with periodic voicemails and texts to their son, their only child, for three full years. Their estrange-ment had begun soon after their son's wedding. Their daughter-in-law refused to see them, and their son explained that she believed they didn't like her and purposely made her feel uncomfortable.

Betty explains, "She was always standoffish, but we tried to be kind to her and make her feel loved." Their apologies and efforts to connect only seemed to make things worse. Wayne and Betty gave the couple space.

Their son was never vicious to them, but he only rarely responded if they reached out. In the last eighteen months, though, he has agreed to four short visits at their home. These occurred when his wife was on work travel. Wayne and Betty empathize with their son's situation.

"That's his wife," says Wayne. "He's loyal to her."

"We'll take what we can get," adds Betty about the visits that their son, who lives half an hour's drive away, has arranged.

Whenever their son plans a visit, Wayne and Betty counsel themselves ahead of time to remain grateful. They discuss what they will talk about and plan topics to keep things light, but they don't go overboard. Betty fixed a meal the last time he came, but it was a simple one.

Although they are careful not to ask questions or discuss their daughter-in-law other than the most benign and generic "hope she is doing well" comments, they make sure they tell their son that she is always welcome and ask him to tell her "hello" from them.

Wayne and Betty never press their son for answers. "We don't want to cause him grief with his wife."

Time will tell if Wayne and Betty will ever enjoy the closer relationship they once shared with their son, or if his wife will ever warm up to them. The couple is committed to the long haul, even if that means long periods of separation or silence in the future. In the meantime, they are busy people. Wayne chairs a Neighborhood

Watch group. Betty volunteers at a local school and, although retired from her hairstylist career, donates her skills to a back-to-work organization.

Other parents are similarly grateful yet lead active lives. Divorced mother, Constance, welcomes her son, now in his forties, for occasional visits when he is in town. He might bring a meal and catches her up to speed on his career and life. Then he's off to stay with relatives who sided with his father in he and Constance's divorce. She knows her son was caught in the dysfunction. When he leaves, she gets back to the life she has been able to build for herself by forgiving her ex-husband and his family, and letting her son go. Constance accepts that her experience of the divorce is different than her son's. She misses him but realizes that, for now, it would be a waste of her energy to fight something she cannot change.

Some parents make themselves content with even more distance. A tenuous social media relationship provides a window to a son or daughter's accomplishments, a way to offer support or pride with a "like," or to get a glimpse of the grandkids. Ginger's daughter was completely estranged for nearly seven years before she suddenly connected via social media. "At least I know she is okay now," says Ginger. "For a long time, I had no idea where she even lived."

"We sometimes talk briefly with replies to each other's Instagram posts," she adds. "But I don't expect much and am careful not to overstep." Ginger ignores any postings she doesn't agree with—same as many do with friends who share differing opinions on social media. "I have no idea why she cut me out originally, but she's an adult. I will respect her boundaries."

These parents all have three important factors in common:

- They are willing to accept a relationship on their adult child's terms.
- Their adult children are not abusive.
- They live fulfilling lives apart from parenthood.

Are Bygones Really Gone?

In many of the reconnection stories I hear, the adult children require parents to let go of the past. Frequently, this is one-sided though, as in Patty's case. She is required to learn from her "mistakes" but has been trained not to put her daughter in any hot seat.

For many families, there has been no clear reason given for the cutoff. Therefore, questions remain: *How do you repair the relationship when you don't understand how it broke? Without revisiting the past to sort out what went wrong, can there ever truly be a fix?* These are valid questions and, when left unanswered against one party's will, may undermine reconciliation, or set the stage for another episode.

Ruth and Terry were surprised when their adult children reconnected. Both their son and daughter had been estranged for two decades. The couple remains cautious but are also open—not so much to stepping back into the familial roles they left behind for their own well-being, but to a relationship with adults whom they hope may have grown up during the long interim of silence. They have also met teenage grandchildren for the first time and are forging tentative relationships with them. Nothing feels certain at this point.

"Why did so many years have to go by without contact?" asks Terry. "I think our daughter was confused or using drugs back then. Her younger brother just followed her lead."

When their son and daughter first contacted them, Ruth's research led to the reconnection techniques trumpeted by Alienated Grandparents Anonymous, Inc. Before the first in-person visit, she and Terry agreed not to bring up the past and decided they would be pleasant, interesting, and fun. In time, they hope to build genuine bonds, but currently, Terry says the interactions feel artificial. Also, the visits dig at hurt and anger he and Ruth put to rest long ago.

The couple uses mindfulness to accept that their feelings are normal echoes of past emotions from unresolved conflict. Terry believes he's coping well but worries about Ruth. "She was once in a very dark place because of our kids. Some days, I wonder if we're doing the right thing. Is it really a good idea to just let them off the hook like this?"

Terry's question is a good one. Here are a few more to consider:

- Can you let bygones be bygones?
- Is it wise to forgive *and* forget?
- Can you survive another round of emotional battering or abandonment?

Terry and Ruth aren't certain of anything. At times, they even wonder if their children only reconciled to try and gain an inheritance. "It's an awful thought," says Terry. "But after so many years, they're actually strangers."

Let's hear more from Julia. In Chapter Six, she shared about reconciling with her son, daughter-in-law, and grandchild—only to have them estrange all over again after two years. Julia and her husband are heartbroken, this time with the added loss of their precious granddaughter.

Looking back, Julia wishes she'd have listened to her husband. He wanted to address every issue and get to the bottom of what caused the estrangement. "I can see now that he was one hundred percent right," says Julia. "But back then, I would have danced on the table and hung from the chandelier just to be *Nana*." So, when they arrived at the restaurant for that first reconciliation meeting, Julia took the list of discussion points her husband had written and sat on it. She says, "I told them we could just talk."

At times, Julia's hindsight torments her. She can't help thinking that if she had just gone along with her husband and insisted on addressing the estrangement and its causes, maybe they could have avoided another split. Of course, there are no guarantees things would be different if she had. When the first estrangement began, Julia and her husband persuaded their son and his wife to see a counselor with them. In that session, their daughter-in-law's inflexibility reigned. This time, then, it's feasible that had they insisted on examining the past, the second estrangement would have started sooner.

Julia still holds a sliver of hope that things might change. However, her husband says this last time was really the last. He can't watch Julia go through such pain again.

Terry feels similarly about his wife. "Ruth is seeing a therapist again," says Terry. "We're taking this a step at a time but if this gets too stressful, we'll quit. We're getting too old for roller coasters."

Terry isn't the only one to come to that conclusion. Let's now meet eighty-one-year-old mother of three, Joan. Her sons remain friendly, but her adult daughter has been estranged for nineteen years.

"I forgave her long ago," says Joan, whose fifty-six-year-old daughter recently reached out to arrange a visit. They agreed to meet for lunch the following week. In the interim, Joan was troubled by a slurry of painful memories. Trembling after a fitful night's sleep, on the morning of the meeting, Joan almost canceled.

At the restaurant, her daughter brought current photographs and shared information about Joan's grandsons, who were sweet little boys when her daughter severed ties. Seeing their photos only intensified Joan's hurt. In them were handsome young men whose chiseled faces were once round, and whose soft cheeks she had once kissed. "I was bereft for all I'd lost," she says. "And for them. They had lost out, too."

Quietly, Joan asked her daughter if she understood how much hurt she had caused. Her daughter offered a weak apology, and then changed the subject to the problems in her life: a recent job loss, her husband's affair, and her younger son's trouble with the law. The lunch ended with a hug, but Joan went away feeling uneasy.

Over the next few weeks, Joan reflected on all that had transpired at the time of the estrangement. She had spent years trying to regain her emotional strength. Joan looked up her grandsons on social media and found them. One is married and lives far away. The other is closer and lives a party-type lifestyle. "I loved the little boys, but so much time has passed, the grown men are strangers to me."

Joan contemplated her daughter's behavior at the lunch, as well as in a subsequent phone call, and several e-mails they exchanged. "She only talked about herself and her problems. Every time I tried to broach the subject of the past to try to figure out why she did what she did, and maybe form some basis for a new relationship, she changed the subject." Meanwhile, Joan's eighty-four-year-old husband has health issues. "I need to be well-rested so I can care for him," she says. "Meeting up with my daughter triggered stress."

The next time her daughter called, COVID-19 was just beginning to cause lockdowns in some parts of the world. "I have concerns because of my age and existing health issues," says Joan. "My daughter dismissed those worries. I don't know how much energy I can expend on someone who doesn't seem to empathize or care."

After much deliberation, Joan told her daughter it was too late for them. "There was a time when I'd have done anything for her," she says. "Now, I just don't have the energy."

Joan forgave her daughter long ago. "So that I could let go of the anger, disbelief, and pain," she says. "I fought hard to regain my peace. I can't let her steal it again."

Reconciling: the Surprises

Many parents are surprised at how their relationships look after "reconciliation." These revealing quotes from parents are grouped by common themes.

A Changed Relationship

- "Forgiveness is a choice. It feels good to have the door opened a crack, but truthfully, I don't know how we can ever come close to being ourselves around one another again."

- "The hurt never goes away. You are just pretending to have a relationship again, but I guess that's better than nothing."

- "I thought reconciling would heal things. She has never been sorry for what she has done, including slander of our family. Without repentance, how can I trust?"

- "I had no idea our separation bothered him as much as it bothered me. I truly thought I was the only one feeling it but learned this truth when we finally got to counseling together. We are now much more open and caring."

The Stress of an Uphill Battle

- "I feel like an old faithful dog that returns, tail wagging, only to be kicked again and again. Just when I think we are doing well with our relationship—*BAM*—his verbal lashings send me into a downward spiral of emotions. At my age, that takes a real toll on me physically and emotionally."

- "I had no idea how humiliating this would be."

- "I thought I'd be happier. Now, I've lost the peace I worked very hard to gain. My daughter is angry at her brother for what he did to us. I struggle now just to relax. I keep thinking he'll disappear again anyway."

- "It's not a comforting experience. Shock, anger, sadness, and bewilderment go along with some relief and joy."

A Change of Heart

- "Despite all the years of sorrow, I feel bland about his coming back. I now realize not speaking to an adult child won't kill me. If it happens again, I will be okay."

- "In a moment of clarity, I realized his coming and going from my life was worse than a full estrangement. I'm tired of him abusing my emotions. Enough is enough."

- "I feel distant. I'm not interested in the type of relationship we had before, but I don't think my daughter will change. I'm also fearful that my reluctance to move quickly in reconciling and trusting her will cause another rift. That wouldn't surprise me at all. My daughter is getting married soon. At this point, the wedding just seems like another complication."

- "I would have done anything for a relationship with my son, but I'm coming to learn that it is more painful to have this untrue, pretend relationship. I'm not sure it's worth the pain to continue on the superficial level he wants."

Fear

- "I'm afraid our son will repeat the estrangement and am guarded because of that."

- "I imagined complete joy. Instead, I dread the contact. She won't discuss the reasons, and I want to protect myself from another estrangement."

- "It's like this: When we're together, I'm constantly wearing my crash helmet and flak jacket, just in case."

- "I'm always careful. I plan what to talk about and mostly just listen and nod. I fear another curtain call on our relationship."

Grandchildren

- "Reconciling brings no relief. It just adds a new kind of hurt. My grandchildren are subjected to bad opinions about me constantly. My eight-year-old granddaughter barely hugs me sometimes, yet we have had some great fun together. The grandchildren are confused."

- "I'm holding back emotionally. I fear my grandson will be taken away again."

- "When I kiss my grandchildren goodbye and wave, I'm always wondering if it will be the last I will see of them for a very long time. It happened before. Rebuilding my relationship with them took a lot of patience. I don't know if I would have it in me again."

- "It's painful that my nine-year-old grandson seems scared of me at times. I wonder what his parents tell him, but I'm afraid to ask."

Letting Go

- "Reconciliation happens when you least expect it. To talk about the past gradually, not all at once, is healing. Some things just didn't matter anymore."

- "I'm surprised how much I trust her not to leave me. I know that if she does, her depression will be the cause. I have kind of forgotten all that happened, and I forgive her."

- "I had to accept that when you're dealing with a Cluster B personality disorder, reconciliation is not possible in the true sense of the word."

- "Just to see him . . . suddenly it didn't matter why the estrangement happened. What was important was going forward."

- "Reconciling set me free. It's like it's one less burden on my soul."

Should Siblings Just Get Along?

Earlier in the book, you heard directly from the siblings of adults who have estranged from their parents or the whole family. Often, the siblings are heartbroken, worried for their parents, and fearful about the future. When parents reconcile, what happens with the siblings? Must they follow suit?

Let's first meet Kirsten, who was sixteen when her oldest

brother, age twenty at the time, got married and disconnected from the family. Kirsten's mother suffered horribly. "She was always crying," says Kirsten. "She went from this bubbly woman who held the family together to someone who could barely get dressed or even eat." Kirsten, her father, and her other two brothers were very worried. They all pulled together to help keep the household running smoothly. "There was a time when I loathed my brother, Barry, for hurting us all," Kirsten says. "Especially Mom and Dad."

Eleven years passed before Barry came back into their lives. At that time, Kirsten was twenty-seven, divorced, and raising two young children on her own. "My brother suddenly waltzed back into the family like he'd done nothing wrong," she says. Kirsten's parents imposed strict demands on her and her other siblings. "Nobody was to do or say anything to make Barry uncomfortable. My parents were afraid he'd leave again, so they'd tell us, 'Don't upset Barry.' Or, 'Make sure you talk nice to him.'"

Kirsten and her other two brothers honored their parents' requests. "We were all expected to suck it in and not talk about it, so we complied," she says. Barry, on the other hand, was treated like visiting royalty. "If he couldn't make it to a gathering until five o'clock, then we waited for him. If he said he wanted burgers, then that's what we had."

By the time Barry rejoined the family, he had divorced and remarried. Eventually, the family learned that Barry's second wife was the one who had encouraged him to reconcile. His daughters were seven and nine when they finally met their relatives from their father's side. "Those girls were afraid of us all," Kirsten says of her standoffish nieces from Barry's first marriage. "They had heard negative stories about us, and it took years for them to realize we aren't the bad people we were built up to be."

The fracture torn into Kirsten's family has had lasting effects. Even today, Barry's daughters, who are now in their thirties, remain guarded. The girls' mother died when they were in their early twenties. At that time, the younger one confided to Kirsten that her mother had been a "scary" person. She no longer visits her mother's family. The older one does still see them and is the more distant of the two girls. "There's probably still some talk about us among them," Kirsten speculates.

With a son of her own, Kirsten understands how much her parents loved her brother and wanted him back. "But he took no responsibility for the hurt he caused us all. For years, our mother blamed herself. She never really recovered from the anguish."

Now age fifty-four, Kirsten admits she still doesn't trust her once-estranged brother. "Barry has been accepted back, and I love him, but my feelings for him aren't the same as for my other brothers. To never acknowledge or take responsibility, to never say you're sorry about what you did and how you hurt your family . . . It's a divide we will never get past."

The divide is probably deeper than it would have been if her parents hadn't insisted that they all just sweep Barry's behavior under the rug and get along. Kirsten understands that parents desperately want their child back, but she advises, "Don't forget your other kids' feelings. I understand not hashing out every detail, but if my brother had been able to hear how much he hurt us, then he'd have had the chance to apologize."

By hearing his side, maybe Kirsten and her siblings could have better understood. "Barry got so tangled up emotionally by his first wife and her family," says Kirsten. "I still don't get how that could happen, but if we'd ever talked about it, maybe I could have worked more on forgiveness." Even today, her parents' very vocal decision that their estate will be equally split when they die fuels some resentment. "It doesn't matter, per se, but it's the principle."

How siblings perceive the fairness in their parents' treatment of them influences how they feel about another sibling and the sibling relationship. When they understand their parents' different or preferential treatment and can justify it, they can often better accept it and their sibling.[1] That might have occurred if the parents hadn't forbidden discussion.

Obviously, it's easier to say that every family member's feelings should be acknowledged, and situations talked through for a happy ending, than it is to accomplish this in real life. Over the years, Kirsten has attempted to broach the subject with her parents, but they only become upset. She doesn't want to hurt them the way Barry did, so she drops the topic. If you're in a similar situation, turn back to the discussions in Chapter Four and read through the discussion tips.

Unfortunately, even today, nearly four decades since her brother first estranged, and nearly three decades since he's been back in the family, Kirsten feels residual effects. When her son became engaged two years ago, she worried he might do what her brother did. "He was madly in love with this girl who was very close to her indulgent parents." They included her son on lavish trips, and as her son's wedding drew near, Kirsten felt left out. "If I asked him to come to his own family's holiday event, he'd get his back up. The girl broke it off a few weeks before the big day, but it was a lot like my brother with his first wife."

Are Kirsten's worries about her son founded? Estrangements run thick through some family trees. If you haven't yet done your genogram (Chapter Four), consider doing that now. Whether genetics or some other family pattern might be at work, Kirsten's concerns are real. She is wise to analyze her firstborn brother's history and compare it to that of her own son and the wider family. Finding nothing can allay her fears. Discovering patterns might enable her to broach the topic with family members, consider possible reasons, and come to conclusions that support herself and perhaps the whole family.

As Kirsten's experience reveals, siblings may act to protect their parents because, as she expressed, the last thing they want to do is cause the family more hurt. You'll recall some of the insights shared by siblings in Chapter Four. Emotionally distraught parents may not realize the depth of their other children's pain over the loss due to estrangement itself, let alone the gravity of the task if they're asked to forgive and forget. Parents don't have to hold family meetings and require everyone to share, but they can empathize and acknowledge everyone's possible distress. Sometimes, that results in a more cohesive future. Other times, it helps the siblings to know their parents care about them and how the estrangement and/or reconciliation impacts them.

For parents to *demand* what they want from their adult children will have consequences. Kirsten believes she was right to go along with her parents' wishes. She holds her head high as a daughter who has shown her parents honor, yet she still harbors uneasy feelings about her brother's character. "At family gatherings, I say 'hello,' but don't spend more than five minutes with him," says Kirsten. When her parents die, she says she will no longer feel the obligation.

Let's turn to Janelle, a divorced mother of two sons. When she reconciled with her youngest son after ten years of estrangement, she wanted her older son, Caleb, to welcome him back too. "He wouldn't," she says. "Years ago, Caleb was the one who traveled to his little brother's college town to persuade him to get in touch with me." Once there, Caleb discovered his brother had dropped out of school. He'd been kicked out of the dorm. For all those years, Janelle never knew where he was. "When he called one day and we reconciled, he didn't want to talk about the past," says Janelle. "I was just so happy to have him back that I let it all go." Caleb was angry. He didn't trust his younger brother.

In the last year, Janelle has seen her previously estranged son several times. His young daughter from an ex-girlfriend visits him one weekend a month, and Janelle enjoys being a grandmother to her. She saw her older son's kids, too, until she suggested Caleb let go of the past and they all come together as a family. "He called his brother 'trash,' and said he loved his wife and children too much to get them involved in what was sure to be a train wreck."

It's possible Janelle's older son is keeping information from her. Among the siblings I surveyed who said they knew facts about the sibling their parents didn't, they mentioned (their words) drug use, lying, immorality, and illegal acts. However, they were torn about telling their parents because the information might cause hurt.

Janelle hopes her older son will come around but says, "I realize I don't have the right to expect Caleb to be friendly with his brother just because I am. He has my best interests at heart. I just didn't expect him to be so vehement."

Janelle's forthright apology helped. "Caleb agreed to visit me soon and bring his family," she says. "I love both of my sons and all my grandchildren. I'm willing to see them separately for now if that's what it takes."

Janelle plans to ask Caleb directly why he is so set against his once-estranged brother. "I'm afraid of the answer," she says. "But I plan to tread lightly and stay calm. I'll let him know I'm willing to listen, and I'll assure him that, no matter what his answer, I will be okay."

Parents can set the tone for any discussion, and that's Janelle's plan. "If I'm okay, Caleb will be, too," she says. Parents can convey that they are strong and that, if needed, they will get support. Their stable demeanor and self-assuredness frees the siblings to also express themselves.

Janelle hopes they can someday be "one big happy family" again. For now, maybe forever, her situation is like some other parents who, though reconciled with an estranged son or daughter, see them separately from other family members.

One mother put it best: "My husband and I chose to accept my estranged daughter back. We owe the same generosity to our son and our other daughter, who want to hold her accountable. Their feelings count." Is this a perfect ending? *No.* "We're careful not to mention this daughter to the other kids because they get angry," she says. "It's a whole new eggshell walk."

As our children grow into adults, with opinions and ideas of their own, we can't expect that they will always want what we want. We may or may not understand their reasons for not wanting to reconcile. Regardless, it may be too much to expect our adult children to just get along or to "play nice" as we may have required of them as children.

Even without estrangement, as siblings develop careers, form committed relationships, and have children, they have less contact. Sibling connections are often held together by those the children have with parents. While it's true that siblings frequently reconnect later in life, the routine gathering of entire families once the kids grow up may be rarer than most of us think or had hoped for.

I once imagined a future where all of my five children, their spouses, and loads of grandchildren would always be around. We bought a home and stayed put, enlarging it as our family grew, with the expectation that we would always stay, and family would always return. Even if Dan had not broken off, our family may not have all been together as often as I once imagined. Just as my siblings and I relocated and got on with our lives, my adult children have spread some. My fantasy about the old homestead was a beautiful one. As my children have aged, I've set my feet firmly in the present—where I can make every moment count.

Forgiveness

Parents are usually ready and willing to forgive, but when estrangement occurs, they do well to work on themselves, gain inner strength, and approach any reconciliation with realistic rather than idealistic views. Those who do often discover that their happiness doesn't depend on a son or daughter returning to them.

There's an old saying that you can't go home again, probably derived from the classic Thomas Wolfe novel of the same name.

Figuratively, that is often true for those who make the choice to sever ties. In the interim, "home" doesn't stay the same. Heartbroken parents face hardships, come to terms, and grow.

Actions have consequences. Parents forgive, but they don't always forget. For their own well-being, maybe that's best. As one mother, whose son reconnected a year ago and now calls every few weeks with his young son for video chats, explains, "I *feel* differently toward my son now. I never thought I would say that, but I do. His lack of concern when his dad was gravely ill two years ago shocked me. He genuinely did not care if his dad lived or died. I *needed* him then . . . and I survived that nightmare without him. I forgive him, but I can't think of a time I will ever need him going forward."

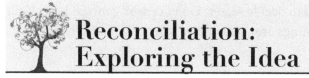

Reconciliation: Exploring the Idea

Reconciling is not as easy as it sounds. It requires four *A*-words and one starting with an *H*. In healthy relationships, reconciling is about:

- **a**dmitting mistakes, relational problems, or disagreement
- **a**pologizing for your part
- **a**greeing . . . to disagree but still value one another, and/or to do better in the future
- **a**cting in ways that honor the other person and/or the relationship
- **h**umility

It's no accident that, when you combine these, the sound is a satisfied sigh: *aaaah.* As a kid, my siblings and I used to make that sound after a long swallow of a cold drink on a hot day. *Aaaah.* That's how the rejoining of kind, humble people who want to connect should feel. Like a refreshing drink on a blistering day.

Ideally, these efforts (admission, apology, agreement, action) are taken up by all parties in a spirit of humility. However, that may not immediately occur. Or one party may decide to let the other off the hook, at least to a degree.

In parent-adult-child relationships, parents frequently must come to terms with changes in how they feel, decide what they want or will settle for in the relationship—as well as what they don't want or will not allow. The parties must negotiate their connections going forward and then renegotiate as needed. Reconciling isn't always how it's dreamt to be, but the reality becomes acceptable, or sometimes even better.

Consider the following questions and write out your thoughts. Sharing with a trusted friend or support group might be helpful, but that's for you to decide—later. Don't censor yourself here. Your thoughts and feelings are valid and worthy of your attention.

- When I consider reconciling, what memories come to mind that fuel my desire to be close again?

- Considering my answers to the previous question, are my thoughts about reconciliation realistic?

- In the past, what advice have I read or heard about reconciling? What parts of that advice, if any, makes sense for my situation? Was any of that advice unsettling or did it anger me, and if so, why?

- When I think about reconciling, what do I envision? *(Be specific.)* How much time do I expect to spend together? What will we do and say? How will our time together feel?

_____

_____

_____

_____

_____

_____

- How much am I willing to bend my vision?

_____

_____

_____

_____

_____

_____

_____

- Is my child's "truth" different than mine? Do I even know? Do I recognize or understand it?

_____

_____

_____

_____

_____

_____

- Can I truly let bygones be bygones? *Should* I?

_____

_____

_____

_____

_____

_____

- Is it wise to forgive *and* forget? What might I need to keep in mind about the past to protect myself in the future?

_____

_____

_____

_____

_____

_____

- Regarding my thoughts about the last question, what can I do to stay safe in the relationship now?

_____

_____

_____

_____

_____

- Given my child's past decisions/actions, what consequences exist, if any, to our relationship? What about my own past decisions or actions?

  _____

  _____

  _____

  _____

  _____

  _____

- In reading through the parents' comments in "Reconciling: the Surprises," which ones stood out to me? Why?

  _____

  _____

  _____

  _____

  _____

- With regard to reconciliation, what are my expectations about my other children and/or other family members? Are these realistic? What issues haven't I considered?

_____

_____

_____

_____

_____

_____

- In this chapter, who and/or what do I most identify with? Why?

_____

_____

_____

_____

_____

_____

If, after reading this chapter and doing this exercise, you feel that *any* relationship with an adult son or daughter, even one in which you feel used or abused, is more desirable than no relationship or perhaps a limited one, consider what may be behind those feelings. Codependency? Low self-esteem? Fear of conflict (even to your own peril)? Fear of the future?

Notes

CHAPTER EIGHT

Reconciling, More to Consider

"If the sun never set, we would have no perception of the vast depths of space, which become visible only at night when we are able to see what is obscured by the bright daylight."
—WILLIAM KEEPIN

Reconciling sometimes requires seeing facts we wish weren't true and digging deep into our stores of parental devotion. We may be required to demonstrate loving patience and remain kind, yet also be tough enough to protect ourselves and help our children. Other times, we must face our biggest fears and failings and hope our children will empathize and care. It's not easy to admit to our own issues, set boundaries, and enforce them, or learn to trust again.

Reconciling When You Suspect (or Know) Your Child Has Mental Illness

Many parents whose adult children "reconcile" use the term lightly. Some come up with other ways to describe the "treaty" that equates to emotional blackmail or keeps them in a state of W.O.E. (walking on eggshells). Recognizing mental instability, whether diagnosed or speculated upon, parents who are committed to staying involved may even adhere to rules their adult children impose upon them. These informed choices are made with purpose. Difficult and complex situations require lots of insight and self-care. Let's look at a few examples.

"They say jump, and we ask, 'how high?'" says Peggy, whose son and daughter-in-law reconnected after three years of estrangement. She and her husband, Roger, are "seeing them again." Among the younger couple's designated rules are strict orders that Peggy and her husband must *never* call on a weekday and must *always* positively support the couple's social media postings. Peggy had previously quit social media because of snide remarks and glimpses of a grandson she hadn't yet met. Now that they've reconnected, Facebook is a part of her everyday life. "Yippee!" she remarks. "I can agree with every opinion, laugh at every joke, and drive myself crazy double-checking that I don't miss a post." She adds, "Don't mind my sarcasm, but it feels silly. My dumb 'like' or emoji makes them seem like the perfect family to their Facebook friends. Reconciling is nothing like I thought."

Peggy's feelings echo those of many who describe a sense of teetering on the edge, knowing that at any moment, they could be out. For Peggy and Roger, staying involved feels like the right thing to do. They have a young grandson they care about.

To manage her emotions, Peggy has come up with some strategies that work for her. "This may sound selfish," she says. "I love my grandson, and when I'm with him, I'm all in, but when we drive away, I get the hand sanitizer and very literally wash my hands of my own son and his family. I detach. Otherwise, my mind strays, and I feel too involved, and they won't let me be."

Peggy is proud of her son's academic and career accomplishments but baffled by who he has become on a personal level. She characterizes his behavior as "rigid" and "demanding," and along with Roger, believes he may suffer some sort of mental illness.

She and Roger are motivated to "behave" (as Peggy puts it) because of their grandson. They've also set their limits. "We only see them about once a month, and not for more than a few hours at a time. Maybe things will change in the future, and if that's for the better, great. If things get worse, then we'll reevaluate. Roger and I went into this reconnection with our eyes wide open."

That's how Bridgette feels about reconciling with her daughter, Megan, after six years of estrangement. Bridgette uses the term "accommodating" for the way she relates to her daughter now. "I know exactly what I'm dealing with," she says. "It's mental illness, and I know that she could turn on me at any time. She has said such vile things to me in the past. I'm aware that can happen again."

Facing reality has allowed Bridgette to take kind care of herself and to avoid being negatively affected by the one-sided relationship. How she reached and maintains her strength can help other parents whose adult children may have mental illness, and who want to stay in touch.

During the silent years, Bridgette met occasionally with a skilled therapist who speculated that her daughter might have a personality disorder. "She's definitely an unstable person," says Bridgette, who has witnessed Megan's mood swings and vicious, sudden turns on Bridgette and other people. "She was sometimes paranoid, too. Liking her coworkers one day, believing they had her best interests at heart, and then deciding they were out to get her fired the next."

Seeing her daughter as unstable allowed Bridgette to empathize more. She's thankful her daughter has a loyal husband. When she looked back on Megan's thirty-two years, she could see that her marriage was her only lasting relationship. "Believing your coworkers are against you doesn't make for a happy life," says Bridgette.

During their estrangement, Bridgette studied *Done With The Crying*, completed the exercises, and committed to reworking her life to support her own well-being. She sought out fulfilling pursuits and cultivated inner peace and personal strength separate from motherhood. After nearly three years, she began to break her daughter's no-contact rule and reach out with occasional electronic cards and "love you" texts. Some were met with vitriol and many ignored.

"I also wrote a letter," she says. "And finally sent it." In the past, Bridgette had shared her letter drafts with her husband and her therapist. "They would pick it apart, add things and delete things, change words, and offer me advice. By the time they were done telling me what to say and how to say things, what was left wasn't truly how I felt. The last time, I just wrote the letter and sent it. Period. No sharing with anyone else."

Bridgette says that, by acknowledging her daughter's summations of her character and apologizing, she threw herself under the bus "at least a little," but she wanted to try. "I did my fair share of eye rolling when I wrote to her, but my daughter is very egocentric. A more balanced letter would have just caused her to feel shame, which would trigger her to slam the door closed rather than allow for the door to open." Bridgette kept the letter short—a smart move. Many parents pour out their hearts, only to find their words return to them in a twisted way.

A month after sending the letter, her daughter e-mailed, saying Bridgette could visit the next time she was in town. During the first visit, they didn't speak about the estrangement. "It's counterintuitive to what I think should happen," Bridgette says. "But I remind myself that she's an unstable personality, so it's okay."

Now, nearly four years later, Bridgette has a granddaughter who is three. About once a month, Bridgette makes the half-day's drive to visit. "I know exactly what I'm dealing with," she says of her daughter. The infrequency of the contact helps Bridgette take care of herself. "When I see Megan, it's all about her. I get my emotional needs met elsewhere and have learned that I can't expect her to be a support for me in any way. But I get to be in my granddaughter's life, and that's very important to me."

Bridgette hasn't forgotten the vile things Megan said to her in the past, nor her erratic behavior that, at its worst, bordered on scary. "Right now, she's doing better," says Bridgette. "If that ever changes, maybe I can help with my granddaughter. Or maybe I'll be kicked to the curb." Bridgette has made inroads with her son-in-law, who she knows got an earful about her from Megan. "He's quietly friendly, and after living with my daughter, he must know how she can be." With a sigh, Bridgette adds, "He loves her as I do. Megan's lucky to have him, and me."

Some parents conclude that *all* adult children who estrange from loving families must be mentally ill. Others believe a society that all but sanctions the abandonment of parents is what is unhealthy. Regardless, parents must not abandon themselves. Neither instability (Bridgette's term), nor a diagnosed mental disorder, excuse abuse by an adult child.

Dr. Bruce Alan Kehr illustrates this point well in his book, *On Becoming Whole* (2018), when he describes his work at a private psychiatric hospital that treated patients with severe mental illness including bipolar disorder and schizophrenia, as well as substance abuse disorders, and even brain injuries. Despite their diagnoses, patients were not allowed to blame their bad behavior on staff, physicians, their medications, or on other patients. Instead, it was made clear to patients that their behavior was their personal responsibility. As a result, behavioral issues were surprisingly infrequent. What is more, the patients were *reassured* by the assignment of personal responsibility. While parents of unstable adult children may demonstrate patience, moderate their own behavior to a degree, and at times make exceptions, *excusing* aggressive, abusive behavior benefits no one.

Further, it is known that some personality disorders remit with time and age. Those with borderline personality disorder and antisocial personality, for example, tend to exhibit fewer symptoms in their thirties, forties, and beyond. Despite a previous diagnosis, the criteria for BPD, over time, is often no longer met. Personality disorders are not always static and fixed. Those with antisocial personality disorder tend to exhibit less criminal behavior in particular with age, while persons with borderline personality disorder enjoy more stable relationships and vocations.[1] These specific changes indicate the ability, even by those with mental illnesses, to learn how to behave better. Dialectical Behavior Therapy (DBT), which is one of the leading treatments for BPD, speeds up the process of managing emotions, dealing with life stress, and functioning. By expecting ethical treatment, parents step away from the role of enabler and assign the adult child responsibility, just as Dr. Kehr's book describes the treatment of patients.

When Help Brings Miracles

Let's look at an example of one adult child who, with age, circumstances, and mental health help, has changed. Earlier, we met Jane and Peter who sent a birthday present to the granddaughter they hadn't seen in years. Their thanks was a text in which their granddaughter blamed them for the family rift. Jane and Peter reasoned she had been coached and still hoped that, one day, she might reach out to them.

The last time their son cut them off, Jane and Peter were so exhausted by the hurt that they vowed, "Never again," to any relationship with their son. His raging temper and vile comments had wreaked havoc on their lives and their health. Their granddaughter's reaction to the gift they mailed to her renewed their *never again* stance. Even so, two years later, the family has reconciled. Let's consider how.

Through the grapevine, Jane and Peter heard their son had lost his long-term job and started over at another company. He was also having marital problems. His wife had given him an ultimatum to either get help for his anger or they were done.

When Jane became sick and underwent a major cancer surgery, she was fearful she'd die and leave Peter all alone. "Our son always had love for his dad," says Jane. "I don't know why he takes his anger out on me and not Peter, but I kept thinking that if I died, Peter wouldn't have a family." So, two weeks before Peter's seventy-fifth birthday, Jane called their son. "I requested he have a special day with his dad and our grandsons," she says. To her surprise, her son agreed. "Peter wouldn't have gone if it weren't for our twin grandsons being there." The four had a pleasant day. Their grandsons were so young at the time of the last break that they were just happy to see their granddad, eat at a restaurant, tell jokes, and laugh. The visit was good for Peter, which was important to Jane.

Several months later, Jane required another surgery. Afterward, while lying in the hospital bed, she made some decisions. Not out-of-the-woods medically yet, she didn't want to die without saying her piece. Maybe her son would hear her out. A couple of weeks after her discharge, she called him, said she'd been sick, and asked if he would come by to talk. He didn't say much on the phone, and Jane doubted he would come, but was later surprised by a knock at the door.

Jane says, "That evening, I let out everything I'd been holding back for years." She told him he had nearly destroyed them when he yanked away the grandchildren they so loved. For the first time in as long as she could remember, her son didn't shout at her. They ended up talking for three hours, and he caught his parents up on his life. He confided that he had nearly lost his wife and children because of his unmanaged anxiety and anger. Medication had helped, and he was in continuing therapy.

The next day, her son posted mean remarks about her on social media. Jane wasn't optimistic for a reconciliation, but she worried about dying and wanted Peter to have a family. Cautiously, she began reaching out to her son, first inviting him over to get some heirlooms from an uncle who had died, and then inviting him again for lunch.

After a couple of solo visits, their son agreed to bring the children over. Jane knew she would be emotional, so she planned a few jokes to keep things light. When her grandchildren walked in, she exclaimed, "Did you guys get taller? Or am I shrinking?" Everyone laughed.

Her son and grandchildren have been back a few times now. Although Jane and Peter have said their daughter-in-law is welcome, she has not come along. They aren't losing any sleep over that but do realize she is part of the reconciliation process. Jane explains, "If she said he couldn't bring the children to see us, he wouldn't. I'm grateful."

Whenever they are with her son, Jane is kind but also firm. "At almost fifty, he has made a turnaround that is nothing short of a miracle," she says. Jane sees him making an effort, but his anger toward her comes out at times.

"Before the last estrangement, I tiptoed around him because of our grandchildren," says Jane. "I now know that doesn't work. He only treated me worse. I won't tolerate that anymore." Recently, their son brought the kids over for a meal. During the visit, he made a comment about his childhood that didn't sit well with Jane. Calmly, she corrected him on the spot. Her son relented, telling her he realized how much she and Peter sacrificed in raising him.

After more than two decades of cycling hurt and hope with a son whose anger issues began in his late teens, Jane admits she may never fully trust her son. However, she reasons that, even if the reconciliation goes bad, the grandchildren are much older now. They won't be so easily convinced that their grandparents are at fault.

Jane and Peter believe that, in the past, they tried too hard to keep the peace. In the end, they lost a big chunk of time with their grandchildren anyway, and their son made their lives miserable in the process. Relationships only work when all parties try.

Jane and Peter once said "never again" about letting their son back into their lives. Now, Jane says they have changed that statement to reflect a sensible approach to reconciling: "We will never walk on eggshells again."

As children grow to adulthood, parents must learn to relate to them as adults. The children, too, must learn to act like adults, and treat well those with whom they have relationships. For successful lives, even those with mental illness must learn to take responsibility. As Jane and Peter have learned, eggshell walks are painful and don't solve anything.

When estrangement first strikes, most parents are so shocked that they immediately look within. *What did I do wrong? What could I have done differently? How can I fix this?* Some get stuck in that mode, which can affect confidence when it comes to parenting their other children and how they manage a reconciliation. It's important to work through the emotional responses as Bridgette did. Parents may moderate their behavior in some circumstances, but there must be limits that serve a purpose. An example is Bridgette's infrequent contact that allows her to know her grandchild, and perhaps be available if her daughter crashes at some future point. Bridgette knows she couldn't maintain their emotionally one-sided and draining relationship if she saw her daughter more frequently.

Most parents who read my writings have been kind and supportive of their children all along. Rather than live in the shadow of an adult child's negative opinions, they do well to remember all the good they did. Jane and Peter do. As it turns out, when Jane recently pressed their son after an expression of anger that didn't settle well with her, he remembered the good they did too, and her reminder defused the situation.

Let's look at another example. For several years, one mother, Corinne, whose adult daughter suffers from bipolar disorder, nevertheless blamed herself for their estrangement. When Corinne finally came across my website, she wrote that, for the first time in years, she remembered who she was: *a good mother.* In time, she was able to move beyond the dark cloud of self-recrimination her estranged daughter had cast over her and reclaim more of herself: *A fun person who is involved in life.*

As many parents say is the case, it wasn't until after accepting her daughter's choice to disconnect that her daughter returned to the family without prompting. By then, Corinne had recognized that, out of a fear that her other two children would abandon her, she'd been too selfless. "I had forgotten that I count," she says. A little at a time, she began to take back her own power. Though scary, she began to tell them "no" sometimes when previously she'd rearrange her schedule to always accommodate theirs. "I have a right to my life, and they're not all that's in it."

One day, during a discussion in which she felt marginalized when she didn't understand the subject matter, she calmly told all of them, including her recently reconciled daughter who is in treatment and managing her bipolar disorder, "I won't take any crap. You're adults now. Not mouthy, self-centered teens." She explains, "I gave them life and then was a good mother to them. We don't have to agree, but they can't throw tantrums or treat me with disrespect. I don't treat them badly either. Mostly, we have fun."

This mother is a lot like I am with my four adult children who remain in contact with me and their dad. Satisfying relationships are based, in part, on mutual respect. We can treat each other kindly.

Mental Health Resources
United States

- National Alliance on Mental Illness (NAMI). Information and support for persons with mental illness, families, and caregivers; United States. (www.nami.org)

- National Institute of Mental Health (NIMH). Research funding agency with help and information. (https://www.nimh.nih.gov/)

- Mental Health.gov. Information to promote awareness and understand mental illness, suicide and its prevention, and related topics. (https://www.mentalhealth.gov/)

Canada

- Canadian Mental Health Association (CMHA). Information and support for mental illness and to promote well-being. (https://cmha.ca/)

- Mental Illness Caregivers Association of Canada (MICA). Resource dedicated to helping family members and caregivers. (https://micaontario.com/)

United Kingdom

- Mental Health UK. Advice, information, and support for those suffering mental health issues and their family and caregivers. (https://mentalhealth-uk.org/).

- MIND. Information and support resource. (https://www.mind.org.uk/)

Australia

- Sane Australia. National mental health information and support charity. (https://www.sane.org/about-sane)

- Mental Health Commission of the Government of Western Australia. Treatment, service, and support-oriented entity concerned with mental illness and substance abuse. (https://www.mhc.wa.gov.au/)

What About Boundaries?

This section uses adult children with mental illness as a backdrop. Even if that's not part of your situation, you'll find the information about how to devise and enforce boundaries relevant and adaptable. Boundaries are vital for all healthy relationships. Read on and be empowered to take charge for your own well-being. You can help those around you in the process.

I often hear from parents whose reconciliation takes place in crisis when a mentally ill child moves home. A son remains emotionally estranged but lives in a van in the driveway with his vicious dogs. A daughter returns with apologies but has erratic moods and odd behavior that prove something is mentally amuck. Stories like these are more common than you might think.

Frequently, a mentally ill adult child is accusatory, lays blame, and manipulates parents' emotions. Drugs and alcohol—perhaps attempts to self-medicate—may be a part of these circumstances, whether expressly stated, strongly suspected, or discovered later. Parents, who are initially thrilled their child wants to be with them, end up shocked, confused, and hurting. When they seek advice, they are often told to assert boundaries, but they may not know how to define or enforce them.

Parents who find themselves in sudden contact with adult children who have become needy, angry, or just plain odd, may be plagued by fears, feel powerless, and experience guilt. Emotionally wrung out, they suffer in shame and step gingerly into a tilting world. They may fall ill from the stress, avoid friends who might question or advise them, and take sleep medications—but still can't rest.

Even the most harmonious, committed relationships can become precarious tightropes where couples snipe and sway above a pit of possible divorce. One spouse is sick and tired of the problems, so checks out emotionally. The other is afraid any confrontation will push the child they're so worried about away. Amidst the turmoil, parents can grow apart and can become hopeless, depressed, and emotionally estranged from one another. They didn't expect to live their "golden years" in a state of chaos.

If any of this sounds familiar, first recognize that you need support. In the U.S., the National Alliance for Mental Illness (NAMI) is a sensible place to begin research, discover others in similar situations, and feel less alone. With local outreach in many cities, NAMI trains crisis counselors who offer empathy, understanding, and solid advice (free). Many NAMI counselors have personal experience with how a loved one's mental illness affects family members.

In addition to their text, chat, and telephone help lines, NAMI hosts informational meetings and support groups.

You can also find help through your local civic offices. Most counties have behavioral/mental health crisis lines, and there is no shame (or commitment) in calling one. A compassionate ear helps parents gain needed information, allay fears, and begin making decisions for their own well-being (which can also benefit the adult child).

Before enforcing any boundaries, you'll need to define them, which requires getting in touch with your feelings. For parents with a troubled adult child who camps out in a vacant room and uses the window to enter and exit just to avoid them, examining their feelings about what's going on may be painful. This may also be true for those whose kids lash out, push guilt buttons, or remember things in accusing ways. These situations erode parents' self-esteem and cause self-doubt. If you need to, seek support in the process. (See the Resources box preceding this section.)

You wouldn't be reading this if you didn't long for change. Mental illness is not an excuse for abuse. You have the right to set up and enforce boundaries.

Here are some of the common emotions that torment parents, as well as the thought processes that can fuel those feelings.

Fear: *What if I require my child to get help and he refuses and ends up homeless and is victimized?* Consider the alternative. If your child will not get the support s/he needs to get well, you commit yourself to the mire and chaos mental illness creates. Further, you allow your child to linger in his current state. What happens when you die? Although this sounds harsh, your demise may come more quickly with all the stress. Weigh everything, seek local advice from trusted sources, and take charge as you can.

Guilt: An acrimonious divorce, a demanding job, lack of money . . . you fill in the blank. Adult children are often remarkable at finding a weak spot and exploiting it. Mental illness often includes manipulative behavior. Adult children may even work to divide parents, so be alert and maintain communication with your partner. Parents of mentally ill children may already feel guilt. You are not to blame.

Worry about what other people will think: This might take the form of not wanting a confrontation that draws attention from the neighbors. The parents with the son and his vicious dogs living in a van in their driveway know that, if they confront him, he's likely to get loud. They hesitate to draw attention to themselves in their quiet, suburban neighborhood where they've lived for less than a year. However, if the dogs get out and bite someone, the parents could be sued since the dogs are on their property.

Concerns about other family relationships: Some will have concerns about what family members think, worries how they'll be characterized, or if others will believe a child's lies or accusations. Or perhaps there are fears of your adult child retaliating against another family member who has somehow been involved. Or, that your mentally ill child will end up on a vulnerable relative's doorstep. Others will fear they (or their spouse) can't or won't follow through, and the child will only gain more power in an already imbalanced relationship.

Avoidance: Parents may be so exhausted that they tiptoe around, hoping things will get better and avoiding the task of facing the issues. The thought of confronting a child about what they see, probing for answers, or making demands, is draining. This is especially true at a time when parents are trying to maintain a bit of distance just to feel normal themselves. Avoiding confrontation and conflict is common in general. How much more so when a family member's mental illness causes chaos? Parents may be worried, embarrassed, or afraid they will be blamed, perhaps even by mental health professionals.

These are just a few of the possible questions and feelings in these complex scenarios that are often glossed over with little more than platitudes and leave parents in places where only doormats should lie. The situations are frequently multi-fanged, and

BEYOND DONE WITH THE CRYING

sometimes require choosing between the lesser of evils. There may be an ex-spouse who also suffers a mental illness, refuses to assist, or enables an adult child's refusal to seek help. Whatever your circumstances, confronting your feelings and defining boundaries is important for your well-being.

We'll get into the specifics of defining boundaries in just a moment. For now, let's take charge of your worries about any confrontation that presses your adult child to seek help, make changes, or move out. What emotions are involved? Being specific is helpful. Now might be a good time to return to the exercise, "Call It What It is," from Chapter Three, to refresh your memory about pinpointing your feelings. Or, if you skipped that exercise, do it before completing this one.

When you consider your situation, what thoughts come to mind? You can use the lines below to reflect and clarify what troubles or concerns you. If you need additional paper, please give yourself that freedom. You deserve the space you need.

_____

_____

_____

_____

_____

_____

Examples of Boundaries

Boundaries are limits you set to define what behavior by another person is (or isn't) acceptable to you in a relationship. Boundaries are personal and devising them depends on your individual concerns in your unique situation. If your adult child is living with you or on your property, you may require no friends come to the house and that no drugs or alcohol be used. Perhaps no sleepovers are allowed, no romantic visitors, or you assert an ultimatum: either get into treatment or find a new place to live.

Your boundaries may come with time constraints, be periodically reevaluated, or require specific cleanliness standards. You might require your adult child to share certain meals with you or in some way contribute to the household. Maybe you draw the line at abuse: no swearing at parents, no physical abuse, no arguments about treatment, continued use of prescribed medicines, or whatever else makes sense—*for the circumstances and for you.*

Boundaries require consequences. It's not enough to assert a boundary and expect compliance. What happens if your boundary is no drinking and your child drinks? Will one misstep (or willful disregard) be allowed before consequences apply? Or are consequences graded such that one incident gets a warning, a second adds another rule, and a third results in losing a place to stay?

These examples are intended only for your own reflection. Your boundaries may be completely different from another parent's. Let's look at a more complete example.

For many years, Rusty suspected the son he shared with his ex-wife suffered from mental illness. Rusty's brother had bipolar disorder, and while Rusty didn't know for sure if his son had the same illness, his alcohol use, moodiness, and erratic behavior was familiar. As his son floundered in his early twenties, going from job to job, Rusty suggested he get help. His son refused and then moved into an old motorhome on his mother's property. He stopped talking to Rusty.

Fast-forward six years to his estranged son calling from the East Coast, saying he was homeless and needing help. Rusty bought him a bus ticket home, with a mental health evaluation as part of the deal. His son arrived skinny, dirty, smelly, and scared. He cleaned up, was fed, and offered new clothes and a soft bed. The next day, when Rusty brought up help, his son became agitated. Within hours, he was in the front yard, ranting and raving "like a mad man," threatening to kill himself with an old machete he found in a garage. Rusty called the sheriff's department and told them it was a mental health emergency. He knew from experiences with his mentally ill brother that the department had specialized officers who were well-trained for such calls. The officers who arrived managed to de-escalate the situation with persuasive words, and his son was carted off to the emergency room and then to a behavioral health hospital. He was treated, in-house, for nearly four weeks. Bipolar disorder was diagnosed.

While his son was gone, Rusty thought through his options. For him, continued treatment was the required boundary. Plus, he wanted his son's permission to make or verify appointments with his outpatient doctor. Rusty also wanted to know at least some details, such as what medications his son was taking and when or if any changes to dosage or type were made. He was surprised when his son agreed, and for the last six months, he has complied with treatment and is improving.

Their relationship is still prickly at times, but Rusty has drawn boundaries against any form of abuse or disrespect. He defines these as verbal or physical assault, as well as any disregard for the value of Rusty's home, which includes dirty dishes piling up in the room where his son stays, smoking indoors, or not properly disposing of cigarette butts or trash. His son can't drink while on his medication, so alcohol use is also against the rules.

Rusty's son recently began working again, and Rusty is hopeful he will continue forward on his wellness path. He also knows from his experience with his brother, and through research, that rebelling against treatment isn't unusual. Rusty allows his son a little leeway about tidiness since he began work and is busy, but he has made clear to his son that he won't bend when it comes to treatment. If his son doesn't comply at some point, Rusty is ready to enforce the consequence and ask that his son leave his home.

Let's also meet Pia, whose twenty-six-year-old daughter has been diagnosed with borderline personality disorder and depression. When her daughter lost several jobs in a row and needed financial help, she reconnected with her mom. Pia let her stay in the spare bedroom for a few weeks. Her daughter's behavior worried Pia. The daughter was angry, admitted to having suffered multiple sexually transmitted diseases since her late teens, and blamed Pia for not having taught her better values.

Pia had been just eighteen when a one-night stand resulted in her pregnancy. She very quickly became a responsible adult. As a single mother, Pia had done her best to raise her daughter on her own. She had expected a lot of her daughter growing up and had been proud that her daughter had been a responsible sort.

Pia says, "My daughter was always capable. She took honors classes in high school, was on the track team, and worked part time herself. It wasn't until after she graduated and moved out to share a house with friends that she started sleeping around, drinking, and using drugs. She was at fault in a car accident when she was twenty. At that time, she got diagnosed with depression and borderline personality disorder but wouldn't stick with any treatment."

When her daughter blamed her for her problems, Pia began to feel guilt. Pia had purposely avoided dating until her daughter was grown and had moved out. At that time, Pia had two boyfriends in close succession, and both relationships also ended. Had she set a poor example?

Deep down, Pia knew her self-doubt was irrational. Her own parents assured her that she had taken responsibility for her daughter and was a wonderful, devoted mother. Her daughter's issues were her own responsibility—not Pia's doing.

Pia did assert some boundaries for her daughter that were quickly disregarded. Her daughter moved out, stayed with her grandparents for a while, and then moved back in with friends. She's currently not in touch with any of the family. At this point, it's Pia's own thinking that most requires boundaries. Her self-doubt and lapses of judgment about being responsible for her daughter's troubles when that is clearly not true reflect the self-blame so many parents feel. If they had only been stricter, required more, expected less, set a better example, had enforced rules more steadily, disallowed back talk, let their kids off the hook more often . . . These are all forms of self-blame, and they are all wrong.

Among the parents of estranged adults, self-recriminatory thoughts abound and often echo the parent-blaming so prevalent among adult children who blast them all over the Internet. The parents did too much or too little, too early or too late. They either were not involved enough or were too involved. The reasons list is endless and circular. For every mother who says she did too much for her kids, there's another who worries she didn't do enough. For every father who was too strict, there's another who thinks he was too lenient.

Pia needs the boundary that all of us do: No what-if thinking. It's sensible and normal for parents to self-examine, try to understand the adult child's perspective, and reasonably consider their own mistakes (and we all made some). What-if thinking only leads to regrets and self-recrimination about what you "should" have done or not done. Here's the truth: Different behavior probably wouldn't have resulted in your child doing anything differently. There is one person who is responsible for your adult child's behavior: *Your adult child.*

Creating Your Own Boundaries

Now that you have read through these potential ideas for boundaries, including Rusty's and Pia's stories, consider your own boundaries. Will you be willing to renegotiate rules you've set at some point, as Rusty did after six months with his son doing well and now working? Go back to the first segment of this section, examine your concerns and emotions, and then consider boundaries of your own. Also, contemplate consequences. Be realistic. Think through how difficult enforcing them will be for you. Mull them over and revise as needed. You may need support. Also consider whether other family members need to know about the boundaries. Can they help? Will they enforce them too?

Use the lines below to jot down your initial thoughts about what boundaries are necessary for your own wellness and peace of mind. What consequences are appropriate and enforceable? You'll also have an opportunity to more fully create boundaries in the exercise at the end of this chapter.

_____

_____

_____

_____

_____

Preparing for a Mental Health Crisis

In times of crisis, having information at your fingertips and knowledge about what to do can calm emotions and clarify what action to take. Your local law enforcement office may have information on their website about mental health emergencies, what you should say if you need help with one, and about their officers' crisis intervention training. Or phone their non-emergency administrative lines and ask—they're used to fielding questions, and this is important.

At a minimum, write down and keep several copies handy, of pertinent information such as:

- *Who to call:* Phone numbers for the individual's caregivers (therapist, psychiatrist, doctor, etc.), others who can offer you or them support (a family member, pastor, etc.), crisis lines for your area (county mental health, law enforcement, etc.), national suicide hotlines.

- *Where to go:* Names and addresses of local behavioral health centers and hospitals that accept walk-ins, nearby emergency rooms.

It's also helpful to know:

- Prescribed medications
- Diagnoses
- History (suicide attempts, psychotic episodes, substance abuse, triggers, etc.)

NAMI (www.nami.org) offers a wealth of information. As of this writing, their website tab labeled "Your Journey" drops to sub-menus chock full of helpful information for specified groups, including family and caregivers. If you're outside the U.S., turn back to "Mental Health Resources," which appears earlier in this chapter, to find sources of local information (or search online for your specific location).

When Reconciling Requires Parents' Change

Sometimes, parents recognize their own mental health issues or ways of communicating require change if they're to reconcile. That's different from parents whose adult children accuse them of some disorder without basis. I hear those stories all too frequently. Parents sometimes see a counselor just in case. Unfortunately, the common scenario is that the parent returns with proof from a mental health provider that the lay diagnosis is wrong. Then, the proverbial goalpost gets moved and some new reason is invented for why the parent can't see the grandchildren or be a part of the adult child's life. These situations are about control, and the parent is not the one with issues.

This section is not meant to excuse estrangement. Cutting someone off is an extreme way to approach a problem and doesn't usually bring positive change. Occasionally, though, a parent will tell me the estrangement shed light on something they needed to fix or change. To that end, I've included a few examples.

Let's start with Elena, who had enjoyed a peaceful relationship with her three daughters. They each married, started families and careers, and moved to nearby areas. This suited Elena, an independent woman who had always had a career. When Elena retired two years after her husband did, they moved her ailing mother into their spare bedroom. The trio socialized some and occasionally visited the busy daughters and their families. Then one day their happy routine was shattered.

Elena stayed home with a stomachache on the morning her husband took her mother to a doctor appointment. They were killed in a multicar pileup. "I was suddenly alone," says Elena.

Her daughters suggested she sell the home where they'd been raised and move to a 55-plus townhome community closer to them. Elena resisted, preferring to let some time pass before piling on additional change. Her daughters didn't press, and as they got on with their lives, Elena tried to do the same. Within a few weeks, though, she could barely leave the house. "I might get in a car wreck," says Elena. The fear made sense given the loss of her husband and mother in the crash, but soon her fears became irrational. "In my own front yard, I'd hear a car engine and worry a driver would lose control, swerve, and hit me."

Concerned for her sanity, Elena didn't confide her fears to anyone. She had her groceries delivered and became increasingly isolated. She made excuses not to attend family events and didn't see her daughters unless they came to her. When her youngest daughter received a promotion that required full-time hours, she asked

Elena to care for her four-year-old. Elena was relieved. She thought having her grandson around would help.

Unfortunately, Elena's fears had become entrenched. She tried to take her grandson places, but as she buckled him into his car seat, her heart would race. "I'd be trembling and dripping with sweat. My stomach would be in knots." The planned trip would be canceled. For Elena, the physical sensations of anxiety only solidified her fears. She'd had a stomachache on the morning of the car accident. She believed that had been her intuition, manifesting in her body.

As Elena's anxiety increased, she couldn't relax. Her grandson would be playing, and she'd find herself obsessed with the thought that he would fall. When he ate, she worried he'd choke.

Eventually, her once carefree grandson also began exhibiting fears, even at home. At bath time, he asked his mom to keep the water low so he wouldn't drown. At the playground, he told other kids not to run because they might trip. Elena's daughter noticed these changes and asked her son and then her mother about them.

Embarrassed, Elena at first hedged. She finally confided what had been happening. When she told her daughter what she thought about her stomachache on the morning of the accident being her intuition, her daughter laughed at her. Then she gave Elena an ultimatum: get help or she'd cut ties. Even when Elena's older daughters intervened, their younger sister refused all contact with Elena and made other arrangements for her son.

Elena's older daughters empathized and encouraged her to seek help. "They felt awful that I'd been so alone," she says. "But it wasn't their fault. I hadn't wanted to bother them."

Admitting she needed psychological help wasn't easy, but after the first phone session, Elena felt hopeful. In that appointment, she even confided what she thought about her intuition on the morning of the car accident. The therapist explained that anxiety can cause physical symptoms. "It was my intuition that day," Elena says. "But after that, my fear took over."

Within six months, Elena had learned to notice and catch her fearful self-talk, change her thinking, and better manage her responses so they didn't manage her. The fears began to subside.

By then, her strong-willed youngest daughter was dug in. Her little boy had suffered, she said, and for that, she refused to forgive her mother.

Elena detailed her therapy in a letter to her younger daughter, who responded by inviting Elena on a trip to an amusement park that required a four-hour drive. Elena wasn't ready to prove herself in that way, and her daughter maintained the estrangement. Hurt, Elena nevertheless remained determined and continued making progress in her recovery. A year later, she could make short driving trips. She began to see her youngest daughter at family events and was glad when her little grandson came running for hugs.

Recently, her youngest daughter apologized but is still a little prickly. "I understand her," says Elena. "She had tried for a long time before getting pregnant. She didn't want her little boy to suffer, and she was angry I didn't tell anyone what was going on. I think it scared her to see me like that. Especially after losing her father and grandmother so suddenly."

Elena's story illustrates how traumatic experiences can deeply affect people and sometimes require professional help. In Elena's case, the estrangement brought a problem to light, but not without creating more discord. Elena's older daughters are critical of their youngest sister. One barely speaks to her now. The choice to estrange from one family member frequently alienates others. (See "Estrangement: It's Catching," in Chapter Five.)

Elena hopes that, in time, her daughters will be close again, but admits, "It's an added worry." She has witnessed some unease among her grandchildren, too. "They aren't as affectionate toward their youngest aunt and even her son, their littlest cousin."

Elena wishes she'd have gotten help sooner but recognizes her limitations. "I wasn't thinking clearly. After such a shock, problems like mine are not as unusual as people might think." She reminds herself that she can't control the other relationships any more than she could control her irrational fears. "I have to let go," she says. "My daughters' journeys are not mine to steer."

Now let's turn to Dodi, who was always close to her only child. When her son grew up and moved out, she believed she would remain part of his everyday life. "He had other ideas," says Dodi, laughing. "I had to stop mothering him so much and let him grow up."

He still came to his parents over bigger things. "Like what sort of mortgage to get or whether we thought he should take a pay cut to accept a position at another firm," she says. "He valued our opinions and advice. We have more life experience, and he recognized that."

The trouble started when Dodi's son eloped. When Dodi and her husband, Fred, were introduced to his bride, they learned he had met her on a company trip. He had maintained a long-distance relationship with her for less than a year, and then suddenly married her.

The pretty, quiet girl made demands on their son. She wanted him to buy a bigger home and have a baby. "Our son had a new job at a company he hadn't been happy with and had planned to move on from," Dodi says. "He would call me and complain about his wife on his way to work." At first, Dodi consulted with her husband, Fred, who said the young couple needed to make their own decisions. Dodi thought so, too, but still listened to her son's complaints. She just didn't share them with Fred anymore.

Dodi felt protective of her son and even admits to feeling a little "puffed up" about the confidences he shared. That is, until knowing so much about his personal life and marital relationship backfired. "He'd tell me his wife was mad at him because he wouldn't agree to some extravagance, and then they'd drop by a few days later, and he'd have given in to her. That upset me."

On one such occasion, the younger couple arrived to show off the wife's new car—which Dodi's son had called her to complain about the week before. Dodi had agreed when he said the payment was too high, and that he had told his wife they needed to wait. When they showed up in the shiny new crossover, Dodi remained silent but says, "Tensions ran high." When the couple left, she told Fred their son had been against getting the car. She told her husband about all the other phone calls, too.

"I'll never forget the look on his face," Dodi says. "He was disgusted. With me and with our son. He said our son shouldn't be confiding any of his misgivings with his wife to his mother. Fred asked me how I would have felt if he'd done that to me." With a small laugh, Dodi says, "I would have been miffed."

Fred reminded Dodi that when they had married, he had bridged the gap between her and his mother. "His mom and I were total opposites," Dodi says. "Fred found things to draw us together because we were both important to him."

A few days after the new car visit, Fred set up a lunch meeting for himself and his son. He planned to give some fatherly advice. Dodi says, "He came home from the restaurant feeling good about their talk, but then we received an e-mail from our son. He asked for some space."

For several years, their son and his wife refused all contact. "I sent birthday and holiday cards at first," says Dodi. "When we found out they had a baby girl, we even called. They never replied or answered. Other than sneaking a peek of the baby on Instagram now and again, we got on with our lives. We had no choice."

When their granddaughter was turning four, their son called his father and apologized. He wanted to reconcile. Fred says, "I met him without Dodi at first. I reiterated what I'd told him before about mothers and their daughters-in-law and laid out some rules about him not hurting his mom again—*or his wife*. And I asked if his wife was on board with the reconciliation." Their son assured his father that she was, and the two men worked to bring the family together.

"It was awkward," says Dodi. "But my son really stepped up. It had been wrong of him to confide in me about her, but I should have corrected him. He needed to talk directly to his wife, or maybe a more neutral person, or a marriage counselor." Of the reconciliation, Dodi says, "We all wanted to try. Our son worked hard to let me see his wife's good qualities. And she is good. I love her."

Dodi's husband was led by common sense but research backs what he already knew. In most cultures today, in-law relationships are not voluntary. When a son or daughter chooses a mate, the new spouse is introduced to the parents, who may not have otherwise ever met or interacted with the spouse. The adult child, then, takes on the role of a linchpin, connecting the people s/he loves. When a mother feels her son is happy in his marriage, she can more easily develop positive feelings about his spouse. She is then more motivated to nurture her own relationship with her daughter-in-law.[2] All of this likely holds true for daughters playing a linchpin role, and of parents forming bonds with their sons-in-law.

By sharing his frustrations about his wife, Dodi's son triangulated the relationship, creating ill-will between his wife and his mother. If your son or daughter has turned to you for advice in the past, listening may have come naturally. However, when airing gripes, the good parts of the marriage aren't shared. Because you love your son or daughter so much, you might take his or her side. It never ends well. If the spouse finds out the intimate details of their arguments were shared with a mom or dad, they'll be angry, embarrassed, or both. If the spouse felt insecure or wasn't sure you liked them before, they'll be even more uncertain.

If you are currently a son or daughter's confidante about a spouse, first, recognize it's a no-win situation. You'll need to delicately put an end to the unhealthy dynamic. Accept some responsibility by saying that you should have halted the confidences to begin with. Explain that the in-law relationship was new to you. It's okay to admit that, in learning to navigate your new role, you made mistakes or even failed.

Dodi reports that after two years, the situation has gone from awkward to much more natural and loving. "I immediately apologized to my daughter-in-law," says Dodi. "I assured her I wanted the best for her and my son, and that I was eager to get to know her and my little granddaughter better, but also my son . . . as the grown up, married man that he was."

If a dynamic such as this has poisoned relationships and added conflict, it's never too late to recognize fault, admit it, and apologize. There's no guarantee the estrangement will end, but clarity is always useful, even if only applied to future situations.

Let's look at a couple of more examples of needed change as it relates to estrangement and reconciliation. Once, a woman joined the peer support forum at RejectedParents.NET to express her anguish. The woman said that her daughter-in-law didn't want her present in the delivery room when she gave birth. This mother railed on about this being her first grandchild, insisting it was her "right" to see the infant as it entered the world.

I immediately disagreed with this woman, who was not yet estranged, but feared she would be soon. Apparently, her daughter-in-law wanted her own mother present, but not her husband's. I understood—and was glad when so many in the forum agreed. We recommended she apologize and make things right while she still could.

I felt likewise when a mother commented that she was the "queen" of her family and believed it was her right to rule the roost—even under her daughter-in-law's roof. I don't know where in the world she was writing from. Perhaps there was a cultural clash between old tradition and new ways of life. I don't know the whole story. Regardless, to maintain peace, mutual respect is required, and I gently told her so.

The queen comment reminds me of an essay in Glennon Doyle's book, *Carry On, Warrior*. Doyle had read Maya Angelou's book, *Letter to My Daughter*, in which Angelou spoke of visiting Senegal. She had purposely walked across a beautiful, expensive rug that other guests were avoiding. She felt proud at her boldness and at helping others see that even the most beautiful rugs were for walking on. Then the rug was removed, and another one laid out and spread with dishes and steaming food. When the hostess asked her guests to sit around the rug, Angelou understood why no one else had stepped on it. In this unfamiliar culture, she had tread on her hostess' tablecloth!

Doyle writes, "Maya Angelou shined a light into the dark part of my heart where I keep my relationship with my mother-in-law." Doyle admits that when she first married, she viewed her in-laws as an unfamiliar culture. She was suspicious, took offense, found fault, offered advice, and tried to change them. Doyle says, "I dragged my dirty shoes all over my mother-in-law's tablecloth. The one she'd spent decades carefully weaving."

Doyle learned that her mother-in-law had spent a lifetime creating a masterpiece in how she lived and raised a family, and then, when her son married, she gave a piece of it away. As Doyle's mother-in-law wisely did, we can let our new daughters- or sons-in-law weave their own homespun masterpieces. We can let them learn their own mistakes without correcting them. We don't have to be the "queen" (or king) of another person's household or tread on the new tapestry they're working to create. In fact, letting go can be quite freeing.

I don't know how things turned out for the woman who insisted on watching her grandchild's birth or the one who thought she should be the queen. Neither woman wrote in again. I hope they recognized their need to change, and by doing so, avoided the estrangements they feared.

Creating Boundaries

Boundaries are needed for various reasons: to protect finances, your peace of mind, or your health. Boundaries might improve confidence and provide an element of safety or even control. Rusty's son has bipolar disorder and came to live with him. Rusty imposed boundaries to feel confident that his son was continuing his treatment and that Rusty had the knowledge to help him in case of an emergency. Rusty also wanted basic respect, as defined by him, with regard to his son's use of his home and their interactions.

With your estranged or reconciled child, or in other relationships, consider the reason(s) you feel you need a boundary. As an example, let's meet Harold. His recently reconciled son, Jay, once stole Harold's passwords and tried to transfer money from Harold's bank account to his. But the bank required a verification. A notice went to Harold's cell phone. When Harold mentioned the oddity, his son became incensed. Angry that Harold was "selfish," he revealed the truth of what he'd done. Harold changed passwords and alerted the bank. He says, "I love Jay, but he won't ever get access to my sensitive information." Harold's need to protect his finances, and his distrust based on history, motivated his boundaries.

Now it's your turn. Write out what motivates your need for a boundary, whether financial or otherwise, including any history to your reasoning. Be as thorough as feels natural or necessary.

_____

_____

_____

_____

_____

_____

_____

Once you have determined your motivations, you'll need to create the boundary. The boundary may require action on your part. Harold locks his office door when his son visits, keeping his computer and personal documents safe. He protects his cell phone with a personal swipe pattern and shields that from his son's view. Recently, Harold enrolled in a fraud protection plan that will alert him to any "funny business."

Reflect on your motivations and come up with one or more boundaries. Also consider how you will enforce them. Harold has told his son that if he were ever to violate his privacy again, the relationship would be over. It's a clear boundary, and one that Jay knows his father will enforce. What is your boundary?

_____

_____

_____

_____

_____

_____

_____

_____

_____

You'll need to address any worries that could become obstacles to you setting boundaries. These might be emotional, such as worry that enforcing a boundary will be viewed as proof that you don't trust or love the affected person(s). You might be concerned that other people will negatively judge you, or that something bad will happen and you'll feel guilty later. Perhaps, because of past relational experiences, you don't fully trust your own judgment and obsess that a boundary you impose will cause a missed opportunity you will later regret.

What are your fears or other feelings about creating and enforcing your boundary? It helps to have a trusted friend, counselor, or family member to help you work through your thoughts. Pia worried her daughter's behavior was ultimately her fault. If that were true, then enforcing a boundary would hurt her daughter more than she already had. Pia's parents helped her weigh reality against her irrational guilt, which stemmed from her daughter's accusations and blame.

You can also counsel yourself. In "Who's in Your Corner?" (Chapter Three), you listed persons you admire for their wisdom. What do you imagine these ideal mentors would say to help?

_____

_____

_____

_____

_____

_____

Harold told his son about the boundary. Whether you need to tell another person depends on your circumstances and who's involved. Boundaries don't always involve another person's behavior. Sometimes, it is your own behavior or thinking you must halt.

For a self-imposed boundary, consider how you will enforce it. Maybe you have come to recognize that looking at social media photos only stimulates rumination and sadness. You've created a boundary around that and have decided you will no longer look. What will you do when the urge hits? Devise a plan for accountability and to distract yourself. Reach out to someone who will remind you of the self-inflicted pain that looking will cause. Or plan an activity to occupy your mind.

Plan around your needs, too. If you look at social media on your cell phone when you lie down each night, you could take the apps off your phone. Change your habits by putting your cell phone in another room. Turn off notifications for social media. You can leave the ringer on high if you need to, to feel secure about important phone calls. Or even silence your phone but program breakthrough rings for calls from certain people.

If your boundaries involve your thoughts, make a practice of noticing them and then doing something to dispel them. Try carrying a small notebook. Jot down your thoughts and then move on. You could devise a plan whereby you only allow thoughts about the person/subject for a few minutes after a healthy breakfast or another time that makes sense.

Another example of a self-imposed boundary is how much you'll reveal or talk about a particular subject to another person. Having a boundary in place, with a plan to enforce it, limits conversations involving awkward questions or a compulsion to share. For help with answers that work as boundaries, consult the "Talking Tips" from Chapter One and the "Ready Answers" in *Done With The Crying*.

What self-imposed boundaries are important to you? Why?
How will you shift behavior and devise plans to change?

_____

_____

_____

_____

_____

_____

_____

_____

_____

_____

Our lives are filled with boundaries we may not consciously consider. Walls and curtains act as borders to deter invasions of privacy. Picture frames are stabilizing structures—boundaries that hold precious photographic memories or artwork. Fences define personal space and deter unwanted visitors. In relationships and in ourselves, boundaries provide limitations and stability that support well-being.

CHAPTER NINE

Potpourri

"The beauty is that through disappointment you can gain clarity, and with clarity comes true conviction and originality."
—CONAN O'BRIEN

After talking with thousands of parents, the siblings of those who estrange, and even some adult children who opted out of family, not much surprises me. At times, I'm still moved to tears by the anguish in parents' voices as they share their suffering. *Always*, I am listening for cues about where I might be able to help. That's why this chapter, with its potpourri mix of subjects, is included.

Even if the covered subjects don't seem pertinent to you now, I encourage you to read these pages. Situations are unique, yet through others' experiences, you will learn information to apply in your own life. Let these wise parents who, among other things, have entered into business with a child, regret decisions made under duress, or have hung on far too long, help you avoid potential pitfalls and protect your future.

Taking Care of Family Business

Entrepreneurial parents often hire their children and train them from the ground up. They derive satisfaction from passing along knowledge, opportunity, and a good work ethic—often believing their dream will live on and support their descendants long after they are gone. As their children mature and take on more responsibility, parents feel pride and have a sense of security. Who better to trust with their hard-earned success than a child?

That's how it was for Rebecca and her husband Doug. After having a daughter and two sons, Doug and Rebecca built a thriving home remodeling business. Rebecca managed the office. During their lucrative years, Rebecca and Doug lived frugally and invested in rental houses. Their daughter, Cecilia, completed an AA degree but wasn't sure which career direction to take. At that time, Rebecca trained Cecilia to keep the company's books. With the parents' backing, Cecilia's brothers opened a successful gym.

Within two years, Doug and Rebecca closed their remodeling business and began buying fixer-uppers. Cecilia often offered design input, and the three of them worked to renovate and flip several houses for a profit. Cecilia encouraged her folks to think bigger, and in 2007, with equity from their existing rentals and recent sales, they closed on two large apartment complexes. They also bought their first commercial property—a quaint tourist spot with a boardwalk, shops, and restaurants—all of which had fallen into disrepair.

When the economy crashed in 2008, Cecilia was still doing the books. With their investments heavily encumbered and the apartment complexes requiring huge amounts of work and money to bring them up to date and solvent, Rebecca and Doug struggled to pay their mortgages. They strategized, and then put their real estate holdings into Cecilia's name. They believed they could stay afloat by leveraging her clean credit slate to finance the work to the apartments and the commercial site. "We trusted her completely," says Rebecca. "And as time went on, she knew our work inside and out. It all made perfect sense. She was building great credit, too, which would help her later. We made Cecilia a partner in our changing business. That was fair. We all worked hard."

The trouble began when their sons befriended a man they hired to work as a personal trainer at their gym. He took a liking to Cecilia, and the two became an item. He quit working for the brothers, and he and Cecilia moved into their own place together. The family saw less of their daughter, but Rebecca says, "We weren't worried. Couples want their own space, and Cecilia could easily keep the books from her house."

As the business moved forward, they sold all but one rental and focused on completing the apartment complexes and rehabilitating the commercial property. Cecilia came up with the idea of using it, with its lovely garden and seasonal creek, for events. The idea was a good one—and immediately lucrative. Everything seemed fine.

Then, Cecilia's youngest brother and his bride-to-be began planning their wedding for the site, and the situation got ugly. Cecilia's boyfriend could be brooding and even rude. One day, the family met at the site, and he became angry for some imagined slight. He threw the sample wedding invitations into the creek and, as those floated away, he stormed off. Cecilia followed him and the couple left. Later, Rebecca and Doug discovered their car had been keyed, but they couldn't be sure who had done that.

"Cecilia's boyfriend seemed over the edge," says Rebecca. "A few months later, she told us she was going to marry him. We reasoned with her to wait, but they eloped not long after."

Cecilia's relationship with the family continued to deteriorate. She said she didn't want to work with her parents anymore. Shocked, they nevertheless agreed to find a way to split the business amicably. They wanted the best for their daughter, and she had been a hard worker. When they asked to see the books, though, Cecilia refused.

For several weeks, she didn't speak to them. Then one day she telephoned in a rage. "She called us lunatics and abusers," says Rebecca. "We just listened. At that point, we were afraid. She was acting crazy and had control of our properties. She could throw us out of our home."

The parents consulted with an attorney and weighed their options. They couldn't imagine testifying against their own daughter, which meant that a lawsuit was out. There would be no guarantees with that anyway.

"So, we were at the mercy of her whims," Rebecca says. She describes herself as an "emotional basket case" during that time and says that she kept thinking if she could just talk to Cecilia, she might come to her senses. But Cecilia wouldn't communicate. Doug was still working on getting the apartment complexes finished, so he did talk to their daughter now and again, but it was strictly business.

Eventually, as the complexes reached completion, Cecilia told them they could keep their own home, a multifamily property where they still lived with her brothers, and she would keep the commercial property, the apartment complexes, and the remaining rental. By then, they had already all been in her name for several years. During that time, unbeknownst to her parents, Cecilia had taken out more loans against the properties and built up her own portfolio. "We never saw the books," says Rebecca. "She had control, and we were afraid. It was extortion. Our daughter extorted us and stole her brothers' inheritance."

In the end, Cecilia and her attorney sent her parents a long letter. They would receive their home free of debt, but with conditions. Doug, Rebecca, and Cecilia's brothers had to relinquish all rights to any of the other properties and agree not to sue her. The deal wasn't equitable, but Rebecca and Doug were exhausted. They wanted the nightmare over.

Another parent, Blythe, who owns a farm with a restaurant and event venue, can relate. "When you're in business with an estranged child, you constantly relive the pain."

From the beginning, Blythe and her husband Bill (her son's stepfather), thought they were doing what was right. They consulted an attorney to incorporate their farm business, and he advised them to give Blythe's son, Luke, 25 percent of the business. This included a home on adjacent, leased property. Luke was twenty-six, single, and learning the business. "It all made sense," says Blythe.

Within a few years, Blythe hired a young woman to work in their farm's restaurant. She was divorced and raising a baby girl on her own. "Tansy immediately had her sights on Luke," says Blythe. "They soon became a couple."

When Luke and Tansy announced their engagement, Bill and Blythe helped Luke buy her a nice diamond. They also paid for the wedding. Tansy's parents and brother traveled from the opposite coast to attend, and Blythe did her best to connect. "That wasn't easy," says Blythe. "They stood out in the parking lot getting stoned and kept to themselves throughout."

After the wedding, Blythe and Bill enjoyed keeping Tansy's little girl while the honeymooners spent a week away. When Luke and Tansy returned, they all worked and socialized as usual. They expanded the farm's acreage, crops, and product line. Blythe was excited about the expansions her son was helping with. The family and its business were growing—literally. She was happy her son was settled with a wonderful wife.

Within a few months, though, Blythe's feelings began to change. "You know how you can think you know someone, and then one day, the veil comes down and it's like there is another person?" asks Blythe. "After dinner one night, that's what happened. Tansy remarked about how everything of ours would be left to Luke one day." Blythe explained to her that he wasn't their only heir. His older sisters would also inherit. "Tansy said to me, 'You can't do that.' Her face and voice changed. I saw someone ugly come out, and I cannot tell you the depth of fear in the pit of my stomach at that moment. I saw this other person, and it terrified me."

Not long after, at an event hosted in the farm's restaurant, Tansy shared a table with Blythe and some others. Over wine, she talked about her childhood and said that she had been molested as a little girl and had never gotten over that.

Blythe felt for Tansy. Having worked as a social worker for many years, Blythe knew the devastation caused by childhood sexual abuse. "When the pain is not resolved somehow, these women seem to have a black hole of emptiness inside them," she says. As the conversation moved forward, and Tansy talked about her ex-husband, her words were like a revelation to Blythe. "She said her ex had told a family member that no matter what he'd done during their marriage, it was never enough. And I thought, *Oh no, my son will be trapped trying to fill her emptiness for the rest of his life.*"

After that night, Tansy avoided Blythe. "I think she regretted letting those details slip," Blythe explains.

Tansy also began keeping her little girl away from Blythe and Bill. When she became pregnant, she quit working at the restaurant. Luke associated with his parents only at work. The young couple's home was within eyeshot of Blythe and Bill's residence. "We saw each other, but Tansy would act coolly superior," says Blythe. "At work, Luke began to criticize me. He'd point his finger at me and say no one that worked for us really liked me. It was a projection. It was Tansy that no one really liked. By then, everyone had seen the real Tansy."

When the baby was born, Blythe tried to visit. "She wouldn't let me," Blythe says. "And my son would scream at me and say that we had never been close."

With all the tension and her son undermining her at work, Blythe was in shock. She began staying away from the farm operations as much as she could and still get things done. "I kept thinking Luke would come around," she says. "But he didn't, and I would see him and Tansy outdoors with the children. It was painful to be so close-by."

When Luke said he wanted Blythe and Bill to sell the business so that he could cash in on his shares, Blythe was reluctant to call an attorney, but says, "We had no other recourse."

Upon reflection, Blythe says her son's turnabout reminds her of abusive men who turn on the women they once loved. Part of her research during her years as a social worker included interviewing men who had killed their spouses. "When she starts pulling away, as often happens, he starts looking at her like an enemy," says Blythe. "All the wonderful things about her become negative. By the time he kills her, she *is* the enemy." Blythe speculates that, with Tansy in his ear, Luke may have come to believe his mother and stepfather owed him everything. Not being their sole heir may have triggered the "pulling away" response Blythe describes from her research.

Luke later told them they wouldn't have to sell if they would buy his shares. Blythe and Bill took their attorney's advice and told Luke no. Since Luke fulfilled a business role, they agreed he would stay on for a year. He quit working soon after anyway, consulted his own attorney, and said they'd fired him.

The farm continued to pay Luke for the agreed-upon year which, as of this writing, is about to expire. They have no legal obligation to buy his shares out, and the farm's lease for the property his home sits on is nearly up. The farm will not renew it. "I think once that happens, the trouble will really begin," says Blythe. "But it isn't the business piece that's the most difficult to deal with. It's the emotional side."

For years now, Blythe watched her son do what she calls "othering" of her and her husband. By making his mother and stepfather into something they're not, Luke can justify his actions. She still has a hard time believing that the man who is now well into his thirties is the same boy she raised and was always close to but says, "I'm getting stronger. I think my son deserves the life that he decides to have. I am sorry we are not included in that life."

After reading these stories, do you believe these mothers bear some responsibility for their adult children's bad behavior? Like most parents, Blythe and Rebecca have reflected upon this question. Both have ideas about how they may have contributed to the problem, or what they could have done better. See what you think.

Rebecca regrets letting Cecilia get away with what she calls a "tone" when she'd say something about her father. "Doug can be bossy if he decides something," says Rebecca. "He's almost always right, but I'd get annoyed with Doug sometimes, too. So, if Cecilia came to me with a complaint, I might kind of side with her. I should have stuck up for Doug. I should have said, 'How dare you put your father down.' Parents, as much as they can, should stay united."

I agree with Rebecca and wrote at length about the concept of a united front in *Done With The Crying*. However, Rebecca never thought the daughter she so trusted would commit such offenses. At the time, she thought she was keeping the peace. Who's to say whether Cecilia might have done what she did anyway?

Blythe has come to different conclusions, mostly to do with her divorce from her three children's father. She wishes she would have gotten legal advice as soon as things began to sour with her son. She explains: "I divorced Luke's father when he was young, and I felt guilty. I understand now that this is the reason I gave and gave and gave. Trying to make up for any pain I had caused Luke. Handing him a life—our life—as penance."

Do these regrets excuse their children's abhorrent treatment of them? *No*. Blythe puts it like this: "I bear some responsibility for Luke's failures, but that responsibility isn't mine alone." Luke, Cecilia, and all adult children who, alone or with a scheming partner, purposely hurt the parents who loved and cared for them, are responsible for their own actions.

Rebecca says that even now, if Cecilia came to her and was genuinely sorry, she would take her back. She referred to a book she often read with her children when they were young: *The Giving Tree* by Shel Silverstein. In the book, the tree loves a little boy so much that she gives of herself to make him happy and, in giving to him, is happy herself. He eats her apples, swings from her limbs, and slides down her trunk. As the boy grows, he forgets about her, but later returns wanting more and more. Her apples to sell for money, her branches to build a house and a boat, and so on. The tree keeps giving, limb-by-limb, until she has nothing left. Rebecca explains, "If Cecilia came to me and said, 'I love you.' If she showed me some respect as her mother and took some responsibility, I would take her back. Even if I'm an old, cut-up tree stump."

Blythe has another view. She is committed to protecting her husband. "From my son and daughter-in-law's greed," she explains. "The son I knew is gone and will not be resurrected. Hope is deadly and so I hope no more. I have learned to say no."

Tips from the Family Business Trenches

When contemplating business with a son or daughter, lovey-dovey feelings and idealistic notions can cloud good judgment. In a business venture with *any* child, be sensible. Wise thinking, measured actions, and resourceful techniques pay off.

Spell Things Out. Without putting the details in writing, family members may not be on the same page. Are in-laws allowed to work for the company? Will a son or daughter *automatically* be the successor CEO? Will innovations (and their profits) created by a second-generation family member belong to the company? Family businesses can have complexities that others do not, and owners too often rely on trust. *Don't!*

When Rebecca and Doug handed control to their daughter, they thought it was temporary and believed Cecilia's intentions matched theirs: to save the business during the failing economy, and then continue forward for the good of the whole family. They skipped the crucial step of hiring an attorney to spell out details, execute written agreements, and protect their assets. With the economy failing and their finances in shambles, they saved a few thousand dollars at the time but paid dearly in the long run.

If you're still in business with an estranged son or daughter, you'll need to separate your fears, longing, and hope from your business decisions. Try thinking of your child as a non-family employee. Then put on your business cap and write out any gaps that require filling or change. Consult with a legal professional. You may still be able to protect yourself.

Don't Avoid Issues. When adult children grow horns and turn on parents, retreating is a natural response. Blythe avoided her son and his tirades by staying out of day-to-day farm management. When seeing his wife and her grandchildren made living so close a heartache, she even moved out of her home and stayed away full time for a while.

It's hard to see the people you love when they're hell-bent on hurting you. The trouble is, running away doesn't fix anything. Your inaction or absence provides free reign for a conniver to wreak more havoc. If you feel you must avoid the issue for your own well-being, at least make the time away productive. Rest up a little, then flex your emotional muscles (Chapter Five), gain a clearer perspective of what must be done, and return stronger and with a plan. When better rested, you can more easily implement sound business strategies.

Blythe says she might have given up fighting completely if she hadn't shifted her perspective to focus on what was most important to her. Her number one goal was to protect her husband. That meant protecting their investment in the farm.

Don't Let Your Fears or Hopes Get the Best of You. Sometimes, parents think if they take an action their adult child won't like, then their offspring will hate them even more. It's a shock to witness your own child's conniving and abuse, but it's a mistake for parents to believe that if they just maintain kindness and continue to love, that their child will snap out of whatever phase they've entered and set things right again. While parents hang back and hope, a child who has the company keys may be changing the locks and the passwords. While stalled in fear or shock, parents' business interests can suffer.

If your son or daughter has worked to undermine you or is laying claim to credit or ownership that oversteps their history, position, or reality, you may be underestimating the rigor with which they'll continue to try. You can't afford to base your business decisions on fear or hope. Get legal assistance and fully disclose the dynamics of the situation. Attorneys hear it all. Find a competent one, well-versed in your area of business, and get help now.

Consider Any Legal Advice Carefully. Cautiously weigh the merit of any guidance. Attorneys have legal expertise, but you know your situation better than anyone. It's okay to think through all possible scenarios for potential solutions. Hypothetical thinking aims to head trouble off at the pass. You're paying for a service. Use it fully.

A second opinion may be wise. After all the trouble with her son, Blythe consulted a new attorney who faulted the previous one's advice. Giving her son so much interest had been a mistake. A second opinion back then might have steered Blythe toward a more sensible plan.

Make Decisions You Can Feel Good About Later. Rebecca couldn't have lived with herself if she'd taken Cecilia to court. She and Doug were willing to lose almost everything to avoid suing their own daughter. Blythe could never have forgiven herself if she didn't protect all her husband's hard work. As a loving stepfather, he'd done everything for her children. She couldn't let Luke deal a fatal wound to the business and her husband's retirement.

Those overarching feelings get at individual integrity and a sense of right and wrong. What thoughts come to mind when you contemplate your family business and consider how a child might sabotage your prosperity? Wisdom can often be defined by decisions you can feel good about later.

Here's another example of a family business dissolution due to estrangement. Bo, whose oldest son had worked hard for the family's distribution company, was heartbroken over the rift that began when his son married. After two years of discord, he could no longer work with his son, but still wanted to honor his contributions. Bo also intended to preserve the family business, which he had started decades ago with his own father, and to protect his assets not only for himself and his wife, but for the benefit of their daughter and her children who remained close to them.

With legal help, Bo presented a plan to split accounts, giving to his son those he had worked hard to procure. This included a large refrigeration account that had increased their profits by 30 percent. Bo considered asking for reimbursement of the company funds spent to procure the buildings and equipment in another city that the account had required. Eager to have the dissolution complete, he decided it was better for his company to absorb the loss. The son protested but eventually took the deal his father felt was generous but also fair, and that protected his whole family—even his wayward son.

Decide Ahead. If you're dissolving business ties with an adult child, make some decisions in advance. Consider ahead how far you will bend. The size or type of business may dictate your decisions. Also, consider what scenarios might take place, and plan a course of action for possible arguments.

Bo and his attorney decided up front how much more to offer if the son put up a fight. With the whole family's well-being in mind, Bo was prepared to give two additional specific accounts, but no more beyond those. He had also devised a strategy wherein he wouldn't immediately offer those if his son balked at the original proposal. His willingness to suffer additional discord, legal threats in front of employees, and embarrassment at his place of business paid off. When Bo didn't waver, his son agreed to the original deal.

Final Passage

Having seen the stress, sadness, and even bullying that can occur when a family member's life is ending or over, I feel strongly that planning for death is each person's duty. Especially when a child is estranged, there's more to do than assigning who gets what. You must choose your advocates carefully so that your wishes will be honored before and after your death. If you haven't already done so, consult the exhaustive section on end-of-life choices in *Done With The Crying* (or the workbook) and get your affairs in order. Here, we'll hear from two mothers of estranged adults and learn from their experiences.

You'll remember Mei, whose husband, Xudong, is ten years her senior. In their culture, one's memorial is of grave importance. Mei has accepted that her older husband will likely be the first of them to die. She has worried that her estranged son will not honor his father or will make some embarrassing scene at the funeral. "Xudong wants a traditional memorial, and he deserves one," she says.

For many couples, discussing the potential problems and solutions is the best course of action. Making peace with an adult child's estrangement can influence how you design your own memorial. Maybe a smaller send-off or even none at all is preferred. Or maybe you will want your spouse to do what works best for him or her since you'll be deceased anyway.

For Mei, consulting a trusted pastor helped put her mind at ease. He assured her that he would talk to the son and daughter-in-law and make certain they would not dishonor Xudong. "I trust the pastor, and I trust God," says Mei.

Regarding her own passing, Mei says she has already arranged for her cremation "in a very private way." There will be no services. "For my few caring friends and relatives, I prefer to say goodbye to them one-by-one in a dedicated way before I enter the very last stage of life in a lonely deathbed." Mei is wise to contemplate these choices early. Making decisions under duress can result in regrets—as mother of one son, Krystyna, knows all too well.

Krystyna was diagnosed with stage four cancer when she first called an attorney to draw up a will. The doctors had told Krystyna she would not live longer than a few more months. Wanting to settle her estate, Krystyna hastily called an attorney from local listings in her area, and the woman agreed to meet in Krystyna's home.

Krystyna's son, Donato, who has hurt her physically on occasion, is routinely abusive verbally and emotionally, and has been episodically estranged over the last two decades, agreed to attend the meeting. Physically weak and in a haze from her most recent hospital stay, Krystyna settled onto the sofa with a blanket when the attorney, an attractive woman in her thirties, arrived. The attorney took an immediate liking to Donato, who has always been a charmer.

"She barely talked to me," says Krystyna, who watched as the attorney flirted with Donato. After finding out he was her only son, the attorney advised Krystyna to make things easy for him. "She talked me into a life estate deed and drew up the paperwork," says Krystyna. The result is a legal arrangement whereby Krystyna will live in the home until her death, at which time the home passes directly to her son. There is no need for probate.

Afterward, with her head clear and her strength returning, Krystyna began to question the decision. When she phoned the attorney to ask for more details, she was put off and told to trust the woman's expertise. "I should have fought it then," says Krystyna. "But it's hard when you're old and sick. I let it go because I thought I was dying so soon."

Four and a half years later, Krystyna is alive and well. "I'd like to sell this place and move somewhere else, a little closer and more walkable," she says. "But I can't." The life estate deed ties her hands. She has consulted with other attorneys and has been told the same thing: Without her son's written agreement, she can't sell. Her son won't reply to her requests. Even if he agreed to a sale, the life estate deed means that her son would get the bulk of the proceeds, leaving Krystyna with fewer resources to acquire another home.

Krystyna's situation underlines the importance of planning for our eventual deaths while we're able. Don't postpone making decisions. Reflect carefully, consider your situation from all angles, and put things in motion that serve your best interests now and in the future.

Krystyna hopes that sharing her experience will prevent other parents from getting into a legally binding agreement that negatively affects them. Consider any advice you receive carefully and do not be rushed.

Krystyna can't do anything about her son inheriting her home, but says, "He won't get anything else." She has begun sorting through her custom jewelry collection, original artwork, and other valuable heirlooms, and matching each item to special people in her life. Taking charge in this way has been empowering and brought her great joy. Clearing space is also practical. Reducing material things creates more space to safely move around, lowering fall risk.

Krystyna is using her money up, too, but not with a vindictive attitude. "I've become a mother again," she says with a laugh, referring to an orphaned baby elephant she "adopted" through an animal care organization. Helping to fund the little elephant's care makes her happy and also brought back good memories. At a time in the early 1970s, when New York City was at a low point due to various problems, a gorilla named Pattycake was born at the Central Park Zoo. The whole city had waited in eager anticipation of the birth and later celebrated the baby gorilla as she grew. At a time when things seemed bleak, focusing on Pattycake distracted New Yorkers from their problems. Likewise, by savoring her memories of that era and of visiting the zoo to see the new addition, Krystyna took her mind off her present circumstances and relived the fun. We can all learn from Krystyna's example of putting our energy toward what's positive.

Krystyna has also made sure that her son will not be called as her default next-of-kin should she become unable to make decisions for herself. We all have the right to choose someone to serve in that capacity. It was Krystyna's medical doctor who helped her with the decision. In fact, I am hearing more and more frequently from people whose medical doctors understand the implications of estrangement and its effects. Often, they are the trusted professionals who offer empathy and sensible advice that parents let go of what they can't control (their adult children) and take action for their own well-being.

Resources for Legal Help

Try your current or past employer for legal help programs through trade unions or as part of pension programs. Also, professional organizations often provide legal assistance for dues-paying members. Do an Internet search for "free legal help" or "legal help for senior citizens" in your area. Or try one of the listings that follow.

In the U.S.

- Eldercare Locator: www.eldercare.acl.gov
  Input your zip code to access your local Area Agency on Aging as well as legal and other resources specifically for senior citizens.

- Law Help.org: www.lawhelp.org
  Helps locate free local legal services as well as provides basic information, forms, etc.

- Legal Hotlines.org: www.legalhotlines.org
  Includes interactive U.S. map to locate hotlines in your area. Hotlines can provide some basic information as well as help individuals locate more comprehensive assistance.

- The American Bar Association: www.americanbar.org
  Can provide contact information for some pro bono and specialized firms.

In the U.K.

- Citizens Advice: https://www.citizensadvice.org.uk/
  Offers lookup for local advice via postcode or town.

- AgeUK Advice line: https://www.ageuk.org.uk/services/age-uk-advice-line/
  Help to locate local legal (and other) assistance.

- The Law Society: www.lawsociety.org.uk
  Can provide contact info, including some low-cost or pro bono workers.

In Canada

- The Canadian Bar Association: https://www.cba.org/
  Includes a pro bono section offering professionals via smaller locations within Canada.

- Clicklaw: https://www.clicklaw.bc.ca/
  Extensive information organized via subject as well as low-cost help.

Are You An "Elder Orphan"?

A scene in the 1985 movie, *The Breakfast Club*, shows the disgruntled teacher who's in charge of the detention students as he shares a beer with the school janitor. The teacher tells the janitor the thought that keeps him up at night is that "these kids" will be the ones taking care of him when he's old. The sharp-witted janitor gives this piece of advice: "I wouldn't count on it."

At a time when the senior citizen population is rapidly increasing, heeding the janitor's advice is wise. Whether you're barely eligible for the discount at the local café or decades beyond, start considering your future now, while you can have some say in it.

The term "elder orphan" is used to describe the growing number of older adults living alone without immediate family or a supportive network. Are you an elder orphan? For obvious reasons, parents of estranged adult children are particularly vulnerable. Even those who are in committed relationships must face the finality of one partner leaving the other behind in death.

Most of the people interviewed for a recent study found the term a practical one.[1] Recognizing reality can be scary, but planning helps.

Aging at home is not a new concept, but how "home" is defined is open to interpretation. As people grow older, and possibly face more physical restrictions, their home can represent safety and independence. Or, the home's location or design could confine and constrain.[2] Too many steps, uneven grounds, narrow hallways, weather that requires upkeep such as snowplowing or gutter clearing, the financial aspect of such upkeep, or isolated areas far from services are a few examples. A once loved place that has become burdensome, isolating, or unsafe is no longer homey.

Most of us remember the television show *The Golden Girls*, which featured three women over fifty, along with the octogenarian mother of one of them, living together, sharing chores and expenses. As roommates, they also became a supportive surrogate family to one another. You may not relish the idea of such close-knit living but at some point, most of us will need help, so we may as well be realistic, thus empowered.

The show, which ran from 1985–1992, was ahead of the times. In the early 2000s, people began to note a coming unprecedented demographic shift that's in full swing now and is known as the "silver tsunami." Groups brainstormed ideas to improve the aging experience and help people grow old in their communities, with like-minded support, as an alternative to ageing in place alone.[3]

Today, co-housing doesn't always mean renting rooms in a large home split with other people. Tiny house communities on shared land are springing up in diverse locales and allow for independence yet foster social connection. Or, there are larger elder co-housing communities, with individual residences centered around a community building for socializing and group activities. Elder communities are becoming more creative and intentional. Some feature skill sharing so residents who know how to grow food, work on cars, or have some other practical talent, can barter with others for the betterment of all.

If we're willing to do research, network, pool resources, and are open to change, we can design new ways of living that benefit us as we age. Be realistic, make sensible decisions, and begin putting them into practice while you can. Like anything worth doing, embracing new concepts of home may require a shift in ideals and include a willingness to adapt. That may mean giving up ideals or expectations but to stay happy, optimistic, and engaged requires mental and emotional flexibility. Besides, stepping out of our comfort zones can be good for us.

Resources for Elders, Whether Orphans or Not
Co-housing

- The Senior Co-housing Handbook: A Community Approach to Independent Living (2d. ed.) by Charles Durrett. Advice for seniors to custom build their own neighborhoods for independence, safety, and social connection.

- *Choose Your Place: Rethinking Home as You Age* by Amanda Lambert and Leslie Eckford. This short, idea-rich volume is a springboard for readers to consider the future in terms of what "home" means and looks like to you.

- Elder Self-directed and Intentional Co-housing (EIC) research and co-housing community listings. Through the Institute of Gerontology at the College of Public Health of the University of Georgia: http://www.geron.uga.edu/eic/elderintentionalcommunities.html

- Find shared housing programs through the National Shared Housing Resource Center: https://nationalsharedhousing.org/

Successful, Happy Aging, Planning for Retirement

- *Who Will Take Care of Me When I'm Old? Plan Now to Safeguard Your Health and Happiness in Old Age* by Joy Loverde. A preparation book to empower readers with new ways of thinking and proactive advice for their medical, financial, and housing plans as they age.

- *Growing Young: How Friendship, Optimism, and Kindness Can Help You Live to 100* by Marta Zaraska. A research-driven look beyond healthy diet and exercise for longevity.

- *Next Stage: In Your Retirement, Create the Life You Want* by Tom Wilson. This well-researched book helps you create a master plan for your later years.

Letting Go for Your Future

Whether you're holding onto an entire room or have relegated an estranged child's things to a set of boxes or bins, consider how holding on may be holding you back. We met Dale and Serena in Chapter Two. Serena joined a cancer support group and began taking action for their future. She wanted to ship their daughter's collectibles to her and get on with their retirement to the sunshine state. Implementing their life plans had become part of Serena's healing, but

Dale was stalling. He got angry and clammed up. Deep down, Dale was afraid he'd lose his wife to cancer. Shipping off their daughter's things seemed so final. If he lost Serena, he'd be all alone.

Dale's refusal to discuss his apprehensions built a wall between him and his wife. He was "alone" already. When Serena learned to better express her emotions and confront Dale, they began taking steps together. That included socializing again. Dale's golf buddies helped him to better understand himself, thus act to support his marriage. "You'd be surprised how deep the talk can get out on the green," says Dale with a laugh.

Serena had come to accept the estrangement. Dale needed to try to reconcile once again before putting their home up for sale. When his efforts were met with their daughter's disdain, both toward her collectibles and any future relationship, he agreed to let the items go. Serena donated them to a thrift store that raises money for women with breast cancer.

Dale and Serena have since moved to Florida. In their new community, they've been surprised to meet several parents of estranged adult children. "But we don't dwell," says Serena, whose cancer is in remission.

The couple recently celebrated their forty-sixth wedding anniversary. Dale says, "We didn't invite our daughter to our party." He doesn't delude himself into thinking she'd have come anyway but says, "She was a big part of our lives. Maybe someday she will be again, but we've learned to live without her." Dale's words capture the sentiment of many parents who continue to hold out hope but prioritize their own lives and happiness.

Now let's meet Janet, a mother of two whose daughter is estranged. Although Janet's daughter "divorced" her ten years ago, her daughter's room is just the same. In contrast, Janet made an exercise room of the space that her son, who remains physically and emotionally close, occupied until he moved out. Janet's is a perfect example of how a typical progression of one's physical space can become arrested after such an emotional fracture as estrangement.

Janet and her husband are working toward the eventual closing of their business and retiring, perhaps to another state. With her daughter's room still decorated in an English-riding theme that represented what was once so important to her, Janet couldn't fully embrace the concept of moving on.

You may have fears similar to Dale's or be afraid that your child will come looking for their belongings and, if you don't have them, you blow the chance at reconciling. Either way, you'll have to deal with those fears. Dale had to try to connect and ask Vannie if she wanted the collectibles. Janet had to revisit the hateful words her daughter said the last time they spoke and finally recognize her little girl no longer existed. To embrace the change needed for her and her husband's future, Janet knew she must let go of the past. Her daughter certainly had.

If you're struggling with whether to hold onto old photographs, mementos from an estranged child's childhood, or even that child's old things, consider how much of a burden they have become. Most parents don't immediately make permanent decisions about material items. Temporary solutions are safe steps forward. Packing things away to a basement bin can be a sensible measure for a time, but as silence yawns out, or intermittent contact is disturbing or stressful, parents recognize that change is needed for their own well-being and future.

Janet determined that she didn't need to try and contact her long-estranged daughter in the clearing process. In thinking this through, Janet realized she no longer knew her daughter, who was now a woman in her thirties. Clearing out the space made sense.

Facing the memories as she went through her daughter's bedroom would be difficult. For Janet, a series of bite-sized actions helped. She scheduled short "clearing appointments" that increased in duration and began with less emotionally charged items like the bedclothes and curtains. Over time, she progressed to her daughter's more personal items. Finally, she fit a childhood teddy bear, a few of her daughter's drawings, and some special photos into a small box she tied with a bow. The box was manageable and wouldn't take up room when she moved, yet allowed space in her heart for a few cherished memories.

Make plans that support your own forward momentum. Janet and her husband have set a goal to dissolve their business in a year and have expanded the scope of their clearing to include other things collected over the years. When the time comes to begin exploring potential retirement locales, they'll be free to take hold of a new life chapter.

Clearing Space

Clearing out abandoned items can be an empowering physical step that sweeps out emotional cobwebs and clears the way toward a freer future. Reflect upon the following questions. Write out your answers to determine your best course of action.

- How is seeing these photographs on the wall, or holding onto these mementos from long ago, pulling me down or keeping me stuck?

- What fears may be keeping me from disposing of abandoned items? How can I move beyond these fears?

_____

_____

_____

_____

_____

_____

- Have I ignored the pain by shutting a bedroom door or avoiding other spaces in my home and leaving things as is? If so, would it be better for me to clear the space/items?

_____

_____

_____

_____

_____

- Does a temporary solution such as a box or bin make sense? Am I ready to make permanent decisions? If not, what *can* I do to help myself right now?

_____

_____

_____

_____

_____

_____

- Do I want to hang onto this stuff forever? If the answer is no, what are some possible actions? (Examples: Have a relative pass the things along or ask if they're wanted. Choose to keep a few special items.)

_____

_____

_____

_____

_____

- What, if anything, must I do before I can feel settled about taking action?

_____

_____

_____

_____

_____

_____

_____

_____

_____

_____

_____

_____

Welcome to the Pocket

When estranged adult children toss a crumb of contact, it can set a cascade of feelings in motion. The lilting joy of hope may not always be grounded in current reality. Even when you sense something is off, you may miss the sweet daughter or kind son you once knew so much that you don't face the truth. That's when you're in what I call "the Pocket." It's a pitiful space that exists in emotionally manipulative relationships.

The Pocket is based on how I felt at one point long ago, when I wondered if my own son was keeping me in his figurative "back pocket," just in case he needed me later. Since then, I've heard thousands of parents describe how they're strung along emotionally. The hope of a relationship is a dangled carrot, and often, parents feel compelled to follow through in some way, even against their better judgment. Caught between hope and fear, they're stuck in repeating dilemmas. Later, they feel like fools, squeezed by emotional extortion.

Learning to take care of yourself and thrive after rejection requires discarding illusions. Not all adult children who reject their parents are manipulative, but some most certainly are. Recognizing emotional manipulation is necessary for the "getting real" of this book's first chapter, which sets the overall tone. Here, I'll offer a few of the most common scenarios where parents end up in the Pocket. Let's take a closer look.

The Pocket: a convenient place where estranged adult children keep parents for a variety of reasons:

a. just in case   c. to maintain control

b. to save face   d. to elicit gifts

Example One, Clarence

After two years of respecting his adult daughter's need for "space," Clarence wonders if it will ever be enough. His daughter, who is away at college, has never explained her issues with him. He has been patient, reaching out lovingly but non-obtrusively with monetary gifts for birthdays and special occasions— usually with no reply. Finally, he mails a Starbuck's gift card with a short note: *Can we get a cup of coffee and talk?* His daughter replies in a text: *Thank you for the card, Daddy. I still love you but need more time.* At first, Clarence's heart sings. In his memory, he hears his darling daughter saying *Daddy* . . . He taps in a quick, *ok, love you, too* and tucks his phone away. Welcome to the Pocket.

Example Two, Amelia

A friend sees Amelia's estranged son at the library with his little girl—the grandchild Amelia has never met. He greets her, they chat, and Amelia's son asks if she knows he and Amelia haven't spoken in several years. When she nods, he tells her it's heartbreaking and that he'd hoped when his daughter was born, his mother would come around and be a grandma to her. Hearing this, Amelia is incensed. Her son made it sound like *she* caused the rift!

Her friend tells Amelia her son is as handsome as always and that her granddaughter is delightful. Amelia imagines her son's dazzling smile and realizes he is as charmingly deceptive as ever. He has always been persuasive. Amelia has seen him use and discard people—even her. But the friend seems to have fallen for his act. Then Amelia imagines the darling little girl and thinks: *Maybe he really does want me in his daughter's life.* Welcome to the Pocket.

Example Three, John

After eighteen months, John's son calls to talk. Because of all the hurt he caused, at first John remains guarded. His son chats, remembering good times they shared, asking about family, and connecting in the old ways only John and he can. John begins to relax. By the end of the conversation, he is smiling. John believes his son when he says he wants a relationship and will call again very soon. For the next few months, he jumps every time his phone rings, but it's never his son. Welcome to the Pocket.

Example Four, Doris

It's mid-December and Doris has been contemplating whether to send a gift to her estranged adult daughter. As the grocery store doors open and Elvis croons, "I'll Be Home for Christmas" over the loudspeakers, her phone beeps a notification. It's her daughter! Doris stops her cart on the welcome mat and reads: *I couldn't let another holiday pass without us talking.* Doris texts that she's happy to hear from her, and then receives another text: *I love you, Mom.* With her heart pounding in her ears, Doris replies: *Won't you come for Christmas? Everyone misses you.*

For several minutes, Doris stands there, waiting. Finally, with her teeth grinding and her shoulders tight, she pushes on. Halfway through the store, her daughter texts. She'll be out of town at her in-laws but: *Maybe for Easter. Gotta go. Miss everyone too.*

Doris texts her a pink heart. At the end of the aisle, she pulls a Sephora gift card from among the holiday variety in the rack. *How convenient that she contacts me at Christmastime again.* Despite the thought, Doris put the gift card in the cart. This will be the fourth year she sends a gift to the daughter she never sees. Welcome to the Pocket.

If you recognize yourself in similar scenarios, read on. You've been where lots of parents have: *the Pocket.* I've spent time there, as have many parents who mistake an ounce of contact, a term of endearment, or a promise for future communication as genuine connection. It's tough to remove the rose-colored glasses and recognize the Pocket for what it is, and that goals a, b, c, or d drive its purpose. No parent wants to think a child they raised could be so calculating, but denial only prolongs our agony. Plus, the Pocket has side effects. Let's look more closely at this disagreeable space.

After his initial joy, Clarence, from example one, starts to seethe. Later, at work, Clarence enters the elevator and pushes his button. A woman about his daughter's age rushes forward, but instead of stopping the doors, he grips his briefcase handle and lets them slide shut. Clarence's displaced anger makes him a jerk.

From example two, deep down, Amelia knows her son was saving face when he ran into her friend. Amelia's history with her son informs her he's cunning enough to seize the moment. He would purposely sow seeds of doubt about who's not talking to whom—*and it works.* As this mom's friend urges her to get in touch, Amelia says, "He could have called me all along." Her friend was fooled. Amelia can forgive her for that. Not everyone can understand estrangement.

Also, Amelia's son was with her granddaughter. *Her granddaughter!* She has longed for that child's hugs, sweet smiles, and a tiny voice to call her "Gran." That desire piles in with Amelia's insecurity. No one *really* understands. Most people think that any parent must be at fault if their own child rejects them. Amelia might very well step backward by reaching out. If she does, her son will encourage her to bond with the child, and then she'll have to walk on eggshells around him.

In example three, John is drawn back in. Many parents would be. His son may have called because he thinks he might need his dad one day. It's also possible he is playing a cruel, "I still got him," game. Or there could be other reasons, like someone in his son's life urging him to try and reconcile. He can now say he called (and perhaps spin the conversation to suit). The hook of renewed hope that snags the parent back into the waiting game often triggers the return to unhealthy coping tools like overeating or overdrinking, too. John tends to throw himself into his work, sometimes neglecting his wife and daughter. Migraines, high blood pressure, insomnia, or other physical manifestations follow due to stress. Even after months or years of silence, a parent who has begun to heal can suffer renewed rumination about past behavior or worry about future abuse.

Among other issues, example four locks parents into spending money they may later regret. Doris recognizes that she's in the Pocket almost as soon as her daughter contacts her, but she gets the gift card anyway. Later, she picks up something for her son-in-law, too. If she doesn't, she knows her daughter will say Doris has never liked him.

Sometimes adult children reach out to genuinely connect. If you're not sure, weigh your situation against past behavior, your child's tone and effort, and your gut feelings. You may be moving toward a reconciliation. However, if you believe it's the Pocket you're hurtling toward, the smartest thing to do is to pause. No need to rush and reply or decide on doing something that will hurt you or be difficult to take back. The gift of a little space and time can help you make sound decisions based on logic and reasoning rather than the emotional lift of (false) hope.

In example one, Clarence saw his reflection in the elevator's mirrored doors and felt disgust. He hadn't done anything terribly horrible, but letting the elevator doors shut in the young woman's face had been unkind. He knew confronting his daughter in anger would be equally unproductive, so he took a breath, faced his workday with intention, and later asked himself:

- *How much time does she need?*

- *How much longer am I supposed to wait?*

- *Should I continue in this sadistic game that robs me of my peace?*

It helped for this dad to realize he couldn't answer the first question, which was beyond his control. The second question wasn't fair. Why was he "supposed" to wait at all? Other than the tuition he committed to and paid each semester, and the gifts he sent her, any relationship with his daughter existed only in his memories. The third question bared the truth Clarence had been avoiding: He'd been in the Pocket the whole two years his daughter had needed "space." He maintained the requested distance while honoring her as he always had and letting her know his door was open to her. Just as people must sometimes alter their diets, the Pocket no longer agreed with Clarence.

He decided not to make further contact—at least for now. He could do that without fanfare, simply shifting the energy he'd spent on his daughter toward his own health and happiness. Or he could send a final note to let her know. Clarence chose the latter. Using her preferred form of communication, a text, he told her he loved her and said that after two years, he was leaving the ball in her court. He didn't bother telling her his other plans. He's cutting back on work hours with an eye toward his own future—with or without her.

In example two, Amelia has been through enough past abuse to know the truth about her son. She's certain that getting to know her granddaughter would bring her great joy but believes that wouldn't be allowed to last. She believes her son would use his own child to hook his mom, make her miserable, and keep her snagged on the line. He'd done similar things over the years.

What would you do? Every situation is different. I hear from parents every day who jumped at the chance to get to know their grandchildren. Many are

330

later heartbroken when, after a period of bonding, they are cut loose without explanation (like Julia was). Still, a grandchild is a huge pull on the heartstrings.

Example three, where John's son calls after a long silence is similar to my experience. I'll never fit in the Pocket again, but in all honesty, I still take a fraction of a step backward with any bit of contact or news of Dan. Over time, though, and with practice, I've learned that self-compassion, recognizing and admitting my feelings, and then using my "Emotional Toolkit," prompts a swifter and swifter reset. With time and practice, you can learn this, too. So can John.

Example four is often easily spotted by discerning parents whose estranged children reach out, like clockwork, close to their own birthday or around Christmas. Doris did. Some parents find it easier just to send gifts. If they enjoy doing that and aren't hurt financially or emotionally, then being in the Pocket is a choice. This can go on for years despite no change in the relationship. However, if you feel compelled to send gifts out of fear your child will be able to say you didn't even remember her birthday (or some such), then you're being manipulated. You're in the Pocket.

For anyone, including parents, remember: *Your worth is not defined by another adult's opinion of you*. Even if that adult is your own child.

Entering the Lion's Den of Tense Events

The days leading up to a funeral, a wedding, a baby shower, or some other family event might be wrought with what-ifs and worries. *What if my estranged daughter starts a fight or ignores me? Does everyone believe the lies my estranged son said about me?*

Decide how important the event is and why. What compels you to go? How is the event's purpose significant for you? Reflection can provide insights that help you commit (or sit the event out).

Juanita, whose estranged daughter keeps her children away, wanted to honor her mother's eighty-fifth birthday, yet she dreaded seeing the hosts, her brother and sister-in-law. They believed the hurtful, manufactured stories Juanita's daughter had used to justify her actions. Juanita figured her daughter would be on her best behavior in front of the other relatives, but she wasn't sure how she should interact with her grandchildren. She had not seen them in almost three years. The thought of them all in the same room overwhelmed her, yet Juanita couldn't bring herself to avoid her mother's special party. "She may not be around much longer," Juanita says. "Being present for her was significant."

You may not feel as committed as Juanita. Or, maybe your family members are just not nice. Over time, one mother realized her compulsion to attend events she dreaded had to do with her codependent nature. Learning to decide based on her own needs and wants rather than always to please other people was a step toward her own independence and self-care. Many of us were raised with ideals of family loyalty and devotion we hold dear. Despite that, there is no need to judge yourself negatively for not wanting to be around people who are unkind. Sometimes people who say they love us don't live up to their words.

Self-care might mean you *don't* attend. Give yourself permission to choose that option first, then weigh an event's significance to others and to yourself. Writing your thoughts out on paper can help you determine the best course of action to take. If you decide to go, make some self-supportive plans for your success and well-being. With a few sensible practices and the right attitude, you can fulfill your commitment unscathed. You might even enjoy yourself. Here are a few tips.

- *Dress for success.* It's tough to be at ease in uncomfortable clothing. For me, physical comfort comes first. I can't be myself with tight waist bands or high heels. Beyond that, think of clothing as a costume that reflects how you want to interact. *I'll be colorful and cheery.* Or, *I'll blend in without calling attention to myself.* Maybe you need protection. I own a tunic with a pattern on front that reminds me of armor, and I wear it to events where I feel vulnerable. My sparkly duck pin reminds me to let the "stuff" roll off my back (like water off a duck's back). For some, a sweater, a scarf, or clothes that cover all skin serve as a security blanket. What can you wear for a psychological boost? Consider your specific needs and dress to support them.

- *Time travel.* One father whose ex-wife badmouths him to their son has attended many tense events. He sets his phone alarm to sound like a ring or text. When it goes off at the pre-chosen interval, he can excuse himself for a work emergency or reset it. A wristwatch also works. If you've decided that two hours is enough time to stay, checking a watch helps you cheer yourself on: *Just twenty more minutes. I'm almost there . . .*

- *Should you stay or should you go?* Flexibility can be a plan. Put an event's structure to use. Split the event into typical phases and reevaluate at each juncture. You might decide to skip out before the cake is served or leave before the presents are opened. Based on how things are going, you can decide on the fly which plan to enact.

- *Grand exit.* Stressful events take start-to-finish plans. Feeling comfortable with how you'll leave may mean coming up with strategies and reasons you can offer to your host. *I can't stay for dessert because of my blood sugar.* Or, *I have an early workday tomorrow.* Consider who you feel you must speak to before leaving—and have a thank you or a compliment planned. One mother tells herself she will slip out whenever she needs to without a word. If anyone stops her, she tells them she's not feeling well. "It's not a lie," she says. "I'm attending an event that causes me angst and heartache."

- *Hold your head high.* One mother checks her posture before entering any event. With her hands on her hips, she stands tall, "like Superman." She's on to something. How we hold our bodies affects our thoughts and feelings. Good posture on the outside translates to more confidence on the inside. It's also true that smiling makes us feel happier. Our bodies and minds are intricately connected, so don't slouch. Paste on a smile and hold your head high.

- *Partner up.* Assign whoever is attending with you the job of wing man and discuss your exit plans before the event. Someone you trust can offer a joke when one is needed most, steer you toward the door at a designated time, or be alert for your agreed upon physical cue or code word that, for you, the party's over and it's time to go.

- *No drama.* One parent has labeled certain relatives and situations as her "drama zones." That means not sitting near a particular relative whose probing questions trigger emotional pain or staying away from gossipy relatives on the kitchen clean-up crew. Reflect upon past events and identify your own drama or danger zones in people or situations. Maybe it's the ones taking alcohol shots after dinner, or a woman whose talk about her hunky-dory life with her grandchildren brings you down. Plan how you can avoid your potential drama zones.

- *Give yourself space.* If you're traveling, consider whether staying with relatives is helpful *for you.* Your own space before and after stressful events frees you to engage in positive self-talk, prayer, or other activities that center and prepare you. Juanita's brother offered his guest bedroom, but she chose a hotel, claiming her virtual workload required concentration and no distractions. Knowing her quiet hotel room was available helped Juanita feel she had more options and was in control.

- *Reward yourself.* If you must travel to get to the event, combine your trip with a bonus you know you'll love. One father visited a college buddy he hadn't seen for many years. The upbeat visit reminded the father who he was at his core: an optimistic person with a zest for life. You might consider a similar visit with someone you know will be uplifting. Or, take a special shopping trip, see a local tourist site, or sample a favorite restaurant or one you've been wanting to try.

Give some forethought to how you'll interact with your estranged adult child, too. When Juanita reflected upon her situation, she could not imagine her daughter starting a scene. Juanita knew that her daughter wasn't about to let any relatives see through the lies she had constructed to paint herself as a victim. The prediction was accurate.

When Juanita arrived at the party, her daughter hugged her lightly, and then avoided her. Juanita had planned some friendly, neutral lines of small talk including congratulating her daughter on a job promotion that family members had told her about, but she didn't get the opportunity to utter them. Even while sitting in the same room, her daughter chatted with other people, and was careful not to look Juanita in the eyes. When someone suggested a four-generation photo, Juanita posed with her mother, daughter, and granddaughter, and was surprised that her daughter slid her arm around her waist. "She was on her best behavior," Juanita says.

You may forecast a similar display of public goodwill or perhaps more spiteful behavior. Has your son or daughter made a public scene in the past? Or are volatility, abusive words, and meanness only a factor when there are no witnesses? Is your adult child invested in playing a role like Juanita's daughter? Will alcohol be present? And does that make a difference in your child's (and perhaps his or her cohorts') behavior? Asking questions that fit your situation allows for educated, imaginal thinking to help you manage reactive emotions and plan your own wise conduct.

Also, consider whether you will approach your son or daughter right away or hang back and wait for your child's cue. You're not a weak raft at the mercy of your child's sea. Taking control where you realistically can is empowering.

No matter what you believe may happen, having a plan in place will help you keep your wits about you. If there's a scene, make sure you're not the one causing it. That may mean avoiding any situation where you could be cornered or walking away rather than engaging. To that end, find out as many details about the upcoming event as you can. Will there be assigned seating? How many guests will be present? Is your host aware of the rift? Will the host be supportive of your needs? Information brings knowledge that can help you feel more confident as well as achieve your goal for a peaceful outcome—at least for yourself.

If you'll be seeing grandchildren, reflect on the facts. Juanita's grandchildren were very young when the rift between her and her daughter began. She knew they wouldn't remember her, so offering hugs would be a mistake. She decided to be friendly but not overly involved. Juanita knew seeing the children would be emotional for her, so planned to stay in the moment and enjoy them.

That day, Juanita carried a large handbag she equipped with a few age-appropriate "busy" items. "The kids were wide-eyed and curious like most young children are with friendly adults in a safe environment," says Juanita. "I was able to pull out a few dollar-store items and see them enjoy those. I also brought a card deck." At one point, in clear view of her daughter and everyone, Juanita joined her grandchildren for a game of "Slap Jack."

If it's important to you to attend an event you know will be stressful, consider how you'll feel once it's done. One couple whose adult daughter is estranged avoided their grandson's sports events all season. Their grandson, who still contacted them from time to time, had been wanting them to go. Finally, they mustered up the courage and steeled themselves against their fears of a possible scene, or more likely, the awkwardness and emotional trauma of their daughter ignoring them from two feet away. Their daughter did ignore them, but their grandson hugged them. The situation saddened them, but as the grandmother says, "I'm glad we went, and we came away stronger because we did."

Sometimes, the strength a parent gains from attending such events means turning the page and moving forward for themselves. For Juanita, that meant closing the door more fully on her relationship with her unsupportive siblings. She hasn't vowed never to see them again but has checked out emotionally. She now says she's "done" with her estranged daughter, who ignored her at the party but later accused her of hateful speech she never said.

For Juanita, the party served as a wakeup call. Seeing how much the grandchildren she last saw as young toddlers had grown over the last several years made her realize how fleeting life is. "My daughter was mad that I'd brought the toys," she says. "But they had fun with me. Maybe they'll know who I am to them one day or maybe they won't, but they'll have a good memory of me. My daughter can't take that away."

Juanita has decided there will be no more waiting and hoping. She is downsizing from the family home where she and her now deceased husband raised their daughter and where she babysat her grandchildren. She had planned on leaving the home to her daughter one day. Now, she plans to sell it and retire to The Villages in Florida, which offers plenty of social opportunities with like-minded retirees. Juanita says, "I've had enough hard work and pain in my life. It's my turn to have fun."

Aftercare

After attending a stressful event, how you take care of yourself matters. Have a plan in place to calm your nerves and tend to your own well-being. Here are a few tips to implement directly or fuel your own creative ideas.

- **Drive safely**. Don't get out on the road immediately if you're emotionally distressed. Know in advance a safe, nearby area where you can park for a few minutes, take purposeful, calming breaths, give yourself a pep talk, and reenergize with a healthful snack you've brought along. If you're with your partner or friend, help them care for their emotional needs, too.

- **Use your words.** Revisit the exercise, "Call It What It Is" from Chapter Three and spell out exactly how you're feeling. Recognize your emotional state with rich language (dismay, relief, worry) and use those identified emotions to journal about how you feel, what went as planned or surprised you, and anything you might have learned that you can use to aid your future well-being. Did you have any epiphanies? Come to conclusions about your future?

- **Be kind to loved ones**. If you live with other people, consider ahead whether you'll want to talk or whether doing so will only drain you. Have kind words or phrasing planned that will allow you to escape if you want. *Traffic was bad so I'm off to get some rest.* Or, *I hope you weren't waiting up for me, I think I'll have a cup of chamomile tea and meltdown quietly while you watch TV.*

- **Use your toolkit**. Ideally, you'll have your toolkit ready (see Chapter Three, "Pack Your Emotional Toolkit"). A first-aid kit is only as good as its contents. Prepare for emotional scrapes and bruises in the same way. If your toolkit is packed, you can draw out healing resources in an emotional emergency without added stress.

- **See clearly**. Parents often have high hopes for a tearful reunion at a family event. This could happen but is unlikely. Also, a hug from an estranged child in front of family doesn't translate into wanting you to call. While family events do bring parents and estranged children together, reconciliation doesn't magically fall into place. Reconciliation takes willingness from all parties. It often comes with hard work or new parameters for any relationship. Planning your words and actions for a calm encounter ahead may be a step in that direction—even if the only result is that you feel less stressed for the next event.

When Only One Parent Is Rejected

At times, parents decide together to go along with the adult child's decision to cut ties with only one of them. Perhaps a young adult is troubled, and the parents figure that one's involvement is better than neither being involved. An arrangement like that has sound reasoning for the short term. Beyond that, parents must ask themselves what purpose is served, if any.

In this section, you will meet three parents who, for various reasons, choose to endure this unenviable, odd-man-out position. I hope you'll read these pages even if the subject doesn't seem relevant to you. Discovering how others come to terms and cope with injustices helps us think creatively about our own circumstances.

First, if you're the in-parent, reflect upon how your actions affect your partner and your relationship. How would you feel if the tables were turned? Your partner is likely to have fears, anger, and feel left out. How might the situation affect the trust in your primary relationship? Life partners look out for one another. Is it fair to expect your spouse to support your continued relationship with the adult child who holds them in disdain?

If you are the outsider, know that your feelings are valid. Insecurity, anguish, anger, envy, worthlessness . . . these and whatever other emotions you feel are normal given the circumstances. It hurts when the one you have committed your life to above all others joins an alliance that excludes you. You have a right to your feelings, regardless of the logic your spouse, friends, and anyone else use to try and shame you. That doesn't mean dwelling on the feelings helps, which we'll get to in a moment.

Now, let's meet a few rejected parents and discover more of their details, as well as perspectives on their partners' continued contact. These are not right or wrong examples. Situations with in- and out-parents can be extremely complex. What works for some is disagreeable to others.

As you read these stories, consider your unique circumstances. Notice any thoughts or feelings that occur, and perhaps provide clues to your expectations, biases, pain, or matters of conscience. Whatever you learn about yourself can help you become stronger and more well-adjusted, and thus make decisions that are right for you (and your spouse).

We'll start with Araceli. She says of her forty-one-year marriage, "I've always been the one to bend."

Araceli worked in hospital admissions when she met her future husband. At the time, he was a busy surgeon. "He was this powerful man who was sixteen years older than me," says Araceli. "Everyone thought he was a catch, and he was interested in me. That felt good."

When they married, Araceli quit working to care for him and start a family. They quickly had a son, but his heart problems led to death by age four. After three more years, they conceived their daughter, and Araceli threw herself into managing her home and family.

"Our daughter inherited her father's strong will," she says. "We were close until her college years. Then, suddenly, I didn't know anything. I didn't have much in common with our go-getter young adult."

In their daughter's growing-up years, it had been Araceli who encouraged her to study and compete. She wanted their daughter to have a good education and go places in life. Araceli fixed meals, drove her daughter to school and extracurricular activities, and saw her through any hardships. "Her dad was always working," she explains. "My role was to support them both."

When their daughter began belittling her, Araceli was devastated. Nevertheless, when her daughter dismissed her entirely, she and her husband agreed that he would keep up the relationship. "We didn't think that would last," says Araceli. "But it has. Our daughter is now a physician with a demanding job and a hospital board position. My husband sees her every other month. He goes to the city, they have dinner out, lunch the next day, and then he comes home. If I ever want to come along, she is suddenly too busy."

Early on, when their daughter's intentions to exclude her became clear, Araceli tried to get her husband to take her side. "He sulked and picked a fight," she explains. "I realized that he isn't going to change. Me giving in to him is how our marriage has always worked. He'll be seventy-three in a few months. At this point, I'm not sure I have the right to expect him to change. And if I insisted, would it hurt him?"

Araceli chooses to put her husband's feelings, needs, and wants ahead of her own, but she has also learned how to make the situation work for her. "At first, I was jealous," she says. "But that was rotten to my bones, like the Bible says." Araceli's couldn't sleep at night and her health suffered. "Me getting sick wouldn't solve anything."

Araceli took charge by recognizing how often her thoughts dwelled on the injustice and betrayal. She noticed the way her muscles clenched, and her chest tightened, and how one sad thought led to another. To combat the responses, she worked at purposefully relaxing her body and catching and reframing her thoughts. She learned to take a breath, let it go, and imagine the distress floating away into the clouds. She also began doing more activities with friends and on her own.

In allowing her husband to spend time with their daughter, Araceli also reaffirmed herself in the supporter role she has always taken pride in. "In that way, nothing has changed." With a laugh, she continues, "But I don't sit around and cry and wish my daughter still loved me. Not anymore anyway. When my husband is gone, I use the time for myself. He comes home from those dates with his daughter to a wife who is happy and relaxed. I might get my nails done, go shopping, take a friend to lunch, or work at the church."

By nurturing herself, Araceli doesn't focus on what she's missing. "Maybe one day our daughter will love me again but for now, she loves my husband . . . and so do I."

If you are in a similar position, how can you support yourself? Can you focus on self-care as Araceli does? Can you view your own and/or your spouse's behavior in a helpful rather than hurtful way?

Let's meet Carol. Her daughter was estranged for three years before granting her father the privilege of a relationship with her children. She brought her first child by the house one day when she knew her mother would be at work. Carol's husband is retired, and for the next two years, the daughter continued to occasionally stop by. When her second child was born, she began initiating planned visits—always when Carol was working.

Father, daughter, and grandchildren go on outings now, which Carol at first found very upsetting. "It didn't bother me so much when she stopped in to see her dad unexpectedly, but to know that he was actively making plans with her without me hurt," says Carol. "We're a team, a unit, and I never thought he would go along with her excluding me."

The grandchildren are three and five, and although Carol wishes she could get to know them, her daughter refuses. "When her dad tried to persuade her, she threatened to cut him off again," Carol explains.

"I guess I'm the bad guy," says Carol. "Our daughter has made vague references to a time when I babysat a neighbor boy and they took baths together, but that was when she was two years old. He was only six months and sat in one of those little plastic forms with the suction cups to support him in the tub. Nothing inappropriate took place."

Carol's husband has made it clear that he believes Carol, but their daughter won't budge. She also will not give more detail about what supposedly took place. "I think maybe she's confused," says Carol. "She stayed with a sitter for a year before she started school, after I went to work. Maybe she has that time with the little boy mixed up with some incident I don't know about."

Because of that uncertainty, Carol sometimes wishes she would have put off going to work for another few years. "Maybe it's partially guilt that keeps me from making a stink about my husband seeing her. Maybe it's because I'm open to the possibility that something happened to her, and that she'll sort that out later and will need her parents at that time. If one of us goes along with this, we can be there for her."

Carol admits to feeling "very down" sometimes. She also has fears. Now and again, Carol's distress builds, and she feels compelled to question her husband. *Has their daughter said more to him? Are they keeping secrets together? Does he still believe Carol?* "He hugs me and reassures me," Carol says. "Then I tuck the fear away again. My husband is so happy after he sees her and the children. I can't bring myself to take that away from him."

Carol adds, "It does hurt, but for now, I can manage my emotions. I'm still working and busy. I may not get to be with my grandchildren, but I love them. And I know that having their granddad in their lives is a plus for them."

Carol uses a journal to vent any negative emotions she feels. "I also keep a gratitude journal," she says. "I write down the good things I feel about the situation and remind myself when I need to."

Hoping to "be there" for her daughter if any *real* traumatic childhood memories surface, Carol has decided that the stress of being left out is worth the security of one parent remaining in contact. Not all would agree. When it comes to trauma, *over*-remembering is a possible memory distortion. Events that were not experienced can mingle with actual memories and fill in gaps.[4] In allowing their daughter to exclude Carol, they may or may not be doing her (or themselves) any favors.

"We both have worries that our daughter might one day turn on her dad and stop the contact," says Carol. After a pause, she adds, "It would be horrible, but better that she cuts him off from the kids than me being the one to take them from him."

Finally, we'll turn to Thad, whose wife remains in contact with their forty-year-old son. "Our boy and I always butted heads," he says. "My wife gave in to him more than I did. She carried him for nine months. I've seen the mother and child bond all these years, so I understand she wants to stay in touch with her only child."

Thad's son believes his dad is set in his ways, was always too strict, and never really loved him. "That's not true, but it was my place to set an example," says Thad. "I provided for my family and required my son to learn how to work for what he needs or wants. He has two sons of his own now who are always on their phones or playing video games. My son is still fit and strong, and he makes a good living. My wife tells me he didn't want to raise his boys like he was raised."

For Thad, his wife's involvement amounts to more of the same. She was always the hugger and comforter. He was the authority in the home. "My son didn't want that, so he chooses the parent who didn't challenge him. I'm not about to beg, and I would never tell my wife she can't see him."

Thad admits to still feeling anger, but he works at channeling that energy into his projects. He wants to support his wife. When she takes the two-hour flight and stays for the weekend, he misses her. She comes home with photographs on her phone and talks about her visit. "It's sad to know my own son wants nothing to do with me, but at least he honors his mother. This way, she gets to see him without me around to rub him the wrong way just by breathing. I just want my wife to be happy."

For two of these couples, the arrangement is a continuation of life-long patterns. When Araceli married, she took on a supporter role. In allowing her husband to see their daughter, she continues to play her part. Thad, too, took his role as a husband and father very seriously. Seeing himself as a role model didn't change when his son disowned him. He derives self-worth in knowing his son is physically strong and provides well for his family. Another parent might forget all the good they did and see only failure because of their child's rejection. By honoring his wife's decision, and by not begging his son to see him, he believes he's still setting a good example.

Carol is strong enough to recognize her daughter's possible memory confusion without becoming overly defensive. For the most part, she trusts that her husband believes she did nothing wrong. They both believe their daughter has issues yet to be addressed, and are willing, for now, to let things stand. Carol is genuinely pleased that her husband gets to be in their grandchildren's lives. By accepting the arrangement, she feels she is helping the grandchildren she loves from afar.

How do you feel about these situations? What can you learn from these parents? Can you challenge their beliefs, weigh them against your own, see other solutions, or applaud them for their resourcefulness?

Consider whether you can accept your partner's involvement, go along with it willingly, and positively change your perspective to support yourself. While it's true that we cannot make another person change, we have that option for ourselves at any time. It's not too late, and sometimes, our own growth has a ripple effect on others.

These rejected parents worked to accept the other parent's continued contact, and then worked at finding ways to cope. If their situations and/or feelings change, they will need to reevaluate, negotiate, and possibly make further adjustments. Emotionally troublesome situations are never a one-and-done.

If you're in a situation such as this, lay down some ground rules. One rejected parent might not want to hear about the other's visits. Another may want to know every detail. What if you're the in-parent, and your adult child forbids you to tell the other parent anything? How will you handle this?

Estrangement is complex enough. A one-parent-in and one-parent-out dynamic makes the challenge even more difficult. If you're contemplating an arrangement such as this, it's best to think through all the possibilities. If you make the choice to go ahead, devise and agree to parameters. Then be open to renegotiation. There should be no secrets.

Coping When You're the Only Rejected Parent

- Nurture yourself. Treat yourself to something you enjoy to make up for the time alone. Do something that makes you feel special (because you are).

- Use a journal to explore your feelings.

- Get the support of a caring friend or counselor who can be objective and offer a useful perspective. Choose someone who will remind you you're a good person and will help you cope.

- Find positive ways to regard the situation if you can. (Page back to "Your Turnaround," in Chapter Two, for rephrasing help.)

- Pat yourself on the back. Sometimes, the most miserable situations allow us to see how "good" we really are (or strong, patient, loving . . . you insert the words that fit). Use the situation as a confidence builder.

- Try new activities that engage your mind and make you feel triumphant. Pushing your own boundaries by learning new skills builds confidence and gives you something all your own.

- Be aware of negative thinking and how it makes you feel. Practice letting negativity go and purposefully shift to thoughts that empower you. "I hate being left out," can become, "Now I have some time for myself."

- If you have agreed to the in- and out-parent situation, don't hold it against your partner.

- Don't forget to laugh. Look up silly jokes, watch YouTube videos, or meet with lighthearted friends.

- Forgive yourself. No one is perfect, and you deserve your own kind regard.

- Be self-compassionate. Being the odd man out isn't easy. Offer yourself the same patience and care you might a friend going through the same thing.

Sects and Cults

At age eighteen, I held a months-long temporary work post in a vast, downtown law office. Attorneys in three-piece-suits sat in leather chairs behind polished wood desks illuminated by banker's lamps. One day, as I hurried up the hallway that encircled a central mezzanine filled with secretary cubicles, I was stopped by a middle-aged attorney. Previously, I had only nodded in passing to this man whose intense blue eyes seemed to look right through me. That day, he was effervescent as he introduced me to a younger man in a leisure suit whose handsome face pinkened as he nodded in hello.

"I don't know how she does it," the attorney said, "but Sheri shows up looking absolutely glamorous each and every day."

Rather than feeling complimented, I shrank back a step, cornered. I muttered a thank you and moved to go around, raising my stack of files. "I have to get these—"

"She's efficient, too." The attorney glanced sideways at the younger man and back to me. "Sheri, you'd be perfect for EST."

I'd overheard the name. Some other attorneys had scoffed about it in the lounge area as I'd made fresh coffee the day before. But EST itself was a mystery to me.

"My friend here is a member, too, and we'd like to invite you personally to join us this afternoon," he went on, his fingers grazing my upper arm. "We'll expect to see you."

When he moved forward, the younger man followed, his dark eyes gentle. "See you later."

Creeped out by the sudden exuberance and familiarity of the attorney who'd never spoken to me before, I left work early that day and didn't attend. A few days later, though, he approached my desk.

"We were disappointed you didn't come the other day," he said, looking at me with the intensity of an eagle eyeing its prey. "Maybe you're not EST material after all."

As he turned and walked away, I felt oddly sad that I'd let him down. And the next week, as applause drifted from one of the meeting rooms, I paused in the hall and looked in. From his chair at the far end of the room where others in smaller chairs faced him, he raised a brow at the sight of me and then asked another young girl to shut the door. She did, and I walked on, feeling dejected, wondering what I was missing and why he didn't want me anymore.

I left the job within a few more days. My position there had been temporary, and as I look back now, I'm grateful for the timing. Some see the now-defunct EST as a cult. Self-made guru, Erhard

Werner, founded the Erhard Seminar Trainings (EST) in 1971. The trainings aren't easily defined, even by graduates, which included well-educated, successful people—doctors, lawyers, psychologists, and other professionals. Graduates became devotees of the training, which was part of the Human Potential Movement of the 1970s.

Reflecting, I wonder if the attorney and group leader may have been (clunkily) trying his hand at intermittent reinforcement. Many cults do use emotional rewards that makes people feel seen, heard, special, and loved—yet inconsistently. The inconsistency keeps the individual hooked, much like a slot machine *might* pay off, so the gambler keeps trying. Cult leaders offer intermittent feel-good moments that trigger an addictive response. And who knows? As a young adult, at the time in a bad marriage, and out in the big world I wasn't effectively prepared for, if I had stayed and he'd have had more opportunities, I might have succumbed.

I sometimes hear from parents who describe groups they believe may be cults, and people who snuck in under the radar, infiltrated their families, and turned their children against them. One such mother, Margit, believes a massage therapist hired to help her teenage daughter, Anja, recover from a sports injury, is part of a cult. Anja was at a low point, after traditional medicine hadn't helped, and her injury forced her to quit the high school sports she loved. Also, the family pet had died, as had her grandmother, Margit's mother. Anja's friends were going on with life, while Anja was often sullen, angry, and feeling left out.

Enter the massage therapist, a woman in her late thirties whom Margit and her husband hired to help with Anja's debilitating pain. She would come to their home with her herbal oils and go to Anja's upstairs room for the treatments. Margit would hear her daughter talking and laughing with the therapist. Anja's good mood would last, too, and Margit was relieved to have her sweet daughter back. The treatments worked, and the parents eventually stopped them. Anja was well, and they were grateful.

After Anja went off to college, Margit discovered her daughter was still in touch with the therapist. She mentioned attending the woman's wedding and staying weekends at her home. Margit wasn't comfortable with the contact, but her daughter was living at school, getting good grades, and doing fine. By then, she was also an adult.

Before Anja graduated from college, she began calling her parents by their first names and developed eating habits that kept her rail thin. She also mentioned wonderful visits with the therapist and her husband, mixed with times when they disapproved of her interests—perhaps in a pattern of intermittent reinforcement. Anja asked her parents not to attend her graduation and invited the therapist instead. After college, she went to live with the woman and her husband in a neighboring city.

For the first year after graduating, Anja returned home for weekends twice. She said the therapist and her husband were traveling but refused to tell them anything about her life with them. She was friendly, though, and the parents tried to keep things light and not pry. However, after each of those visits, she sent e-mails insisting they become vegan, and saying they needed to repent. They weren't sure where this was coming from but were worried. Eventually, Anja refused all contact and changed her last name to match that of the therapist and her husband and began calling them Mom and Dad.

Margit has since discovered that the therapist has a website targeting young women much like Anja. She has come to suspect the therapist and her husband run a cult, and that she and her husband were victims right along with their daughter.

Margit is among other parents who speak of individuals, families, and groups that are often unwittingly invited into their homes or social spheres. It isn't until after their adult child disowns them that they suspect a cult. Parents are often embarrassed as well, which makes them reluctant to speak out.

One father, Ari, confided that his daughter joined a sect she first found online. Led by a man and woman who claim a direct connection with God, the group's purported focus is love. They match up romantic soulmates and also help them find life purpose that aligns with their ideals of love.

At first, Ari thought his daughter was studying the Bible. "She said it was an online church," Ari says. "But they found my daughter a man, her 'twin flame.' Before I had a sense of what was happening, she had moved to another state and rejected our whole family. They both work for the sect now. I believe she is under mind control."

Destiny, a single mother of two, says that her oldest child married at age eighteen and then went through a rough divorce two years later. Her daughter, Jesse, then saw a therapist. "After a few months, Jesse's feet seemed more on the ground than ever," Destiny says. "She was living back at home with me, and I encouraged her to attend college."

Jesse did begin school, but quickly met a couple pushing a multilevel marketing business. She quit her classes and pursued that instead. "I wished she'd have stayed in college, but she'd been so sad after her divorce. It was good to see her so happy and confident."

Within a few months, though, Destiny saw a concerning transformation in Jesse, and she began to ask her daughter questions. "I never called it a cult," says Destiny, "but that's what it was. Jesse quit going to therapy and said the business group was everything she ever wanted. They had all sorts of meetings and classes. Jesse went through personality changes that erased her morals and beliefs. She was no longer lonely but had become a stranger."

Today, loneliness is known to be more widespread among millennials than any other generation.[5] In the three examples mentioned, loneliness played a role. Margit's daughter had an injury that left her an outsider in her previously busy athletic life. Ari's daughter had suffered several breakups and a stream of dead-end dates before finding the group that introduced her to her spiritual soulmate. Jesse's marriage at an early age ended badly, and as Destiny says, "She was vulnerable."

In *Done With The Crying*, I talked about cult-like families that become third-party adversaries and help adult children to become estranged. Those do exist, and I hear from parents all the time who have experienced them. Until recently, I didn't know how plentiful more formalized cults and sects are. You may be surprised as well, although they are becoming more exposed. Ones involving sex or celebrities get the most airtime, such as sex cult, NXIVM, which is the focus of a recent STARZ documentary.

Actress Catherine Oxenberg attended an introductory session for what was billed as a group to promote professional success as well as more meaning in one's personal life. She took her nineteen-year-old daughter with her. Catherine quickly realized she wasn't interested, but her daughter was persuaded to join the group. Oxenberg worked tirelessly to get her daughter untangled from NXIVM, and the founder has since been prosecuted.

Typically, people don't knowingly join cults. Scary, destructive, or criminal cults often masquerade as innocuous spiritual or self-development groups. They offer help for the troubled, injured, or those looking for answers. You might have been, at first, relieved to see your child getting involved in something you believed was good—and you're not alone in being duped by those who are masters at their game.

Resource

- Cult Education Institute. A nonprofit education and research organization studying destructive cults and movements. Provides vast archives of information about varying groups over time, an alphabetic listing, a forum, and links to help educate the public. Information for those doing research, looking for help, or considering legal action. The "about" page is a good place to start. https://www.culteducation.com

Intermittent Reinforcement

Intermittent Reinforcement is an inconsistent relational pattern that can consist of:

- reward and punishment
- approval and disapproval
- attention and disinterest

Often, it's done unintentionally. For example, one day, you let your kids choose toys to keep them quiet in the store. The next time, you tell them "no," but they won't stop crying for toys. The next time, you tire of their whining and let them choose toys. You *inadvertently* hooked them on the belief that their crying *might* be rewarded, much the way a gambler is addicted to the possibility of a win. By rewarding the kids with toys, you reinforced unwanted behavior.

My kids once had a little dog they taught to say "I'm-hun-gry" with three sharp barks. When she started barking three times repeatedly at the dinner table, we got irritated and told her to stop. She'd keep barking, though, and we'd end up giving her scraps . . . It was a dumb trick we have never taught another pet since.

Intermittent reinforcement is effective as a means of control, which is why it's used by some manipulative figures (cult leaders, abusers, narcissists . . .) to keep others hooked. Anja may have been subject to it when the massage therapist and her husband sometimes treated her wonderfully and other times expressed disapproval. It's also common in relationships where one partner isn't so great, yet behaves adoringly, or at least well enough on some days, that the other gets hooked on hope and confused into staying. I believe intermittent reinforcement explains a lot of the compulsion felt by persons who are committed to an ideal and strung along by people who are only sometimes nice.

Many divorced parents tell the tales of ex-spouses whose attention toward their minor-aged children was intermittent at best. Sometimes months or even years passed without a bit of interest in their kids. Then the absentee parent would show up with teddy bears, trips to Disneyland, and lots of sweet talk. These inconsistent parents were sometimes worshipped by the same children they stood up on visitation days and let down with numerous broken promises. Whether intentional or not, the inconsistent parent carries out intermittent reinforcement. Like how abused partners or cult recruits get hooked, the child gets attached to the inconsistent parent.

Supportive, attentive parents are sometimes baffled when their adult children reject them for the inconsistent deadbeat one who has suddenly expressed renewed interest. Often, these relationships include revisionist history and bad-mouthing by the worshipped parent that's akin to the parental alienation tactics that one divorcing parent uses against the other with children who are minors. Even when that's not the case, in some of these situations, patterns of intermittent reinforcement, perhaps ingrained over a lifetime, are likely at work.

Choose Your Focus

Just as a potpourri has fragrant dried flowers or pretty pinecones among wood shavings and spicy bits of bark, this chapter includes a mix of subjects. Some probably resonate more than others. Potpourri ingredients have a purpose: to build volume, hold fragrance, and create texture. This chapter is much the same.

Lessons in trust and values infused the tales of children's business betrayal. Our blind trust that other people have our same values can make us vulnerable. The messy business of disentanglement requires measuring what is the most important to preserve against what we can—or must—let go. With regard to adult children, or anyone, what can you glean from the chapter's family business stories? What can you apply in your own life right now or consider for your future?

_____

_____

_____

_____

This chapter's end-of-life discussions are reminiscent of two well-known sayings:

- Never put off until tomorrow what you can do today.
- Haste makes waste.

Planning early for the inevitable is a reasonable middle ground to protect yourself and your assets. Whether you have never completed estate documents, need to review and update them, or have only just begun to consider the subject, what can you do now to prepare for your final passage? Where else can you apply these ideas in your life?

_____

_____

_____

_____

The word "home" may bring up fond memories, represent security or your own independence. Whether or not you're an elder orphan, what are your thoughts about your current residence in terms of your future? What doable steps can you take now to make changes, decisions, or devise plans?

_____

_____

_____

_____

Moving forward always requires some letting go. In contemplating that truth, what material items, expectations, or emotional struggles come to mind? What resistance, such as fear or guilt, springs up to try and hold you back?

_____

_____

_____

_____

_____

_____

The tips for before and after attending tense events are a model for treating ourselves with kind, thoughtful care *anytime*. What situations or advice stood out to you? How can you treat yourself with more self-compassion, remain safe in your day-to-day life, and be your own best friend?

_____

_____

_____

_____

_____

We all must stand alone at some point, in some life situation. What did you learn from the in- and out-parents in the chapter? Did any light bulbs come on for you? Whatever your situation, how can you apply the tips to build your own confidence and personal fulfillment (in any part or in your life as a whole)?

_____

_____

_____

People who are lonely or otherwise vulnerable are more susceptible to malignant persuasion—from a cult or anyone. Thinking about the entire chapter (or whatever you may have been reminded of), what possible weak points come to mind? What practical steps can you take now to shore up any weak areas and/or build strength to protect yourself?

_____

_____

_____

Each of our lives is a potpourri of favorites mixed with less desirable bits. We can choose to focus on the wood shavings and bark—and let those overshadow the pretty pinecones. Or we can infuse the filler with our hard-won wisdom, enjoy the preserved flowers with their colors softened by years of wisdom, and relish the dried curlicues now freed of their vines. We can look forward to the next ingredient in life's mixed bag of potpourri, hope for the best, and breathe in the fragrance of purposeful peace.

CHAPTER TEN

Permission to Stop

"Holding on is believing that there's only a past.
Letting go is knowing that there's a future."
—Daphne Rose Kingma

My stomach flipped as we came over the top on the historic replica of an early Ferris wheel and started down. I squeezed my eyes shut. It was the first turn of five. I knew from counting during two ride cycles before agreeing to get on board with my then preteen son.

As we neared the ground, the ride paused. I opened my eyes to see the operator, his head tilted in concern. "Are you okay? Do you want to get off?"

I did want to, but my eager boy in the seat beside me begged, "Please, Mom."

To the operator, I shook my head. It was just a ride, a mechanical wheel with a specific, spherical route. Four more turns, and I could step off and be done.

The ride whooshed us up and around again. I tried to smile as my son pointed out this or that. By the fourth turn, with the end in sight, my son asked me to go around again. "No," I said decisively. I'd faced my fears and joined him. It was enough.

Too bad stopping is not that easy with estrangement. Most parents stay on the emotional "ride" for years, clambering back aboard if their son or daughter asks. Even without contact, hope can bring the tilting whirl of optimism when sending a text or card. Then comes the downward spiral of only silence, or worse, cruelty or hate, in reply.

Even when parents come to a decision to disembark, to walk away and not look back, forces exist to push them to try again. Family members, friends, society, or idealistic views of a parent's love that hold them hostage. I know all of these. At one point, even my ex-daughter-in-law was among them.

They had been apart about a year when she phoned. At hearing her slightly strained but familiar voice, I pictured the same cute-as-a-button face from long ago. I had already heard about their parting ways. The grapevine is all too quick to spill its secrets. Hearing the news had made me sad—for her, for him, for all of us.

Years earlier, I might have rejoiced to discover they'd split, thinking the news would open a pathway for the rest of us to reunite. But the day she called, I knew a reunion wasn't imminent, or even likely. She said she'd processed her emotions over what happened between them but was troubled. Our child was alone. Things between us might change, she said, if we would just reach out, because she knew our child never would.

I didn't tell her that Dan *had* reached out—with unkind communications that had only moved us further apart. I also didn't tell her that just a few months earlier, *I* had been the one to initiate contact. In a brief but friendly text, I had provided some financial information that might be of help. *I don't know your circumstances*, I had texted and explained about some COVID assistance available under certain circumstances through our Native American tribe, and also about an insurance policy I'd been paying since my child's birth. The policy had reached maturity. All that was needed was a call to the company, maybe some paperwork, and the money would go to the rightful owner, which had apparently shifted from parent to child at age eighteen. There had been no chit-chat, but also no animosity. The last text I received about that information had been a *thanks*, the words between us like those of business associates. We had become strangers.

After those texts, I swiped my phone back to its starting point and got on with my day . . . *and my life*. The habits of joy and fulfillment I have had many years to perfect rejoined me, old friends to urge me onward. Our cordial exchange had been enough.

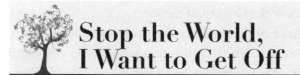

Stop the World, I Want to Get Off

The chaos of estrangement can feel like you're stuck on a wild ride. In Chapter One, I introduced you to "The Boat" as a useful analogy. Parents of estranged adult children can see themselves as resilient survivors who leap from the boat their estranged children steer. They clearly see the toxic waste they're drowning in and finally swim to shore. Here are few more analogies for parents. Which ride are you on, and how can you get off?

The Merry-Go-Round reduces life to a repetitive blur. You reach for the brass ring and don't snag it, but still get on the ride again. The music plays but it's too loud and not your choice. You're up, down, and all around, but going in circles. That's how it is for parents of estranged adult children who keep returning to the same old defeatist thoughts or actions. As long as you're on board, nothing changes and your path keeps spinning. However, you don't have to sit tight until the music stops. You can hop off and walk away from the same old repeating cycles of hope and pain, hello and goodbye, or effort expended for nothing gained.

The Seesaw requires balance. To work well, no one can play the heavy. Yet for most parents, the adult child holds all the weight. Like the scrawny kid in the playground, parents get caught up in

the air. The heavy weight controls what happens next, and sometimes, they jump off and leave you plummeting. *Down you go!*

Are you still climbing aboard the seesaw?

The Roller Coaster offers the heights of hope as well as the depths
of despair. In the middle of these high and low points come unan-
ticipated twists and turns. You're white-knuckling it all through
the ride. No parent wants to get on the estrangement coaster again,
but when they disembark, their land legs are still wobbly. When
presented with the opportunity to go again, the memory of the
high may overshadow the sinking of the low.

Does one or more of these rides match your experience? If so,
consider what you can learn from the comparison. Do you jump
back on the roller coaster despite knowing what's ahead? Even
those who escape The Boat of estrangement and swim to shore
may watch the horizon for a while and consider jumping back into
choppy, toxic waters. Is it clear to you that the seesaw is unevenly
weighted? What else can you see about the relationship (or lack
thereof) between you and your estranged adult children? What
about the merry-go-round? Has life since estrangement become a
blur where you're going through the motions but going nowhere?

Use one of the rides here or come up with another that represents
what estrangement has been like for you. Playground equipment, a
circus act, a form of transportation, a carnival ride. Use what comes to
mind and learn from it. What's similar about your estrangement experience and how you respond? Write your thoughts on the lines below.

Consider what it takes to get off the ride. What fears or worries come to mind? What sadness or happiness? Maybe you have a mixture of emotions. Identify them here.

_____

_____

_____

_____

_____

What ways of thinking must you change? What actions will you need to stop or start? Write down your ideas, then initiate some success steps. Keep them simple enough to achieve but tough enough to get you off the ride. Forgive yourself for emotional wobbles and occasional backslides but catch yourself before you go too far. Your life is your ride. You're the one at the wheel, so steer.

_____

_____

_____

_____

_____

_____

Onward

Last year, as the breezy spring days faded into the heat of summer, cherries on the trees at the home we'd begun moving to hung in clutches, their yellow skin blushing to red. One evening, as a brilliant sunset painted the sky violet, we realized the cherries were finally ripe. My husband and I pulled a few and savored their juicy sweetness straight from the tree. What a thrill that was. As twilight faded into darkness, we reluctantly headed back to the house. That night, I drifted off to sleep dreaming of the basketsful we'd pick the next day.

When morning came, we awakened to a chattering commotion. I looked out the back window to see squirrels squabbling. Tails flicking, they chased each other along the branching highways of the towering oaks, leaping from tree to tree, and chattering. Bleary eyed, my husband and I took our coffee cups and wandered outdoors. In the tiny, unkempt orchard at the far side of our property, the squirrels stopped to stare. We walked down the hill, only to find that, instead of cherries, clutches of seeds hung from the trees!

At first, we stood dumbfounded, mouths agape at the seeds stripped of the fruit by squirrel teeth. Then anger set in. They had eaten the fruit and left the pits. Nearby, the squirrels scuttled off into the leafy boughs of the oak trees, their chattering now like laughter. They had come in unexpectedly to steal our cherries and, for a little while, even our joy.

This spring, the graceful limbs of the cherry trees with their spearhead-shaped leaves are again heavy with ripening fruit. So far, the squirrels are quiet, probably waiting, watching for signs of bird pecks, or testing the highest fruit themselves for its sweetness. Meanwhile, I've been reading about how to outsmart them.

My husband likes to tease that he'll get out a BB gun but neither of us could really kill them. Those who blog about the wily creatures say distractions work best. *Roll big balls of peanut butter in nuts*, advises one funny blog that tells readers they should place the sticky balls as far away from the cherry trees as possible. The idea is to lure the varmints away, then keep them busy chewing and with peanut butter stuck to the roofs of their mouths.

I'm not sure this idea, or any of the distractions I've read about, are intended for more than a laugh. But for me, those squirrels, and my response to their cherry stealing, have become a metaphor for life and how I respond to its follies. Even when I've worked my hardest, enjoying the expected rewards wasn't always guaranteed.

If you're reading this book, then you know all too well that many good parents who work diligently and do their best sometimes end up *without* the sweet fruits of their labor. Adult children sometimes still decide to thumb their noses at us. It's in our responses that we can move forward, still find joy, and live a meaningful and fulfilled life. The pivot to distracting ourselves and having fun while we do is really what all the silly Internet advice about battling squirrels conveys. We can spend hours trying to outwit the squirrels, or *lifetimes* trying to get our children to act as we want, both without guarantees that anything we do will work. We can let them steal our energy and joy. Or we can accept them as they are, recognize we can't change them, and learn to live and laugh despite them.

If we're honest, most of us can look back on our lives and identify things we tried to force, knew were pointless, or allowed to make us miserable for far too long. We must decide how best to spend our time, energy, and devotion. For our second or third acts, let's choose wisely, learn quickly, and let go when needed. We may not get to enjoy the fruits we expected to enjoy, but we can still put good out into the world. We can make a difference, for others and for ourselves.

Look How Far You've Come

Looking back is part of any journey. We buy mementos, take pictures, and recount our experiences from along the way. For me, writing this book has been a journey. By reading, answering the questions, and doing the exercises you've undertaken a similar course. Thank you for joining me. Let's look back now, reflect, and enlighten our continuing paths.

You began in Chapter One by *Getting Real* about the far-reaching effects of estrangement and used the first exercise to "Shine a Light" on hindrances to your well-being. You gained insight into ramifications such as negative self-talk or overinvolvement into others' problems, as well as physical insults to your wellness including insomnia or binge eating. By chronicling these effects specifically and in writing, you set the stage to overcome them.

Getting real about the trauma of estrangement requires dropping the rose-colored glasses not only about your child but about yourself. Most people are familiar with the term "fight or flight" as it relates to the body's response to stress. You learned two lesser-known facets that could apply to estrangement in "Freeze and Fawn." You may be familiar with zoning out, or "freezing," in activities that become ways to escape an uncomfortable reality. Or you may be more of a "fawner" like Roy, who repeatedly opened his wallet to the daughter he feared he'd lose. Ultimately, striving to please another to your own detriment is unwise and won't fix any relationships. Becoming more self-aware promotes *your own* growth for *your own* fulfillment, peace, and joy.

"The Boat" illustrated five aspects of resilience and applied them to estranged parents' lives. Did you recognize yourself treading water in a toxic sea? Perhaps you've begun the journey forward, yet still look back and long for what once was or what you'd hoped for. Will you free yourself and swim to shore?

Finally, the "Lifetime Map" helped you see yourself from a new vantage point to provide insights and motivate self-compassion. Beth saw how her circumstances coupled with her personality had shaped her as a caregiver and nurturer. But she also identified the need to speak up more often and, sometimes, to put herself first. Gabe noted how his lifelong love of bicycling had helped him grow and get through troubled times. He could use the hobby for his future well-being and even to grow closer to his wife. What revelations did you discover? How were you helped? What will you carry into your future . . . or leave behind?

In Chapter Two, the physical manifestations caused by the emotional stress in divorced mother of two, Linda, helped you see that it's vital to *Take Care of Your Mind, Body, and Spirit.* How you think about the estrangement either causes distress or provides relief. You can exercise "Your Turnaround" over defeatist self-talk. Wisely "Mind Your Mind" to habituate strong thinking that inspires.

Dale's anger illustrated how a temper clouds judgment, confounds decision-making, and stalls momentum. However, social support helps pave a forward path. When his wife Serena joined a support group, talking with others helped her stand up for herself. She could then also help Dale move beyond blinding rage and toward their future.

Myrna provided a powerful example of overcoming estrangement-induced stress and resulting poor health. As her weight ballooned and she suffered the sudden onset of allergies and asthma, she became depressed. Nevertheless, Myrna took small steps to get herself back in order. As she did, she contemplated her future: *What do I want for myself? What can I do? What expectations will I need to let go of?* With more clarity, an improved outlook, and better health, she took bigger steps to move to a new location and build new social connections.

"Friends Forever?" explored the fact that not all friendships are lasting. "Making New Friends" helped you consider the nature of friendships and what you seek from them. You can use those insights to meet like-minded people who will respect your boundaries. For some, professional counseling, coaching, or therapy is desired. "Tips for Finding Support" and "Is a Life Coach Right for You?" explored differences in purpose and working styles, and guidelines to choose the most sensible form of professional support for your individual needs.

Reminders to take good care of yourself led you back to the chapter's focus on wellness of the mind, body, and spirit. That includes disallowing abuse and being aware that estrangement stress can pop up for many years, often when you're least expecting it. News from afar can be unsettling and set you back. Specific examples helped you to take charge of your own well-being, stay proactive, recover quickly, and make yourself a priority.

In Chapter Three, a *Face-Off* with the monster in the mirror revealed the ugly thoughts about one's own children that can torment parents, yet are natural responses given the circumstances. With the help of Gigi and Brad, you learned ways to curb emotional displays in inappropriate settings and how to prepare mentally, physically, and in your environment, to find humor and cope. You also chose an imaginary dream team to support you and learned how to reinterpret frustrations to tamp down anger rather than fuel its fire.

Bonnie and Mike shared the complex emotional landscape surrounding a child's sexual abuse. Perpetrators may be school chums, a family member, or someone else. Survivors often don't tell. Childhood sexual abuse may play a silent role in estrangement. Bonnie and Mike demonstrated how to lean on your individualized history and personal strengths to regain emotional balance—and you can do this, too—even if your circumstances are different.

"The Bitter Truth" helped you root out any bitterness that's crept into your outlook to cause distrust, impair your health, and make you unlikeable. Ebenezer Scrooge and my septic system helped you contemplate your legacy and take steps toward positive change. Finally, you learned to "Pack Your Emotional Toolkit" for your own kind, loving care.

Chapter Four sees you *Shaping the Family* as if it's a song. Adjusting notes for a well-balanced tune despite the loss is good composition. *Over*compensating (as I did for my broken toe) throws your family out of whack. The whole family can get stuck in an echoing tunnel that always chimes back to the person who left. A decision to change and honest discussions from a place of love bring awareness that help the family grow.

In "Siblings Say," you heard from brothers and sisters who suffer the consequences of being left behind, feeling responsible for their broken parents, and trying to compensate for the estranged ones' bad behavior and absence. By taking care of ourselves, parents model healthy coping and wise living that frees these precious sons and daughters to pursue their own satisfying lives.

"Family Culture" showed how our history can complicate our growing families and contribute to estrangement. And in "The Straw that Breaks the Camel's Back," I related more of my ongoing story. You saw how relatives' wishes for happy endings occludes their full understanding and can influence us. Hope is a beautiful expression of human nature but not always reflective of reality. You learned to temper hope with reason, history, and others' influence. If you reach out and are rebuffed, you can reinterpret the experience as a reminder about what is real and worthy of your efforts and focus.

"Healing in the Family Tree" discussed intergenerational trauma and its basis in science as well as in family secrets. Inherited stress is real. So is how people interpret and fill in the uncertainties and unknowns of family history. These may have a role in estrangement. Finally, in "Warning! Genograms Are Addicting," you chose a focus and began to identify patterns in your family tree.

In Chapter Five, we looked at *The Wider Family*, beginning with "A Grandchild's Point of View." Cynthia, now an adult, shared her memories from early childhood when her mother trashed her beloved grandmother. She wished her grandmother would have been stronger. Then, instead of young Cynthia seeing her own sense of powerlessness echoed, she and her grandmother could have enjoyed their brief moments together. A strong, self-possessed role model could have helped Cynthia cope.

A discussion of grandparents' rights revealed the hidden costs of fighting for them. "Has the Grandparenting Role Changed?" shed light on the changing role of grandparents in society and revealed ageist myths and their possible consequences. "A Grandparent's Legacy" explored smart, proactive measures to convey love, provide history, and share knowledge despite the distance. You learned about leaving a legacy will, its roots and function.

"Supporting Your Marriage and Your Spouse" shared Vera's worries over how she might be judged by in-laws in her second marriage. It's unwise to suffer in silence, guess others' thoughts, and attribute motivations to them based on our fears. With communication, we may discover that our fears are irrational. Catriona, too, is in a second marriage. Long ago, she made the decision to let her manipulative estranged sons be. Her husband still gets sucked in and gives money to his own narcissistic adult child. Catriona found a way to protect hers and her husband's assets. You can, too. Financial abuse of elders is common, and married partners must protect one another and themselves.

In "Estrangement: It's Catching," Mitch, Wallace, and Myrna related their experiences to highlight the ways your other relationships (with friends, family, or outside groups) may have changed. With the help of Margaret and Sukie, you sought conclusions about relatives' behavior and solutions for "When Others Interfere." Using the "Triage" exercise, you began to sift through your needs and values, order their importance, and make sensible decisions about extended family.

Sometimes, you must stand alone, even when it means you don't take relatives' (or experts') advice, or they perhaps judge you. You can "Be Discerning, Not Desperate" when you seek advice or receive unbidden input, recognize how your family's story of you may still exert influence, and grow stronger as an individual who knows what's best for yourself.

Chapter Six makes clear that *There Are No Perfect Parents*. The dynamics of estrangement are different when parents feel responsible because of their bigger than typical mistakes. Yet there are also similarities. Parents such as those in Chapter Six look inward and soul search for the cause of estrangement the same as most parents do. Often there is no clear-cut or sensible answer.

By way of these parents' shame and regret, you learned more about how to forgive (even yourself), hope, and heal. In "Your Turn," you explored important questions about when parents' love and contrition make them easy targets and gluttons for punishment, and how to use self-compassion to take kind care of yourself.

Is Reconciliation Possible? is answered in Chapter Seven. Consider whether you will "Bend . . . Or Break?" Apologizing for shortcomings is wise but buying into "A Shared Delusion" of revisionist history that puts undeserved blame on you *isn't.* You looked realistically at whether you might be "guilting" your adult child—a concept that heaps fault on already vulnerable parents who are taught, once again, to walk on eggshells. Remember, the acronym? Walking on eggshells = W.O.E.

"Can *Some* Contact Work for You?" Wayne, Betty, and Ginger accepted less contact than their ideal. These parents had three vital things in common that make the "some contact" approach work. Even so, bygones may not really be gone. Estrangement fosters distrust and uncertainty. Those feelings don't just disappear—*poof!*—with an apology. Reconciling takes work by all parties. You may be like Joan, who, after many years and late in life, no longer has the energy to put effort in with a daughter who says she wants a relationship but whose attitude and behavior demonstrate that she hasn't changed.

"Should Siblings Just Get Along?" provided insight into how siblings feel when an estranged one returns to the fold. Kirsten's parents welcomed her estranged brother with open arms—and no accountability—creating an atmosphere of resentment. In some families, "A Sibling's Longing" for reunion causes concern. Denise and Chico helped you learn ways to handle tense conversations that may ensue. In "Reconciling: the Surprises," you heard parents' unvarnished feelings about reconciling. Finally, you contemplated the concept of consequences, which exist despite "Forgiveness," and used the questions in "Reconciliation: Exploring the Idea," to contemplate reconciling realistically.

Chapter Eight, *Reconciling, More to Consider* explores additional challenges and complexities. In "Reconciling When You Suspect (or Know) Your Child Has Mental Illness," Peggy and Bridgette illustrated useful mind-sets in order to stay in touch with grandchildren and cope: a healthy sense of humor, remaining cognizant of instability, and measured contact help. You learned that mental illness is no excuse for abuse. With the help of Jane and Peter, you saw how an adult child who gets mental health support can change. Reconciliation requires parents' patience but also their strength. With Rusty and Pia as examples, you learned how to set boundaries—and enforce them.

"When Reconciling Requires Change" detailed needed adjustments on the part of parents. If your child confides negatively about their spouse, as Dodi's son did, it's a recipe for disaster. If you suffer out-of-control anxiety like Elena did, or have some attitude problem, get the support you need and improve. Parents who take care of their own health and can look honestly at their own behavior can better help others, be positive role models, and live well for themselves.

Chapter Nine, *Potpourri* provides a mix of topics, starting with family business. Rebecca, Doug, and Blythe confided about adult children they completely trusted yet who betrayed them. With their regrets and lessons, some "Tips from the Family Business Trenches," and the help of multi-generational businessman, Bo, you learned possible ways to end work-related ties while protecting your assets, your dignity, and your grace. Legal help is prudent, but as Blythe's story reveals, not all attorneys are created equal.

In "Final Passage," you heard how Mei calmed her worries over shame and embarrassment about her husband's memorial service. Krystyna revealed the potential damage, and subsequent regrets, that can occur when you put off end-of-life decisions and act under duress. Pro bono and inexpensive options are suggested in "Resources for Legal Help."

People fare better when they face their own aging head-on. "Are You an 'Elder Orphan'?" addresses the increasing numbers of older adults living without a supportive network. Reflect upon what you want out of life in later years, the possible limitations you fear or know you will face, and what sort of community will be agreeable—and then act. "Resources for Elders, Whether Orphans or Not" offers choices.

Part of embracing a new phase of a life means "Letting Go for Your Future." You learned from Janet that keeping an estranged child's room intact, or otherwise holding things, may be an outer reflection of stalled emotional space. Dale and Serena showed how letting go lets *you* go. By reaching out one more time, offering their daughter her collectibles, and then accepting her refusal and donating them, they launched their own unburdened, fun-loving retirement phase. Questions you answer mark a roadmap to sweep out emotional cobwebs and clear your way to a freer future.

With the help of Clarence, Amelia, John, and Doris, you recognized manipulative behavior and escaped "The Pocket." This pitiful space imprisons parents with false hope, keeps them stalled in denial, or motivated by fear about what others might think or say about them. And there are side effects such as a diminishing bank account and displaced anger.

Chapter Nine's potpourri mix contained planning tips and self-care for before, during, and after "The Lion's Den of Tense Events." Occasions that bring estranged family members face-to-face are sometimes inevitable. The chapter also offered advice from Araceli, Carol, and Thad for "When Only One Parent Is Rejected," and the other remains in contact with the estranger. "Coping When You're the Only Rejected Parent" helps with positive viewpoints, self-nurturing, forgiveness, and strengthening self-esteem.

In "Sects and Cults," I shared my brush with a cultish group from the 1970s Human Potential Movement and how intermittent reinforcement is used as a means for control. Margit, Ari, and Destiny shared their stories of groups that came in under the radar and all but stole their adult children. For various reasons, their kids were at vulnerable life points. These parents were happy to see their children involved with something they at first believed was good. Their experiences shed light on the wolf-in-sheep's-clothing techniques of those who are masters at their game. Also, cult-like families exist and contribute to estrangements.

Finally, we arrive at Chapter Ten, *Permission to Stop*. Most of you can recognize the "ride" analogy in your own merry-go-round, roller coaster, or up-down seesaw of estrangement. Strapped in as an unwilling passenger, you grew sad, weary, or sick. If you're like most parents, you know that, at some point, for your own well-being, you must disembark, get your land legs back, and recover. You know when the most sensible choice is "Onward." Not all work brings sweet rewards in expected ways. Search for any positive aspects, recognize anything you gained along the way, and do something good with what you've learned—for others and for yourself.

Your Basket

Sometimes, when I reflect on the mix of circumstances that have filled my life, I'm reminded of a Food Network television show where competitors open a basket of odd, mismatched ingredients. Some competing chefs make entrees that cover over the bitter bits. Others embrace and even feature them. Some make not-so-tasty dishes. Others mix up masterpieces.

Consider your life's basket and especially the estrangement. Reflect on how you've handled its effect on you, the people around you, and your overall life. Those competing chefs sometime change their minds, throw out what didn't work and start fresh, or mold a failed entrée into something different—and better—than the original plan.

In Chapter One, we met Donna, whose history involves an abusive, deadbeat dad ex-husband who is now the favored parent. In doing the Lifetime Map and reflecting, Donna came to realize she had stopped trusting her own judgment. That's why she isolated herself and avoided close relationships of any kind. "It's no way to live," says Donna, who is taking steps now to "rejoin the human race."

Like Donna, the Lifetime Map you started in Chapter One still has room to roam and grow. Among all your life's ingredients, what have you covered over, embraced, or featured? What can you discard, substitute, add, or perhaps even learn to like? Write down a few thoughts.

_____

_____

_____

_____

_____

Estrangement from your adult child(ren) thrust you into unexpected circumstances. How you view those circumstances, what you pinch into the mix, heap on top, or cook up, shapes your life. Maybe you can't do anything to change your adult children's decisions, but you can own your personal journey despite them.

To own something means to hold power and have mastery over its use and effects. That's where you come in, making choices and handling the ingredients you've been dealt. Even in estrangement, you can own your life—the bitter and the sweet. Make it a masterpiece.

Connecting

The day my ex-daughter-in-law called, she briefly caught me up to speed from her perspective. Their ride together had been unpredictable, the twists and turns too far beyond expectations for them to remain united. Ultimately, they had both walked away. On the telephone, she urged me to get in touch. Yet in the same breath, she said that the man she married didn't exist, and the individual she divorced was a person she no longer knew.

The reality is that none of the family Dan once referred to as "your side" (meaning "my" side) rather than his own loving clan know that person anymore. Huge gaps in time, space, and identity have taken place. The person we once saw as a son we would know forever has become a stranger. It's probably sad to read these lines, but at this point, it isn't debilitatingly sad for me to write them. They are facts, written by a mother who remembers a sweet young man she knew and loved, but has come to terms with how things are now.

Some parents tell me that, even after years of repeated rejection, they *can't* let go. A few have been insightful enough to identify why: Pain is all they have left. Holding the pain tight, they say, keeps the connection alive. In their child's absence, they keep reaching out or ruminating because stoking the flames of continued pain is how they relate. Pain becomes a practice. For me there's a better way. Maybe for you, too.

In Chapter Five, we talked about our connections to family members throughout the ages by way of DNA. Many who practice family constellations believe that on an unconscious level, repeating old patterns is a way to connect, identify with, or even to show love to those in our history. I'm not trying to convince you of that, but the *practice* of pain *is* repetitive. In holding pain tight, you honor your child—yet you dishonor yourself. You hurt your health, your psyche, and your potential.

Much of this book has been about the discovery of patterns, and the mining of our own histories to make sense of our lives. That applies to the topic of connecting, too. You can let the pain go yet remain connected.

Parents of estranged adult children remember their youngsters from earlier times. They cherish sweet moments, darling smiles, family togetherness, and the two-way love that flowed like strands of silk, connecting us even when we were apart. That those memories remain alive is a beautiful reminder of all that was and assure you of their permanence. The threads to that history remain for parents even when the children sever ties.

It's counterintuitive to think of our children, who came *after* us, as our past. But estrangement changes everything. The shift ripples through the continuum of time, changes the relationship, us, and our children. Even for parents who successfully reconcile, nothing is ever the same. When a person walks away, the space they left changes. Should the person return, the home and family they left no longer exists. This is what is meant by the saying: *You can never go home again.*

Our children, the bond we once knew or expected to enhance and give new shape in the future, is *behind* us. If we think of our estranged adult children as our past, even if just for now, we can change how we connect. We can leave the pain and adopt ways of relating to ourselves that help rather than hurt us. We can see our place in a child's life from a new vantage point. We can exist in their lives as part of their history, the rich, dark soil that gave them life, regardless how they despise or find the good in it.

Let me pause here and say that this is not intended as an end. Your children may circle back. Perhaps in this life, in Heaven, or if your belief system allows or dictates, in some other form.

Even for those with stepchildren or adopted children, the idea of connecting in a new way is relevant. In *Done With The Crying*, I shared my own hard work to visualize my son in a life he chose for himself, to see him as willfully walking forward on his own path, without me and without our family, by his choice. I could stand in a distant space and wish him well (as I continue to do).

By seeing him in that way, my relationship with him began to change. I could shake away the pain or shame, honor myself, and move forward *for me*. That's why so many years later, I could contact Dan with some financial information and the facts of that insurance policy without expectations or needs. The currency of family love exists in a new way. Despite Dan's decision to separate, I could embrace my loving intentions to help.

The threads of love with which I raised Dan still exist. By letting go of the pain, I could connect in a way that allowed him his wings—and also honored my own. I don't have to remain sad, bound to a tumultuous end. In time and with practice, the cutoff could become a new beginning.

Every so often, my old pain surfaces. I might hear another parent's story that stirs up echoes of my own shock and hurt. In a way, writing this book required touching those old wounds and dragging them out for another look. Deep pain is like that. Healing in layers that can require re-opening, cutting away, and clearing by repeated care. But pain doesn't feel good. Nor does holding it *do* good—for me or for anyone else. In all the years since those early days of hard work to regain my footing in unknown territory and carry on, I have learned that gripping tightly to the sorrow, shame, and devastation of what happened hurts me and spreads to those around me. It's no way to connect.

Will Dan and the rest of us ever reconcile in the flesh, eye-to-eye, and in the same room? I can't know for sure, but I have long since reconciled to the facts: I was a good mother who loved a son. He exists in my treasured history, a sweet boy who grew into a strong, handsome man. Somewhere along the way, he made decisions and chose a new path without his family, in a new way of life. I have no choice but to accept the decisions made by a child who is

BEYOND DONE WITH THE CRYING

now grown up, raised by parents to become independent. Despite that, whether acknowledged or not, the silken threads of our years together, our beautiful, *connected* memories remain. I choose to see those threads in sunlight, permanent as they are, and gleaming. Maybe my child does too.

Endnotes

CHAPTER ONE: Getting Real

1. Conti, R.P. (2015). Family estrangement: Establishing a prevalence rate. *Journal of Psychology and Behavioral Science*, 3(2), pp. 28–35, doi:0.15640/jpbs.v3n2a4

2. Gilligan, M., Suitor, J. J., & Pillemer, K. (2015). Estrangement Between Mothers and Adult Children: The Role of Norms and Values. *Journal of Marriage and the Family*, 77(4), 908–920. doi:10.1111/jomf.12207

3. Silverstein, M., & Bengston, V. L. (1997). Intergenerational solidarity and the structure of adult child-parent relationships in American families. *American Journal of Sociology*, 103(2), 429–460).

4. Pascoe, E. A., & Smart Richman, L. (2009). Perceived discrimination and health: a meta-analytic review. *Psychological Bulletin*, 135(4), 531–54. doi: 10.1037/a0016059

5. Blake, L., Bland, B., & Imrie, S. (2020). The Counseling Experiences of Individuals Who Are Estranged From a Family Member. *Family Relations*, 69(4), 820–831. https://doi.org/10.1111/fare.12385

6. Myers, H. F., Wyatt, G. E., Ullman, J. B., Loeb, T. B., Chin, D., Prause, N., Zhang, M., Williams, J. K., Slavich, G. M., and Liu, H. (2015). Cumulative burden of lifetime adversities: Trauma and mental health in low-SES African Americans and Latino/as. *Psychological Trauma: theory, research, practice and policy*, 7(3), 243–51. doi: 10.1037/a0039077

7. Kimron, L., & Cohen, M. (2012). Coping and emotional distress during acute hospitalization in older persons with earlier trauma: the case of Holocaust survivors. *Quality of Life Research,* 21(5):783-94. doi: 10.1007/s11136-011-9984-6. doi: 10.1007/s11136-011-9984-6

8. Walker, P. (2017). Emotional flashback management in the treatment of PTSD. Psychotherapy.net: Resources to Inspire Therapists. https://www.psychotherapy.net/article/complex-ptsd

9. Southwick, S. M., Bonanno, G. A., Masten, A. S., Panter-Brick, C., & Yehuda, R. (2014). Resilience definitions, theory, and challenges: interdisciplinary perspectives. *European Journal of Psychotraumatology,* 5, 10.3402/ejpt.v5.25338. doi:10.3402/ejpt.v5.25338

CHAPTER TWO: Take Care of Your Mind, Body, and Spirit

1. Yu L, Chiu C, Lin Y, Wang H, & Chen J. (2007). Testing a model of stress and health using meta-analytic path analysis. *Journal of Nursing Research (Taiwan Nurses Association),* 15(3), 202–214. doi: 10.1097/01.jnr.0000387616.64812.60

2. Wood, A. M., Maltby, J., Gillett, R., Linley, P. A., & Joseph, S. (2008). The role of gratitude in the development of social support, stress, and depression: Two longitudinal studies. *Journal of Research in Personality,* 42(4), 854–871. https://doi.org/10.1016/j.jrp.2007.11.003

3. Chapman, B. P., Fiscella, K., Kawachi, I., Duberstein, P., & Muennig, P. (2013). Emotion suppression and mortality risk over a 12-year follow-up. *Journal of Psychosomatic Research,* 75(4), 381–385. https://doi.org/10.1016/j.jpsychores.2013.07.014

4. Chopik, W. J., O'Brien, E. (2017). Happy you, healthy me? Having a happy partner is independently associated with better health in oneself. *Health Psychology,* 36, 21–30. doi: 10.1037/hea0000432

5. Siew Maan Diong, George D. Bishop, Hwee Chong Enkelmann, Eddie M.W. Tong, Yong Peng Why, Jansen C.H. Ang & Majeed Khader (2005) Anger, stress, coping, social support and health: Modelling the relationships. *Psychology & Health,* 20:4, 467–495. doi: 10.1080/08870440405 12331333960

6. Bowen, K. S., Uchino, B. N., Birmingham, W., Carlisle, M., Smith, T. W., & Light, K. C. (2013). The stress-buffering effects of functional social support on ambulatory blood pressure. *Health Psychology: Official Journal of the Division of Health Psychology, American Psychological Association*, 33(11), 1440–1443. doi:10.1037/hea0000005

7. Hall, Jeffrey A (2018). How many hours does it take to make a friend? *Journal of Social and Personal Relationships.* https://doi.org/10.1177/0265407518761225

8. Luong, G., Charles, S. T., & Fingerman, K. L. (2011). Better With Age: Social Relationships Across Adulthood. *Journal of Social and Personal Relationships*, 28(1), 9–23. doi:10.1177/0265407510391362

9. Charles S. T. (2010). Strength and vulnerability integration: a model of emotional well-being across adulthood. *Psychological Bulletin*, 136(6), 1068–1091. doi:10.1037/a0021232

10. Lee I, Shiroma EJ, Kamada M, Bassett DR, Matthews CE, Buring JE. Association of Step Volume and Intensity With All-Cause Mortality in Older Women. *JAMA Intern Med.* Published online May 29, 2019, 179(8):1105–1112. doi:10.1001/jamainternmed.2019.0899

11. Loidl, B., & Leipold, B. (2019). Facets of accommodative coping in adulthood. *Psychology and Aging*, 34(5), 640–654. http://dx.doi.org/10.1037/pag0000378

12. Hicks, J. A., Trent, J., Davis, W. E., & King, L. A. (2011, June 27). Positive Affect, Meaning in Life, and Future Time Perspective: An Application of Socioemotional Selectivity Theory. *Psychology and Aging.* Advance online publication. doi: 10.1037/a0023965

13. Marina Arkkukangas, Annelie J Sundler, Anne Söderlund, Staffan Eriksson & Ann-Christin Johansson (2017) Older persons' experiences of a home-based exercise program with behavioral change support. *Physiotherapy Theory and Practice*, 33:12, 905–913. doi: 10.1080/09593985.2017.1359869

CHAPTER THREE: Face-Off

1. Lieberman MD, Eisenberger NI, Crockett MJ, Tom SM, Pfeifer JH, Way BM. Putting feelings into words: affect labeling disrupts amygdala activity in response to affective stimuli. *Psychol Sci.* 2007 May; *18*(5):421–8. doi: 10.1111/j.1467-9280.2007.01916.x. PMID: 17576282.

2. University of California - Los Angeles. (2007, June 22). Putting Feelings Into Words Produces Therapeutic Effects In The Brain. *ScienceDaily.* Retrieved January 17, 2021. www.sciencedaily.com/ releases/2007/06/070622090727.htm

3. McGregor, S. (2016). *Done With The Crying: Help and Healing for Mothers of Estranged Adult Children* (1st Ed.). San Marcos, CA: Sowing Creek Press.

BOX: Keeping the Secret—This topic is written about exhaustively. I have offered these two resources as representative of overall information:

4. O'Grady, R.L. & Matthews-Creech, N. (n.d.). Why children don't tell: Sandusky case sheds light on complexities of child sex abuse. https://lacasacenter.org/why-child-abuse-victims-dont-tell/

5. Why don't they tell? Teens and sexual assault disclosure (n.d.). https://www.nctsn.org/sites/default/files/resources/fact-sheet/ why_dont_they_tell_teens_and_sexual_assault_disclosure.pdf

BOX: By the Numbers

6. Townsend, C., Rheingold, A., Haviland, M.L. (2016). Estimating a child sexual abuse prevalence rate for practitioners: An updated review of child sexual abuse prevalence studies. Charleston SC: Darkness to Light. Retrieved from www.D2L.org/1in10 (www. D2L.org) To get to this article, go to www.D2L.org and scroll down. Click on the box that says "Research," and then you click on the "prevalence rate white paper."

7. Martine Hébert, Marc Tourigny, Mireille Cyr, Pierre McDuff, Jacques Joly. Prevalence of Childhood Sexual Abuse and Timing of Disclosure in a Representative Sample of Adults From Quebec. *The Canadian Journal of Psychiatry*, 2009;54(9):631–636

8. Daigneault et al. Men's and women's childhood sexual abuse and victimization in adult partner relationships: A study of risk factors. *Child Abuse & Neglect*, 2009; 33 (9): 638 doi: 10.1016/j.chiabu.2009.04.003

9. Rohde, P., Ichikawa, L., Simon, G. E., Ludman, E. J., Linde, J. A. Jeffery, R. W., & Operskalski, B. H. (2008). Associations of child sexual and physical abuse with obesity and depression in middle-aged women. *Child Abuse & Neglect*, 32, 878–887.

10. Kendler, K., Bulik, C., Silberg, J., Hettema, J., Myers, J., & Prescott, C. (2000). Childhood sexual abuse and adult psychiatric and substance use disorders in women: An epidemiological and Cotwin Control Analysis. *Archives of General Psychiatry*, 57, 953–959.

11. Dube, S. A., Anda, R. F., Whitfield, C. L., Brown, D. W., Felitti, D. J., Dong, M., & Giles, W. (2005). Long-term consequences of childhood sexual abuse by gender of the victim. *American Journal of Preventive Medicine*, 28, 430–437.

12. Stitt, Seán (2007) "Non-offending Mothers of Sexually Abused Children: the Hidden Victims," The ITB Journal: Vol. 8: Iss. 1, Article 3. doi:10.21427/D7016T Available at: https://arrow.dit.ie/itbj/vol8/iss1/3

CHAPTER FOUR: Shaping the Family

1. Schreiber, K. (May/June, 2007). Poison People. *Psychology Today Magazine*.

2. Singer, Margaret (2003). Cults in our midst: The continuing fight against their hidden menace. Jossey-Bass: San Francisco.

3. Woke, Dieter & Skew, Alexandra (2012). Bullying among siblings. *International Journal of Adolescent Medicine and Health*. 24, 17-25. doi:10.1515/ijamh.2012.004.

4. Shulevitz, J. (2014). The Science of Suffering. *The New Republic*. https://newrepublic.com/article/120144/trauma-genetic-scientists-say-parents-are-passing-ptsd-kids

5. Glausiusz, J. (2014). Searching chromosomes for the legacy of trauma. *Nature* (2014). https://doi.org/10.1038/nature.2014.15369

6. Yehuda, R., Daskalakis, N. P., Lehrner, A., Desarnaud, F., Bader, H. N., Makotkine, I., Flory, J. D., Bierer, L. M., & Meaney, M. J. (2014). Influences of maternal and paternal PTSD on epigenetic regulation of the glucocorticoid receptor gene in Holocaust survivor offspring. *The American journal of psychiatry*, 171(8), 872–880. https://doi.org/10.1176/appi.ajp.2014.13121571

7. Dias, B., Ressler, K. Parental olfactory experience influences behavior and neural structure in subsequent generations. *Nat Neurosci 17*, 89–96 (2014). https://doi.org/10.1038/nn.3594

CHAPTER FIVE: The Wider Family

1. Sonja Hilbrand, David A. Coall, Denis Gerstorf, Ralph Hertwig (2017). Caregiving within and beyond the family is associated with lower mortality for the caregiver: A prospective study. *Evolution and Human Behavior*, Volume 38, Issue 3, May 2017, Pages 397–403. https://doi.org/10.1016/j.evolhumbehav.2016.11.010

2. Esposito, L. (2017, September 13). The Health benefits of having (and being) grandparents. *U.S. News And World Report*. Downloaded from: https://health.usnews.com/wellness/articles/2017-09-13/the-health-benefits-of-having-and-being-grandparents

3. Grandparents contribute to grandchildren's well-being. Retrieved from: https://www.ox.ac.uk/research/research-impact/grandparents-contribute-childrens-wellbeing

4. Sara M. Moorman, PhD, Jeffrey E. Stokes, MA, Solidarity in the Grandparent–Adult Grandchild Relationship and Trajectories of Depressive Symptoms, *The Gerontologist*, Volume 56, Issue 3, June 2016, Pages 408–420, https://doi.org/10.1093/geront/gnu056

5. Yon Y, Mikton CR, Gassoumis ZD, Wilber KH. Elder abuse prevalence in community settings: a systematic review and meta-analysis. *Lancet Glob Health*. 2017 Feb;5(2):e147-e156. doi: 10.1016/S2214-109X(17)30006-2. PMID: 28104184.

6. Fullen, M. C. (2018). Ageism and the counseling profession: Causes, consequences, and methods for counteraction. *Professional Counselor*, 8(2), 104–114. https://doi.org/10.15241/mcf.8.2.104

7. Whitbourne, S. K., & Sneed, J. R. (2002). The paradox of well-being, identity processes, and steretoype threat: Ageism and its potential relationships to the self in later life. In T. D. Nelson (Ed.), *Ageism: Stereotyping and prejudice against older persons* (2nd ed.) pp. 247–273. Cambridge, MA: MIT Press.

CHAPTER SEVEN: Is Reconciliation Possible?

1. Young, L.C. (2006). *Young adults' perceptions of parental differential treatment: Measurement and relation to psychological adjustment, attachment style, and close relationships.* University of Victoria. https://dspace.library.uvic.ca/handle/1828/3529.

CHAPTER EIGHT: Reconciling, More to Consider

1. American Psychiatric Association. (2013). *Diagnostic and statistical manual of mental disorders* (5th ed.). https://doi.org/10.1176/appi.books.9780890425596

2. Woolley, M. E., & Greif, G. L. (2019). Mother-in-Law Reports of Closeness to Daughter-in-Law: The Determinant Triangle with the Son and Husband. *Social Work*, 64(1), 73–82. https://doi.org/10.1093/sw/swy055

CHAPTER NINE: Potpourri

1. Montayre, J., Thaggard, S., & Carney, M. (2020). Views on the use of the term "elder orphans": A qualitative study. *Health & Social Care in the Community*, 28(2), 341–346. https://doi-org.nuls.idm.oclc.org/10.1111/hsc.12865

2. Barry, A., Heale, R., Pilon, R., & Lavoie, A. M. (2018). The meaning of home for ageing women living alone: An evolutionary concept analysis. *Health & Social Care in the Community*, 26(3), e337–e344. https://doi-org.nuls.idm.oclc.org/10.1111/hsc.12470

3. Blanchard, J. (2013). Aging in community: Communitarian alternative to aging in place alone. *Generations*, 37(4), 6–13.

4. Strange, D. and Takarangi, MKD (2015). Memory distortion for traumatic events: The role of mental imagery. *Frontiers in Psychiatry*, 6:27, doi: 10.3389/fpsyt.2015.00027

5. Ballard, J. (2019). Millennials are the loneliest generation. https://today.yougov.com/topics/lifestyle/articles-reports/2019/07/30/loneliness-friendship-new-friends-poll-survey

Mentioned Books
(in the order they appear)

- *Codependent No More: How to Stop Controlling Others and Start Caring for Yourself* by Melody Beattie (1986)
- *The New Codependency: Help and Guidance for Today's Generation* by Melody Beattie (2008)
- *Connecting to Our Ancestral Past: Healing through Family Constellations, Ceremony, and Ritual* by Francesca Mason Boring (2012)
- *Family and Other Constellations Revealed* by Indra Torsten Preiss (2012)
- *It Didn't Start with You: How Inherited Family Trauma Shapes Who We Are and How to End the Cycle* by Mark Wolynn (2016)
- *The Canadian Grandparents Story* by Daphne Jennings (2019).
- *Invisible Grandparenting* by Pat Hanson (2013)
- *Banished: A Grandmother Alone: Surviving Alienation and Estrangement* by Nancy Lee Klune (2018)
- *On Becoming Whole: A Healing Companion to Ease Emotional Pain and Find Self-Love* by Bruce Alan Kehr M.D. (2018)
- *Carry On, Warrior: The Power of Embracing Your Messy, Beautiful Life* by Glennon Doyle (2014)
- *Letter to My Daughter* by Maya Angelou (2009)
- *The Giving Tree* by Shel Silverstein (1964)
- *The Senior Cohousing Handbook: A Community Approach to Independent Living (2d. ed.)* by Charles Durrett (2009)
- *Choose Your Place: Rethinking Home as You Age* by Amanda Lambert and Leslie Eckford (2020).
- *Who Will Take Care of Me When I'm Old? Plan Now to Safeguard Your Health and Happiness in Old Age* by Joy Loverde (2017)
- *Growing Young: How Friendship, Optimism, and Kindness Can Help You Live to 100* by Marta Zaraska (2020)
- *Next Stage: In Your Retirement, Create the Life You Want* by Tom Wilson (2019)

Acknowledgments

First, thank you to those who have so generously shared their stories. Through your pain, honesty, and wisdom, others gain the courage to persevere.

As always, I'm grateful for the encouragement of my wonderful family. Thank you for your patience and support.

A few fellow writers and friends have been particularly instrumental in helping me bring this book to fruition. It is with much gratitude that I mention (in alphabetical order):

Country music historian and memoirist, Diane Diekman, author of books including *Live Fast, Love Hard: The Faron Young Story*. Diane is a retired U.S. Navy Captain, and her no-nonsense thoughts and rare pep talks helped keep me on track. I hope to return the favor as she works on her next book.

My vocabulary is no "match" for tennis author Paul Fein's (www.feinpointsoftennis.com). I have appreciated his quick, precise feedback on my work—often offering a different word to replace one of mine.

William Grote, who is working on an update to *Helping Your Aging Parent: A Step-By-Step Guide*. Bill's keen eye made sense of my occasionally incomplete thoughts, while his silly sense of humor helped me laugh at myself.

Lori Hall-McNary, whose *Rockin' L Ranch Mysteries* series for children is sure to be a hit. The coincidental connections within our lives demonstrate a divine plan for our enduring friendship— and Lori's ready scissors help my writing be more concise.

Mona Leeson Vanek, historical nonfiction author of the fascinating *Behind These Mountains* volumes. Mona's honesty and enduringly cheery spirit infused our decades-long friendship with trust. She passed away just before this book went to print. I'll miss her commentary on my future writing and will fondly remember her.

Indian author Janaki Lenin (*Every Creature Has a Story: What Science Reveals About Animal Behavior*) offered a sensible viewpoint that caught my use of colloquialisms as the book progressed—hopefully making this work more suitable to a global audience.

Catharine Moser, whose book-in-progress, commissioned by Oklahoma University Press, is about late-nineteenth century Thoroughbred breeding in Montana and its contribution to national horse racing. Cathy often spotted subtle, unintended nuances in a simple phrase or how two sentences were joined. Her perspective was sometimes surprising and allowed me a new view.

Julie Wininger, who is working on a novel series based on her Slovak roots. Her critical insight, contrasting opinions, and sparse praise were a gift to this work. I am grateful for our long-term friendship.

Sala Wyman (www.wordshavecolor.com). Sala's writing often mixes some sharp spices of life with the staples of food and family. Kindness tempers her thoughts—which sometimes stirred up my own—and the book is better for it.

A lot of work goes into a book such as this. Special thanks to editor Natalie Hanemann for her sharp eyes and expertise, interior designer Lorie DeWorken for her style sense and graphics, and to cover designer Cathi Stevenson who deserves a medal for her patience. Much gratitude also to literary agent Judy Klein for her enthusiasm.

I can't possibly name everyone! Thank you to all the people who have offered an encouraging word or listened patiently as I worked through this book.

Thank you to my mother and father, whose memories live on and continue to inspire me.

Finally, thank you to God, who is actually first on this list.

About the Author

Sheri McGregor knows the pain of an adult child's rejection. One of her five adult children disengaged from the family, which set her on a quest to find answers, reclaim her happiness, and help other parents of estranged children. In late 2013, she founded RejectedParents.NET where she connects with hurting parents from around the world.

McGregor holds a bachelor's degree in psychology, a master's degree in human behavior, and has recently completed two years toward a doctorate degree in psychology. McGregor works as a life coach and has served on the advisory board for National University's College of Letters and Sciences. Her long career as a writer includes articles on psychology, health, and a variety of other topics, which have appeared in dozens of national and international publications. She has also written for anthologies, websites, and organizations including the non-profit Families for Depression Awareness. Sheri McGregor has been a repeat guest on a San Diego FOX Television affiliate, on KUSI TV, and on a variety of radio shows and podcasts. Her quotes and books have appeared or been featured in publications and at sites including *CNN, HuffPost,* Ask Ellie, *Good Housekeeping, AARP, The Saturday Evening Post, Vanity Fair, PsychCentral, Self Help Daily, The Star, Portsmouth Daily Times, Great Senior Living,* and *Considerable.*

Sheri McGregor has become a powerful voice for the parents of estranged adult children. Her highly regarded book *Done With The Crying: Help and Healing for Mothers of Estranged Adult Children* helps parents break free from emotional pain and move forward in their own lives. As of this date, approximately 60,000 copies are in circulation, and in 2019, an accompanying workbook was released for repeat readers or those using the e-book or audiobook. *Done With The Crying* was a *Foreword Reviews* Finalist and a winner of a *Living Now* Book Award. McGregor's latest offering, *Beyond Done With The Crying: More Answers and Advice for Parents of Estranged Adult Children* is a must-have for those enduring this unique sorrow.

Sheri McGregor lives in the Sierra foothills where she loves to hike, is inspired by nature, and is grateful for every moment. She has recently brought her love for gardening to houseplants and may soon be writing from an indoor jungle.

Index

Made in the USA
Las Vegas, NV
16 October 2023

79150014R00226